Innovation, Technology, and Knowledge Management

Series Editor

Elias G. Carayannis, George Washington University, Washington, DC, USA

This series highlights emerging research and practice at the dynamic intersection of innovation, technology, and knowledge management, where individuals, organizations, industries, regions, and nations are harnessing creativity and invention to achieve and sustain growth. Volumes in the series explore the impact of innovation at the "macro" (economies, markets), "meso" (industries, firms), and "micro" levels (teams, individuals), drawing from such related disciplines as finance, organizational psychology, R&D, science policy, information systems, and strategy, with the underlying theme that in order for innovation to be useful it must involve the sharing and application of knowledge.

This book series is indexed in Scopus.

Israel Patiño-Galván

Innovation and Entrepreneurship Ecosystems

An Evolutionary Vision in the Creation of Local Ecosystems

Springer

Israel Patiño-Galván
Department of Accounting and Administration
Tecnológico de Estudios Superiores de Ecatepec
Ecatepec de Morelos, Estado de México, Mexico

ISSN 2197-5698 ISSN 2197-5701 (electronic)
Innovation, Technology, and Knowledge Management
ISBN 978-3-031-24516-9 ISBN 978-3-031-24517-6 (eBook)
https://doi.org/10.1007/978-3-031-24517-6

This Springer imprint is published by the registered company Springer Nature Switzerland AG
The registered company address is: Gewerbestrasse 11, 6330 Cham, Switzerland

The development of this work is dedicated to Ambar Yotzin, mom Gloria, and my aunt Florecita.
Thanks to my family for the motivation, in particular my brothers Laura, Paco, and Mary, and my nephews Hazel, Joselyn, Esmeralda, and Rubén.

Preface

This work seeks to offer an alternative for the creation and evolution of local innovation and entrepreneurship ecosystems, taking advantage of the resources and infrastructure of universities as the main source of infrastructure through an entity that operates and is the leader of the ecosystem. To have the possibility of taking advantage of and directing the talent of citizens so that they generate new and sustainable Startups, which collaborate with the growth and development of existing companies; so that together with the rest of the stakeholders of the ecosystem they promote its evolution, generating as a result the sustainable social and economic development of the locality. However, it is important to generate solid foundations in the creation of the ecosystem that allows its permanence and evolution, identifying and projecting the necessary resources in the long term, identifying its natural and social wealth, and seeking care for the environment, create and development the culture of entrepreneurship, ensure the commitment to freedom of creativity and search for solutions with social responsibility.

Ecatepec de Morelos, Mexico Israel Patiño-Galván

Contents

About the Author

Israel Patiño-Galván received his Bachelor's degrees in Computer Science and SME Management from Technological of Higher Studies from Ecatepec, Mexico and Open and Distance University of Mexico, Mexico; PhD degrees in Administrative Sciences and Computer Systems from National Polytechnic Institute, Mexico and Da Vinci University, Mexico, respectively; Master of Science degree from National Polytechnic Institute, Mexico; and Master of Computer Systems degree from Technological of Higher Studies from Ecatepec, Mexico. In relation to the Work Experience, it is presented in five blocks: Professional, Academic, Research, Social, and Entrepreneurship. In the Professional, he has been Scrum Master, Project Manager, Systems Developer, Coordinator, and *Information Technologies (IT)* Manager in the public and private sector. In Academic experience, has taught administration, accounting, innovation, statistics and probability, information technology, and undergraduate and graduate programming languages, collaborated as coordinator and president of graduate school, and participated in the design and updating of undergraduate and graduate courses. Regarding Research, has specialized in the lines of research on innovation and entrepreneurship ecosystems, application of Information Technologies and Intelligent Systems in public and private administration, and whose results have been published in articles, books, national conferences and international; he collaborates on editorial boards and is a reviewer of articles in scientific and technological journals; he participates as an evaluating jury in academic and governmental projects on innovation, education, management and entrepreneurship. He belongs to different research groups in the national and international context. Regarding the experience of the Social Sector, he has participated as an advisor representing the academic, professional, scientific, and cultural sectors of the Technical Advisory Council of the Federal Law. He was coordinator of the Technological Innovation Commission to contribute proposals and technological solutions that collaborate with the optimization of administrative processes inside and outside the *Civil Society Organizations (OCS)*. Finally, in relation to the experience in Entrepreneurship, he focuses on the creation and development of ventures, from their ideation, planning, design, prototype development, implementation, and operation.

Chapter 1
Introduction

This paper focuses on a flexible proposal for the creation and evolution of local innovation and entrepreneurship ecosystems, where the central and operational role is led by the university through an *entity that operates the ecosystem* (*EOE*). Its development, field research, documentary, and experience applied by the author were carried out to substantiate the proposal.

To develop this document, three sections were considered. In the first section, the innovation and entrepreneurship ecosystems are contextualized, where their concept, typologies, and characteristics are shown, in addition to making a search of the existing ecosystems worldwide, as well as the identification of methodologies that are used for the creation and measurement that allows assessing the degree of development of ecosystems. The variety of *EOE* that can be assumed by the operation of the ecosystem is also exposed, to know how some countries develop their ecosystems and how the *EOE* intervenes to ensure their development and interaction between stakeholders. On the other hand, the role that universities have within the ecosystem is also presented and how through the *EOE* its infrastructure and resources are used by the ecosystem, which, far from interrupting its objective of academic training and research, is integrated into the ecosystem, in addition to being an agent for linking and interacting with the pillars of the government and enterprises which collaborate with the development of activities of the ecosystem. Finally, the success factors and criteria that have been presented by various successful ecosystems are listed, which serve as a reference for the new ecosystems to identify and assess said factors in their implementation.

In the second section of the work, phase 1 of the proposed ecosystem is presented, a vital phase for its creation, since it starts from an adequate planning, where the development and alignment of the institutional mission and vision are crucial for the design of the objectives, goals, strategies, and indicators of the ecosystem, without forgetting the investigation of the state of the locality where the ecosystem will be created. In this second section, six stages are considered. The first of them shows

I. Patiño-Galván, *Innovation and Entrepreneurship Ecosystems*, Innovation, Technology, and Knowledge Management,
https://doi.org/10.1007/978-3-031-24517-6_1

and suggests the planning of the ecosystem. Once the planning is developed, the second stage is the search for and obtaining sources of financing without return on investment, an aspect to be considered for investors since the payment of interest or income is not contemplated, since priority is given to ensuring the process of creating enterprises, their start-up, and permanence. In the second stage of this phase, the inclusion of calls and reception of entrepreneurship projects is suggested, followed by the stage of implementation of undertakings where business plans, designs, prototypes, and other entrepreneurship proposals are implemented. Finally, in the last closing stage, the company is given "independence" to be managed and operated by the entrepreneur (before-entrepreneur).

In the third and last section, phase 2 of the ecosystem is developed, which refers to the evolution of the ecosystem. In this phase, there are four stages, starting with the stage of financing sources with return on investment. Unlike the first phase, in this, there are already returns for investors, since for this phase the startups are stable with the capacity to deal with these kinds of compromises. Later, stage two is shown, which refers to the calls, reception, and selection of already established startups and interested investors. At this stage, there are various factors to be able to participate. For this, the participating companies are categorized, and certain information is requested to give certainty to the interested parties. Subsequently, the stage of the funding rounds is presented, the operational stage of the financing, where the already stable startup intervenes, and the investors interested in collaborating with capital to collaborate with its development, in addition to obtaining returns on their investment. Also, the closing stage is presented, which ends phase 2, which concludes by obtaining more than 50% of the capital required by startups. Finally, the conclusions, recommendations, and expected benefits are developed once the proposal is implemented.

On the other hand, it is important to mention that, given the flexibility of the proposal, the phases and stages are cyclical, which must respond to the planning and operation developed by the EOE in conjunction with the interested parties. Flexibility allows the horizontal and vertical functions of the EOE to be adjusted according to the degree of maturity and growth of the ecosystem to allow its evolution.

Finally, it is important to mention that given the complexity of the subject, some sections of this work are mentioned in a general way to demonstrate their importance and role within the phases and stages, which will surely be detailed in future works.

Chapter 2
Context of Innovation and Entrepreneurship Ecosystems

2.1 What Is an Innovation and Entrepreneurship Ecosystem?

Innovation ecosystems are spaces promoted by institutions, enterprises, or other organizations to investigate and develop solutions to new, old problems and/or needs. In them, not only research and technology are developed but also advances in management, economics, biology, and health, among others. This space serves as a stimulus to adopt the most innovative technologies in companies and society (Zavala, 2015). According to Smart Social City (2014), an innovation ecosystem is an open network of knowledge, where companies, governments, universities, and society support and accompany initiatives in the identification and resolution of their challenges and opportunities for improvement, from innovation and sustainability.

From author's point of view, an **ecosystem of innovation and entrepreneurship** is how the talent, creativity, and ideas of individuals manage to refine and create logical or physical things or objects, consuming the available resources of the ecosystem, thus achieving the materialization of ideas, turning them into innovation.

- In this sense, an ecosystem has different components, such as:
- The talent of people (ideas, creativity)
- Collaboration/feedback between the actors
- Access to capital/investment
- An adequate legal framework to regulate their actions

I. Patiño-Galván, *Innovation and Entrepreneurship Ecosystems*, Innovation, Technology, and Knowledge Management,
https://doi.org/10.1007/978-3-031-24517-6_2

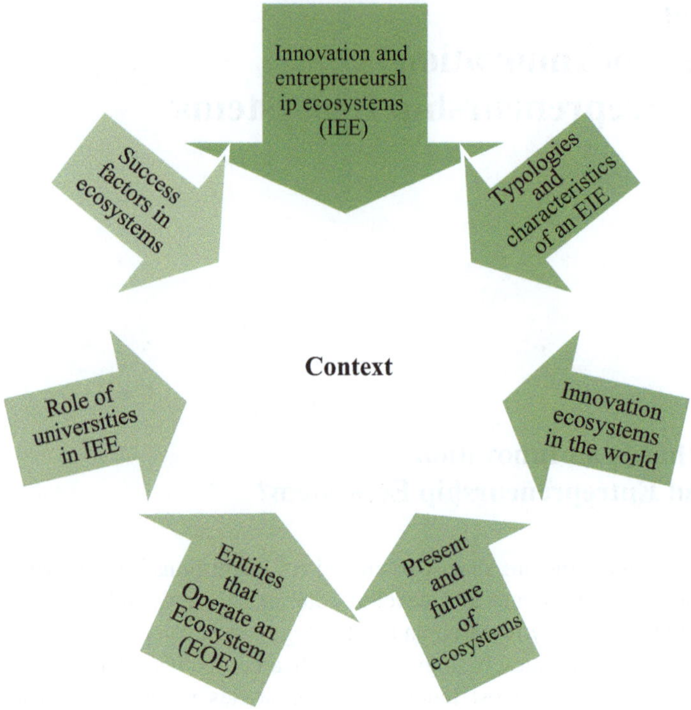

Fig. 2.1 Context of innovation and entrepreneurship ecosystems. (Source: Author, 2021)

However, the most important condition for an ecosystem to be successful is the society/community or, in other words, a knowledge network that eliminates hierarchies, that is in constant contact, and that shares ideas and experiences to offer alternative solutions to existing problems or to improve products or services (see Fig. 2.2). In this sense, universities function as diffusers and amplifiers of the said knowledge network, since they are the ones that provide support and collaborate to link actors, ideas, and necessary infrastructure. In addition, they create opportunities for the community to access resources that are normally inaccessible. The most important thing is that the core of the community is always made up of intellectual capital, that is, entrepreneurs. It is important to mention that an institution should not assume the center of the community, since if this happens, the community would have a good diffusion, but the activity and growth would decrease. In the same way, in an ecosystem of innovation and entrepreneurship, enterprises cannot be absent, which support each other to make the market grow. Finally, the government also interacts in the ecosystem as a diffuser of the knowledge network that collaborates with infrastructure in coordination with the university (Smart Social City, 2014).

To have a clearer idea of the concept of an innovation and entrepreneurship ecosystem, some concepts are presented in Table 2.1.

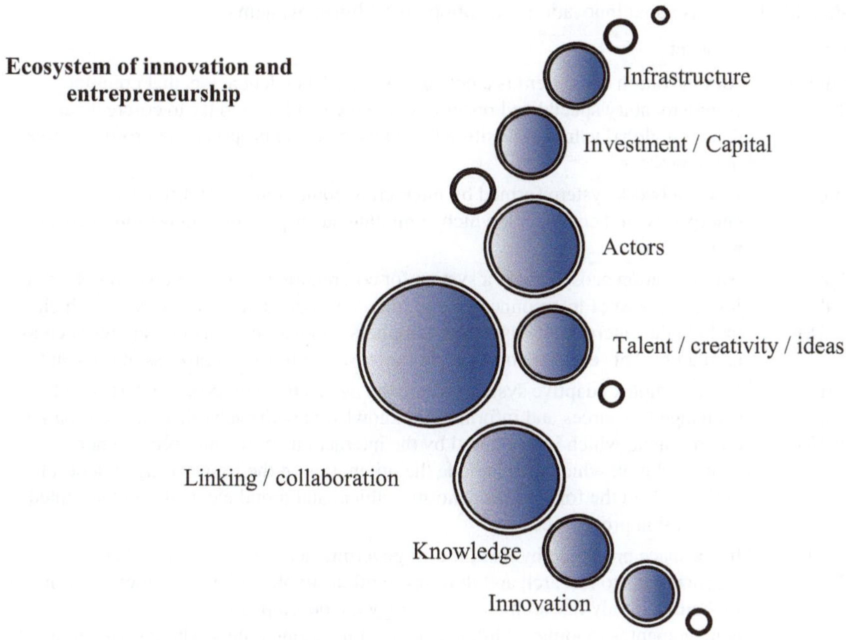

Fig. 2.2 Processes and actors of the innovation and entrepreneurship ecosystem. (Source: Author, 2021)

It is important to highlight the words that are repeated the most in Table 2.1, to identify the possible dimensions of an innovation and entrepreneurship ecosystem:

- Actors
- Artifacts
- Coevolution/specialization
- Collaboration/complement
- Competitiveness
- Talent/creativity/ideas
- Capital/investment
- Legal framework
- Knowledge and infrastructure

The foregoing will allow the visualization of the elements susceptible to being integrated into the innovation and entrepreneurship ecosystems.

Table 2.1 Concepts about innovation and entrepreneurship ecosystems

Author	Concept
Witte et al. (2018)	An innovation ecosystem is a network of interdependent actors that combine complementary specialized resources and/or capabilities to try to co-create and deliver a global value proposition to end users and appropriate the profits received in the process.
Ding and Wu (2018)	It is a network system formed by interacting communities, governments, enterprises, and customers, which communicate or promote innovation to create new products.
Gomes et al. (2018)	An innovation ecosystem is a system for co-creation or the joint creation of value. It is composed of interconnected and interdependent actors in a network, which include the enterprises, customers, suppliers, innovators, and other agents such as regulators. This ecosystem has a life cycle, which follows a process of coevolution.
Vargas et al. (2018)	It is a complex adaptive system, where the agents that compose it interact and exchange (resources and information) knowledge with each other, in each spatial environment, which is structured by the interactions of the different elements contained in it, which also include the orientation of the frameworks of action for individuals in the form of laws, norms, ethical and moral elements, and accepted intervention procedures.
Zavala (2015)	It is a space promoted by institutions, governments, enterprises, or other organizations to research and develop solutions to old and new problems and needs. In them, not only research and technology are developed but also advances in management, economics, biology, and health, among others. These ecosystems serve as a stimulus to adopt the most innovative technologies in companies and in society.
Nambisan and Baron (2013)	An innovation ecosystem refers to an interconnected network of companies and other entities that coevolve capabilities around a shared set of technologies, knowledge, or skills and work cooperatively and competitively to develop new products and services. The three defining characteristics of an innovation ecosystem are the dependencies established between the members (the performance and survival of the members are closely linked to the ecosystem), who share a common set of goals and objectives (shaped by the approach at the level of the innovation system), ecosystem in a unique value proposition for the customer, and knowledge and skills (complementary set of technologies and capabilities).
Smart Social City (2014).	An innovation ecosystem is an *Open Knowledge Network (OKN)*, where companies, governments, universities, and society support and accompany organizations in the identification and resolution of challenges from innovation and sustainability.
Carayannis and Campbell (2009)	An innovation and entrepreneurship ecosystem are a set of multilevel, multimodal, and multi-agent systems. The systems consist of meta-networks of innovation and knowledge as building blocks and organized in a self-referential or chaotic architecture of knowledge and innovation, which in turn constitute agglomerations of reserves and flows of human, social, intellectual, and financial capital, as well as cultural and technological artifacts and modalities continually coevolving, co-specializing and co-creating. These innovation networks and knowledge groups also form and dissolve within various institutional, political, technological, and socioeconomic domains, including government, university, industry, nongovernmental organizations, and information and communication technologies, biotechnologies, advanced materials, nanotechnologies, and next-generation energy technologies.

Source: Author (2021), taken from the list of definitions of an innovation ecosystem (Granstranda & Holgersson, 2020)

2.2 Components, Typologies, and Characteristics of Innovation and Entrepreneurship Ecosystems

Innovation ecosystems are made up of several areas, which allow the identification of ecosystems that develop worldwide, in addition to knowing the factors that intervene in their creation. Some of these items are its components, typologies, and characteristics. On the one hand, some of its components are made up of the size and type of actors, sectors of specialization, and scales of operation of the ecosystems. In relation to its typologies and characteristics, there is diversity depending on its scope, the type of leading entity of the ecosystem, its objective, and finally the interaction of the actors and their connection, which results in the growth, development, and evolution of ecosystems. To identify these items and their importance, they are addressed in the following subtopics.

2.2.1 Ecosystem Components

According to the research developed by Komorowski (2019), the components of innovation ecosystems are the size, number, and type of actors, sectors of specialization, stages of development of the ecosystems, scales of operation, central entities that operate the ecosystem, ecosystem leaders, and their scope, actions, and goals. The results of this investigation are presented below:

1. Size of city

   Cities are distinguished by different categories based on the average number of inhabitants according to the following ranges.

   According to Fig. 2.3 more than 26% of the ecosystems are in large cities (L), followed by medium (M) and very large (XXL), which means that the bigger the city, the greater the number of ecosystems.

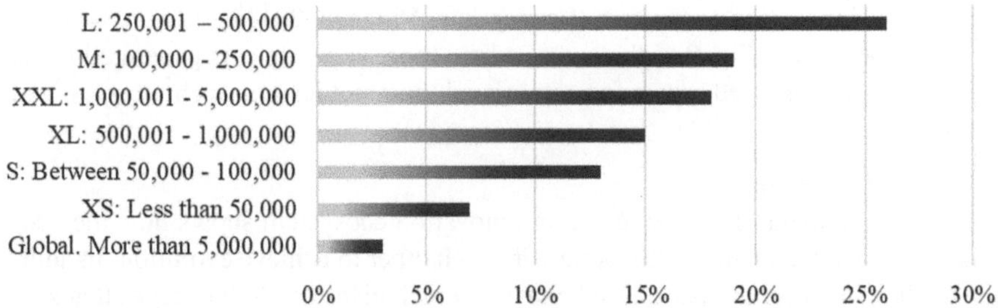

Fig. 2.3 Number of ecosystems identified by city size. Source: Author (2021), taken from Innovation Ecosystems in Europe: First outline of an innovation ecosystem index (Komorowski, 2019)

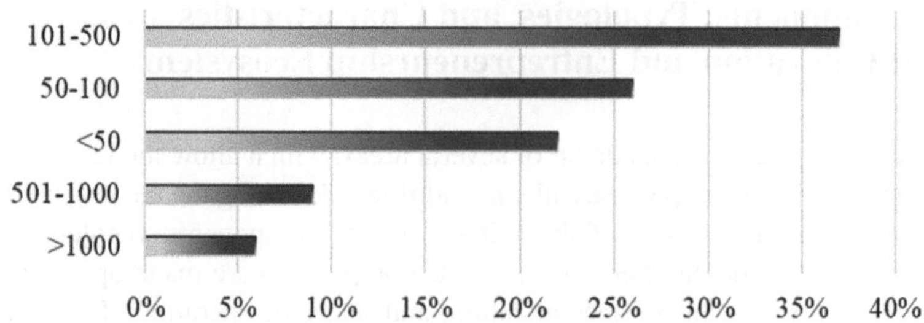

Fig. 2.4 Number of actors involved in innovation and entrepreneurship ecosystems. Source: Author (2021), taken from Innovation Ecosystems in Europe: First outline of an innovation ecosystem index (Komorowski, 2019)

2. Number of actors in the innovation system

The functioning of innovation ecosystems is conditioned by the number of actors involved. Therefore, it takes different sizes. According to the results, ecosystems can be created from two actors.

According to Fig. 2.4, most innovation ecosystems concentrate between 101 and 500 actors with 36%, followed by 50–100 and less than 50 representing 26% and 22%, respectively.

3. Type of actors involved

The actors involved in the innovation and entrepreneurship ecosystems are represented by different organizations with their respective roles, which contributes to defining the organization, sector, and type of ecosystem.

According to Fig. 2.5, the main actors in the construction of *innovation ecosystems (IE)* are the universities, followed by *small and medium enterprises (SME).*

4. Sectors of specialization and industry

In this area, according to Komorowski (2019), innovation ecosystems are identified by the generation of experts. In the case of the European Union, they have made the creation of smart specializations for the creation of innovation a relevant factor. Therefore, experience in certain industries becomes an important criterion for the design of an innovation ecosystem (Launonen & Viitanen, 2011).

As can be seen in Fig. 2.6, the sector where more experience is generated is the energy sector, followed by information and communication technologies and health care.

5. Stages of development

The development of the stages of an innovation ecosystem shows how the ecosystem actors interact and collaborate with each other to achieve evolution, in addition to allowing a certain pattern of behavior, which gives rise to the stages that said ecosystem goes through. In general, a cluster integrates and develops these stages which are emerging, growing, permanent, and transformation as seen in Fig. 2.7 (Rong et al., 2015; Menzel et al., 2010).

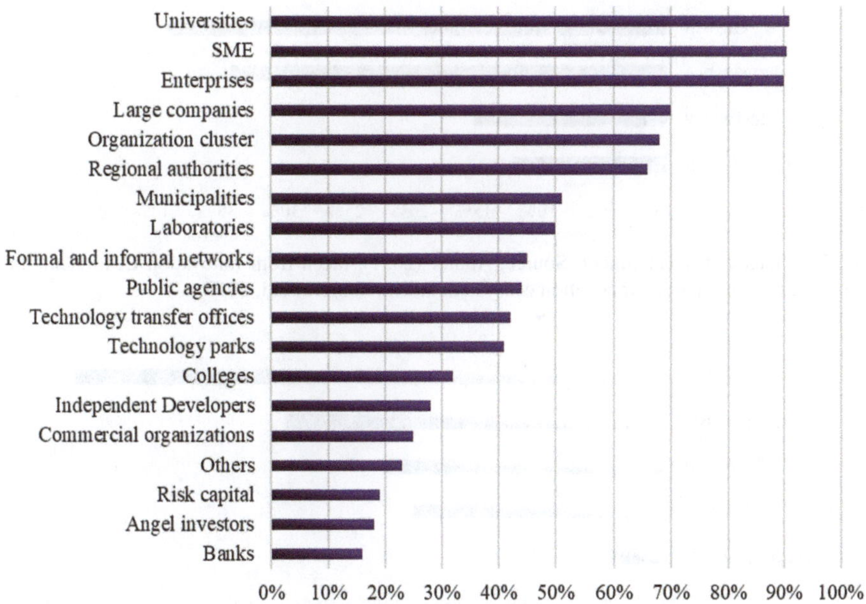

Fig. 2.5 Type of actors involved in innovation and entrepreneurship ecosystems. Source: Author (2021), taken from Innovation Ecosystems in Europe: First outline of an innovation ecosystem index (Komorowski, 2019)

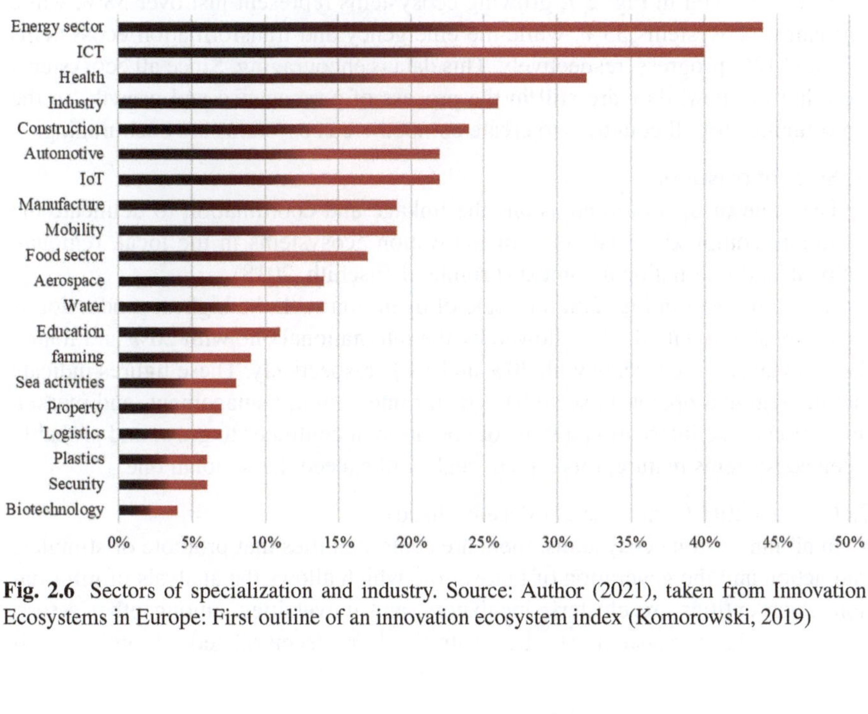

Fig. 2.6 Sectors of specialization and industry. Source: Author (2021), taken from Innovation Ecosystems in Europe: First outline of an innovation ecosystem index (Komorowski, 2019)

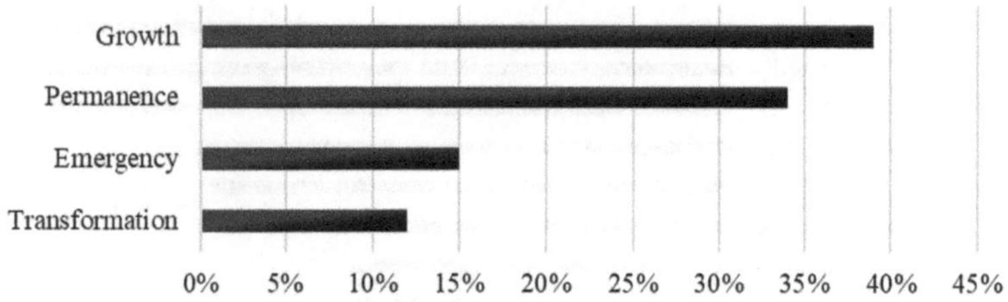

Fig. 2.7 Stages of development. Source: Author (2021), taken from Innovation Ecosystems in Europe: First outline of an innovation ecosystem index (Komorowski, 2019)

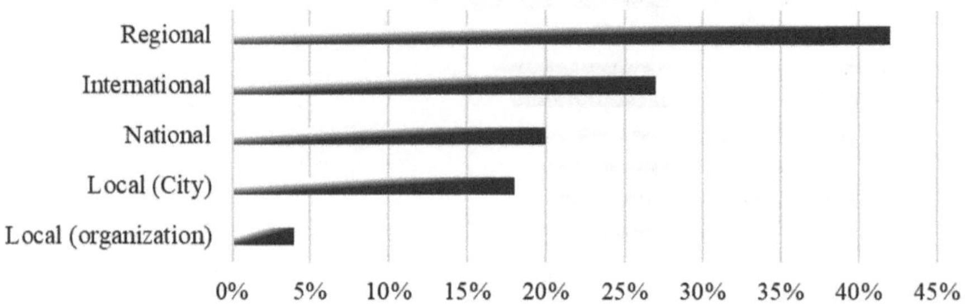

Fig. 2.8 Scale of operation. Source: Author (2021), taken from Innovation Ecosystems in Europe: First outline of an innovation ecosystem index (Komorowski, 2019)

As can be seen in Fig. 2.7, growing ecosystems represent just over 38%, while permanent ecosystems 33%, while the emergency and transformation ecosystems 15% and 12% progress, respectively. This data is encouraging. Since all ecosystems are relatively new, they are still in the process of permanence and growth, so the opportunities for all countries to create competitive ecosystems are encouraging.

6. Scale of operation

The scale of operation envisions the linkage and coordination to delineate the operation, complexity, and types of innovation ecosystems in the local, regional, national, and international context (Fromhold-Eisebith, 2018).

As can be seen in Fig. 2.8, the scale of operation with the highest production is the regional one with 45%, followed by the international one with 26% and finally the national and local scale with 20% and 18%, respectively. These figures indicate that the regional operation scale has greater interaction, management, and market. In relation to the international scale of operation, it continues to grow, and probably when ecosystems mature, this type of scale will exceed the regional one.

7. Central entity (centralized or decentralized)

In all innovation ecosystems, there are central entities that promote or stimulate interaction and the generation of innovation, which allows the analysis of information. Such entities are clusters, incubators, and universities, among other actors. Therefore, the ecosystem can be centralized or decentralized, if and only if collaboration structures are allowed to be created between different actors and levels of intervention in the processes. In this context, financial structures, talent generation, and organization are important to understand the type and functioning of innovation ecosystems as observed in Fig. 2.9 (Autio & Thomas, 2014).

As can be seen in Fig. 2.9, 50% of the organization, linkage, collaboration, and management between the actors are concentrated in the clusters, a question that is understandable by the knowledge, grade of experience, and specialization that they develop. On the other hand, it is followed by associations and communities with just over 10%.

8. Leadership of key actors

In the emerging context of innovation ecosystems, it is important to target the leading actors. The more roles of the different actors within the innovation ecosystem, the more important leadership will be. The knowledge acquired by the leader will be essential, and even more so in the birth of the innovation ecosystem. The main actors assume roles of governance, association creation, platform management, and the value of management (Dedehayir et al., 2018).

As can be seen in Fig. 2.10, government leadership represents more than 50% of the cases, followed by the leadership of the universities and later by individual initiatives. This is an advantage, if the government actor has a well-defined long-term objective and ensures the continuity of the ecosystem, relying on universities, experts, and enterprises as part of the interested actors.

9. Actions and goals

The main objective should be innovation and entrepreneurship; however, environments for innovation and support can be created through actions and goals where these are not always defined, so it is suggested to build them progressively according to the general and specific objectives set out. To do this, the objectives must be accompanied by specific common or shared objectives among the actors. These

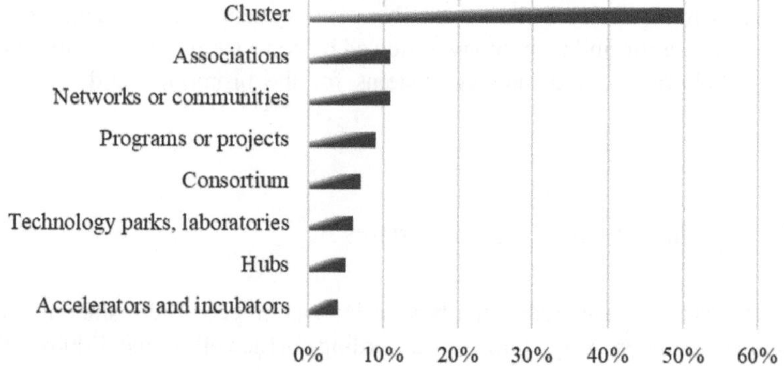

Fig. 2.9 Central entity. Source: Author (2021), taken from Innovation Ecosystems in Europe: First outline of an innovation ecosystem index (Komorowski, 2019)

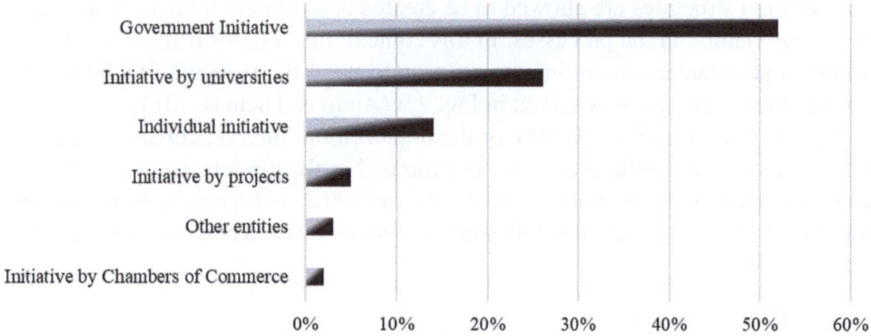

Fig. 2.10 Leadership of key actors. Source: Author (2021), taken from Innovation Ecosystems in Europe: First outline of an innovation ecosystem index (Komorowski, 2019)

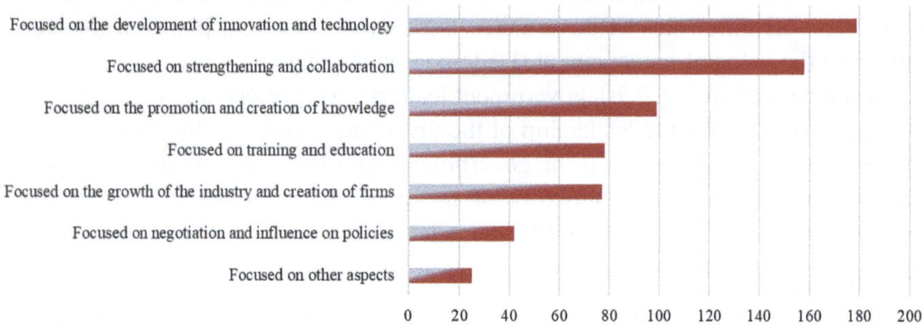

Fig. 2.11 Number of ecosystems identified by actions and objectives. Source: Author (2021), taken from Innovation Ecosystems in Europe: First outline of an innovation ecosystem index (Komorowski, 2019)

actions define the types of innovation ecosystems and collaborate in classifying direct actions and broad objectives (Sölvell et al., 2008).

According to Fig. 2.11, the largest number of ecosystems is focused on the development of innovation and technology, followed by ecosystems aimed at strengthening and collaboration, and later ecosystems for the promotion and creation of knowledge.

2.2.2 Typologies and Characteristics

The characteristics are linked to the type of innovation ecosystem since its objectives and stakeholders vary; however, according to Llewellyn and Erkko (2019), there are generic characteristics such as:

- Heterogeneity of the actors. It generally arises as the actors involved in innovation ecosystems come from a variety of industries and sectors. This heterogeneity is accentuated by the role-based governance that characterizes ecosystems.
- Outbound products or services. Innovation ecosystems facilitate the generation of products or services. In this sense, the outputs of innovation ecosystems are products or services that are compatible with each other, adhering to the production chain in a modular way.
- Interdependence of the participants. It is perhaps the most outstanding characteristic since information flows in ecosystems. In this regard, the first interdependence is technology since the ecosystem requires technological infrastructure to operate. The second interdependence is the economic aspect, due to the ability to invest in infrastructure, and due to all the products or services that are generated in innovation ecosystems, and finally the third interdependence is cognitive, that is, the participants of the ecosystem have patterns of historical practices, experiences, philosophies, values, and beliefs that provide the formal and informal rules of action, interaction, and interpretation that guide decision-makers.

On the other hand, according to Klimas and Czakon (2020), around 49 types of innovation ecosystems are considered worldwide, grouped into 5 categories and 14 typologies, where each ecosystem has its own characteristics as shown in Table 2.2.

As can be seen in Table 2.2, there are different types, criteria, and categories of innovation ecosystems; however, it is important to note that within this categorization, local and hierarchical innovation ecosystems led by universities tend to be more successful, because the seed intellectual capital is formed and polished in these, in addition to having infrastructure to support them, such as facilities, teachers, researchers, minimal infrastructure to operate the enterprises of students or entrepreneurs, and links on which interested actors add efforts and capacities to materialize innovations. This does not mean that any other actor can assume this role; however, by their nature, universities have a greater projection and reduce the risk of failure. In fact, the leadership of the universities in the beginning stage and the learning process and maturity of the ecosystem, the leadership roles, may change according to the interests and strategic plan in the medium and long term. Finally, the archetypes of innovation systems are delineated by the size and complexity of the cities, characteristics, and linkages that are observed in Table 2.3 in such a way that greater complexity requires greater and better interaction between stakeholders, as well as increase the number of specialists and resources. This will result in a greater response capacity and available resources, which increase the probability that innovation and entrepreneurship projects emanating from the ecosystem will be successful, in addition to reducing the risks of failure. From the above, according to Table 2.3, it can be observed in a general way how these archetypes require greater capacities as their complexity increases (Klimas & Czakon, 2020).

Table 2.2 Typologies and characteristics of innovation and entrepreneurship ecosystems

Category	Typology of the criterion	Type of innovation ecosystem	Characteristics
1. Genesis and existence of innovation ecosystems	1. Birth of the ecosystem	1. Intentional (deliberate, planned)	Created by focal companies or market players. The moment of birth of an ecosystem depends on the decision of the actors.
		2. Emergent (implicit)	The system is created to solve problems or urgent needs. It is difficult to identify the moment of his birth.
	2. Governance mechanism	3. Hierarchical	The ecosystem is led by the main actor, usually a producer. This type of ecosystem is managed strictly and autonomously by the firm.
		4. Collective	They are collectively coordinated by a set of actors, generally companies with access to strategic resources.
		5. Self-coordination	Each actor manages his roles within the ecosystem, joining the general objective.
	3. Stages of the life cycle	6. Emergent	In this stage of the ecosystem, the preparation and training for the stages or phases of operation (planning) can be divided.
		7. Development	At this stage, stakeholders participate in the co-carried out innovation processes.
		8. Mature	At this stage, the activity of the innovation ecosystem and its structure stabilizes. The behaviors and interactions of the actors are co-adaptive and coevolutive.
		9. Decline (decline)	The number of actors and the co-creation of innovation decrease. The interaction between the actors is weak.
		10. Finished	The innovation ecosystem ceases to exist, and some of the players are operating in the market independently, without interaction.

Category	Typology of the criterion	Type of innovation ecosystem	Characteristics
2. Structure of the innovation ecosystem	4. Actors	11. Symmetric	Actors manifest interactions, objectives, and projects in common.
		12. Asymmetric	The actors involved participate in a diversified way in co-innovation processes with the integration of the private initiative with the support of the universities as pillars of innovation.
		13. Centralized	One of the actors that leads the ecosystem, assumes the main role of leadership. The essence of this ecosystem is the coordination between the actors.
		14. Decentralized	There is no dominant actor.
	5. Innovation co-creation relationships	15. Egocentric	This ecosystem is considered from a responsible company perspective for product launches. Increases innovation co-creation relationships, developed by stakeholders
		16. Ecocentric	This ecosystem starts from the coexistence of direct or indirect actors, generating co-creative relationships of innovation focused on the initiatives of the actors.

(continued)

Table 2.2 (continued)

Category	Typology of the criterion	Type of innovation ecosystem	Characteristics
3. Innovation ecosystem with a focus on innovation leadership	6. Scope of innovation	17. Microscopic	The focus falls on the elements, its implementation, and results of collaborative co-innovation or open innovation at the organizational level.
		18. Middlescopic	The focus is on open innovation at the industrial and regional level.
		19. Macroscopic	The focus is on open innovation at the national and international level.
	7. Type of innovation	20. Focused on disruptive innovation	Orientation to revolutionary innovations in the market
		21. Focused on radical innovation	Orientation to innovations based on new technologies
		22. Focused on incremental innovation	Orientation to innovations based on changes, adjustments, or development of existing solutions
		23. Focused on social innovation	Emphasizes on social innovations, focused on social needs
		24. Focused on pioneering (exploratory) innovations	Orientation to simultaneous innovations for current technology, market structure, and how to satisfy social needs
	8. Intensity of the co-innovation process	25. Redirect co-innovation	Prioritizes cooperation and co-creation of innovation, their relationships, and the greatest impact on co-creation of value in the discovery stage of the innovation process
		26. Redirect co-development	It prioritizes cooperation and joint innovation creation relationships, where the greatest impact lies in the joint creation of value, in the development, and in the implementation stage of the innovation process.
		27. Redirect co-delivery (impact products)	It lies in generating relationships with a greater impact on the co-creation of value in the innovation delivery process.
		28. Redirect dissemination	Prioritizes cooperation, relationships, and the impact of co-creation of innovation in its diffusion stage.
		29. Focused on the adoption of multistage co-innovation	This ecosystem is characterized by multistage cooperation throughout the process of innovation and exploitation of joint creation relationships.

Category	Typology of the criterion	Type of innovation ecosystem	Characteristics
4. Degree of innovation ecosystems	9. Technological scope	30. High technology	It operates in high-tech industries in accordance with the regulations implemented by the *Organization for Economic Cooperation and Development (OECD).*
		31. Medium technology	It operates in medium- to high- or medium- to low-technology industries in accordance with *OECD* regulations.
		32. Low technology	It operates in low-tech industries according to the *OECD*.
		33. Mono platform	Operates under a single technological platform
		34. Multi-platform	Operate on more than one technology platform
	10. Spatial scope	35. Based on cities or municipalities/districts of innovation	In general, this type of ecosystem is led by municipal or district authorities.
		36. Locals	Its structure belongs to a locality; it can be a district or city.
		37. Regionals	Its structure belongs to a region; it can contain several local ecosystems.
		38. Nationals	This ecosystem belongs to a complete country; it may contain regional ecosystems belonging to the same country.
		39. International	This ecosystem is made up of national ecosystems from various countries.
		40. Global	This ecosystem is made up of several international ecosystems.
	11. Physical scope	41. Digital	It operates on the network on collective cooperation platforms. Digital innovation ecosystems include mobile and virtual digital ecosystems.
		42. Mixed	It operates under technological and administrative structures virtually and physically.

(continued)

Table 2.2 (continued)

Category	Typology of the criterion	Type of innovation ecosystem	Characteristics
5. Performance of the innovation ecosystem	12. Performance in innovation	43. Successful	Ecosystems that have achieved their proposed objectives
		44. Failure	Ecosystems that did not achieve their objectives and put the success of the innovations developed at risk
		45. Promising	This ecosystem develops ecosystems with high innovation potential, since it integrates actors with organizational and technological innovation capacity, so the value chain in the market is fully integrated.
	13. Economic performance	46. Profitable	It constantly transforms technology and other contributions to innovation including the market. It is known as a healthy ecosystem.
		47. Not profitable	This ecosystem presents problems to generate competitive innovations.
	14. Strategic performance	48. Sustainable	The actors are characterized by an adequate level of proximity/linkage (cognitive, social proximity, institutional proximity, and geographic proximity), which delivers long-term results.
		49. Not sustainable	The actors involved do not manage to have a multidimensional approach, which generates tensions, lack of communication, and an increase in risk for the co-innovation processes.

Source: Author (2021), taken from typologies of innovation ecosystems (Klimas & Czakon, 2020) and definitions and characteristics of innovation ecosystems – entrepreneurship (Aarikka-Stenroos & Ritala, 2017; Autio & Thomas, 2014; Arena et al., 2018; Arora et al. 2019; Dattee et al., 2018; Dedehayir et al., 2018; Durst & Poutanen, 2013; Ferasso et al., 2018; Iyer & Davenport, 2008; Gomes et al., 2018; Jucevicius et al., 2016; Kapoor & Lee, 2013; Luo, 2018; Mazzucato & Robinson, 2018; Oh et al., 2016; Phillips & Srai, 2018; Planko et al., 2017; Pombo-Juárez et al., 2017; Rabelo & Bernus, 2015; Radziwon, 2018; Reynolds & Uygun, 2018; Rocha et al., 2019; Russell & Smorodinskaya, 2018; Schroth et al., 2018; Spelmeyer & Lingens, 2018; Su et al., 2018, Sun et al., 2017; Walrave et al., 2018; Ding & Wu, 2018; Xu et al., 2018; Yaghmaie & Vanhaverbeke, 2019)

Table 2.3 Main archetypes of innovation ecosystems in Europe

Small cities	Medium cities
Organizations dedicated to research Public agencies Technology parks	Laboratories Large enterprises Municipal governments Comprised of less than 50 stakeholders
Large cities	**Extra-large cities**
Formal and complex framework Autonomous actors More than 1000 stakeholders	Universities Risk capital More than 1000 actors Banks Clusters of organizations

Source: Author (2021), taken from innovation systems in Europe: First draft of an index of innovation ecosystems (Klimas & Czakon, 2020; European Commission, 2020)

2.2.3 Typologies of Ecosystems Focused on Leadership

According to the literature, there are various types of ecosystems based on that they produce, emphasizing the leading role of the actors who are leaders in the ecosystems. One of those actors, given their strategic position in the ecosystem, are the universities that support ecosystems. These typologies are the following (Llewellyn & Erkko, 2019):

- Business ecosystem (Adner, 2017; Teece, 2018). This type of ecosystem is characterized by the type of actors that are involved, since they operate under an environment of co-responsibility, under agreed work standards, share information, and co-create in the form of value offers. They share experiences, strategic information from clients, suppliers, regulatory authorities, and educational and research institutions. They form communities of organizations, institutions, and individuals to assess the information and take actions for the benefit of the actors. In this sense, according to Carayannis et al. (2018), a business ecosystem is an organizational goal composed of resources and competencies sustained by actors that cooperate and, in some cases, compete to encourage the creation of value. This implies that within this type of ecosystems, enterprises take advantages so that among all and depending on their skills they can solve internal challenges, and this generates experience among the ecosystems.
- Platform or digital ecosystems (McIntyre & Srinivasan, 2018; Thomas & Tee, 2019; Spigel, 2017). This type of ecosystems emphasizes technological interdependencies within the ecosystem. They share technological architectures and connectivity. This environment is known as a platform. They are organized and interact through structures that subdivide tasks or activities, forming a complementary network where they generate value to their offer of services or products. The challenge in this type of ecosystem is the leadership role, since it requires coordination and improvement of capacities, so one of the actors involved must assume this role. There is flexibility among the members of the ecosystem if it does not interfere with the interests of those involved in seeking

the growth of all actors. Normally, the interactions lead to the development of capacities to improve their infrastructures and the adoption of technological tools that allow better analysis and decision-making.

- Entrepreneurship ecosystems (Autio & Thomas, 2014; Colombelli et al., 2019). This ecosystem facilitates the creation of strengthened business models, thanks to inherent actors such as available infrastructure (provided by the ecosystem leader), human resources, and newly created enterprises (collective enterprises) with complementary value chains ready to be used. This ecosystem serves the growing demand for entrepreneurship professionals and regional communities interested in creating new enterprises. A mature entrepreneurship ecosystem gives rise to knowledge, industrial and innovation clusters, as part of regional and national innovation environments. The actors involved become linkage and support agents for the ventures, adding value, by involving experts in the required disciplines, in addition to accelerating the search for internal or external sources of financing and business accelerators.
- Knowledge ecosystems (Bogers et al., 2017; Järvi et al., 2018). This ecosystem presents the knowledge generated as a product of research and is reflected in open research + development and innovation processes. The actors in this ecosystem participate in the joint creation of normally commercial knowledge to create shared, normally pre-commercial products. These ecosystems facilitate the cogeneration of macro products (at the ecosystem level) to give an opportunity to consume or take advantage of the research and knowledge generated.
- Innovation ecosystems (Adner, 2017; Constantinides et al., 2018; Jacobides et al., 2019; Teece, 2018; Hannah & Eisenhardt, 2018). These ecosystems emphasize the output that is produced and the benefits that will be obtained not necessarily or exclusively for profit. They are spaces where multiple actors collaborate for the generation and production of value, share standards, which allows collaboration for the creation of new products, services or methods, or improvements to them.

2.2.4 *Typologies of Ecosystems According to Their Spatial Scope*

Although it is true that innovation and entrepreneurship ecosystems are formed, interact, and coordinate with various actors and/or elements, the end result is the knowledge process that is generated, in addition to success and materialization in innovation through products, services, and processes/methodologies that are created to meet a public, private, social, or academic needs. Thanks to this we can distinguish in practice different types of innovation ecosystems that obey their dimensions, capacity, region, or segment in which they are developed that collaborate in said materialization in products/services or solution to problems. We can see the above in Table 2.4

Table 2.4 Types of innovation and entrepreneurship ecosystems

Author	Type	Concept
Edquist (1997)	Innovation system	They are all economic, social, political, organizational, institutional, and other factors that influence the development, diffusion, and use of innovations.
Lundvall (1992)	National innovation system	All parts and aspects of the economic structure and institutional configuration that affect learning, as well as search and exploration, such as the production system, the marketing system, and the finance system, which are presented as subsystems in the learning takes place.
Asheim and Gertler (2005)	Regional innovation system	The institutional infrastructure that supports innovation within the production structure of a region
Breschi and Malerba (1997)	Sector innovation system	That system (group) of enterprises active in the development and manufacture of the products of a sector and in the generation and use of technologies. This system is related in two different ways: through interaction and cooperation processes in the development of technological artifacts and through competition and selection processes in innovative and market activities.
Granstrand (2000)	Corporate innovation system	The set of actors, activities, resources, and institutions and the causal interrelationships that are in a certain sense important for the innovative performance of a corporation or groups of collaborating companies and other actors (for example, universities, institutes, agencies)

Source: Author (2021), taken from definitions of innovation ecosystems (Granstranda & Holgersson, 2020)

According to what is presented in Table 2.4, the different types of innovation ecosystems can be visualized, all of them similar in context and objective. However, some follow their nature, interests, and other issues as part of their goal and evolution. In relation to evolution and given that the proposal of this book focuses on an ecosystem of innovation and local entrepreneurship, Table 2.5 presents the concept of ecosystems of local innovation without leaving aside the ecosystem of international innovation.

Table 2.5 Ecosystems of local and international innovation

Type	Concept
Local Innovation Systems (LIS)	They are the means and resources through which the talent, creativity, and ideas of individuals are improved and oriented so that they can create and solve problems, optimally and sustainably consuming the available resources of the environment, thus achieving the materialization of initiatives, turning them into innovation and entrepreneurship. The central factor being the talent of the individual as a natural generator of ideas and solutions. This allows to generate knowledge and own resources, in addition to progressively improving the interaction between the actors. Once the ecosystem matures, it integrates with other ecosystems, turning them into regional and international innovation ecosystems.
International Innovation Systems (IIS)	It is the cluster of regional and national innovation systems that have collaborations with clusters from other countries, through which it is possible to generate knowledge not only of the local and regional but also international context where problems are addressed considering knowledge, innovation, and technologies generated in different areas/regions. This allows to accelerate solutions and significantly improve final innovations. The *IIS* are very complex, and maturity is required to achieve them since too much information flows, which needs to be processed by all the actors to make the best decisions that are translated into development and economic and social growth for the ecosystems involved.

Source: Author (2021)

2.3 Ecosystems of Innovation and Entrepreneurship in the World

Innovation ecosystems as of 2000 accelerated in certain regions of the world, focusing on ensuring their development and growth, in addition to adapting existing resources and infrastructure to guarantee their evolution, starting with entrepreneurship ecosystems, redefining their local potential and regional. However, each ecosystem is characterized by certain aspects that guarantee its degree of success to a greater or lesser extent, considering its local characteristics, skills, and national and international experience to successfully enable ecosystems.

To identify these characteristics, the following comparison is presented in Table 2.6 of the three main innovation and entrepreneurship ecosystems (Galdino de Barros & Almeida, 2020).

According to Table 2.6, the following frequent characteristics are observed in the ecosystems shown:

- Encourage the culture of innovation, the importance of the link and interaction between the triple helices
- Involve stakeholders to identify needs in public and private innovations
- Have the necessary infrastructure and financing to support innovations
- Support for university and social talent
- Strategies to generate disruptive innovation
- Adjustment to public policies that concern the context of the innovation and entrepreneurship ecosystem

Table 2.6 General comparison of the top three innovation ecosystems in the world

Ecosystems	Characteristics	Interaction	Innovative solutions
United State	Encourage with the culture of innovation Build progressively the entrepreneurial spirit directed and linked by the triple helix Industry as a driver and practical support Success in the university-enterprise link, originated by Silicon Valley	Creation of infrastructure and links with the business sector Interaction with the government sector for the creation of public policies	Increase in financing to the ecosystem Increase in the number of successful ventures There are startup scalability programs. Improve life quality. Access to financing cycles Access to university and social talent Comprehensive support for new ventures and entrepreneurs Access to specialist researchers
Israel	Entrepreneurship culture based on patents Integration of society in the identification of public and private innovations	The number of successful ventures increases to the point of generating one for every 2000 inhabitants. Integration of universities to the innovation cycle	Adoption of products derived from innovation by foreign countries Increase in financing for innovations and ecosystem infrastructure Strategies to generate disruptive innovation Development of innovations for small cities Start with the export of innovations in the world.
China	Eliminate the belief in copying innovation, through programs based on global innovation led by expert intellectual capital Incremental participation of universities contributing to innovation with intellectual capital	Interaction with world ecosystems for the creation of innovations and successful startups Limit innovation with the government sector and on the contrary increase innovation through universities	Identify the regional and sectoral potential Creation of innovation to generate local and regional solutions Start with innovations for the global market Exponential increase for the ecosystem infrastructure

Source: Author (2021), taken from comparative study of innovation ecosystems to integrate the success of entrepreneurship ecosystems (Galdino de Barros & Almeida, 2020)

Continuing with the innovation and entrepreneurship ecosystems, according to Ziyaad (2018) and Startup Genome (2017), an evaluation framework was created to classify them, taking a methodology that groups metrics into five categories: performance, financing, market research, talent, and startup experience. These favors measuring the performance of the smallest, medium, and large ecosystems, with which all ecosystems can be compared and opportunities for improvement can be identified, as shown in Table 2.7 and Fig. 2.12.

Table 2.7 Top 20 ecosystems of innovation and entrepreneurship worldwide

Rank[a]	Ecosystem	Positions					Growth rate
		Performance/ performance	Funds/ financing	Market research	Talent	Experience in startups	
1.	Silicon Valley	1	1	1	2	1	4.2
2.	New York City	3	2	3	7	4	4.5
3.	London	4	4	2	10	5	4.8
4.	Beijing	2	5	19	8	2	4.4
5.	Boston	6	6	12	4	3	4.0
6.	Tel Aviv	9	8	4	11	7	4.5
7.	Berlin	7	9	6	5	10	4.6
8.	Shanghai	8	3	10	9	13	5.5
9.	Los Angeles	5	7	15	14	11	4.2
10.	Seattle	12	13	14	3	6	4.5
11.	Paris	14	14	9	16	8	4.2
12.	Singapore	16	16	11	1	20	4.6
13.	Austin	15	11	18	6	9	4.3
14.	Stockholm	17	20	8	18	12	5.3
15.	Vancouver	19	19	7	15	15	4.3
16.	Toronto	18	12	5	20	18	4.7
17.	Sydney	20	10	13	12	17	6.3
18.	Chicago	13	15	20	13	14	3.9
19.	Amsterdam	10	17	17	19	16	4.8
20.	Bangalore	11	18	16	17	19	4.7

Source: Author (2021), taken from Global Ranking of Entrepreneurship Ecosystems (Ziyaad, 2018)
[a]The ranking methodology is made up of a weighted average of the following factor scores: 30% return, 25% financing

As can be seen in Table 2.7, the ecosystems of Silicon Valley, New York City, and London are in the top three with the highest performance, and on the other hand, Shanghai, Stockholm, and Sydney are the ones with the highest growth rates. Given the above, it is suggested to form solid innovation and entrepreneurship ecosystems that develop the five indicators. This will allow better development and long-term growth. Additionally, the index considers the links between these ecosystems, with Silicon Valley being the one with the greatest interaction with ecosystems on practically all continents, followed by Shanghai. These links allow collaborations, technology transfer, and development of local technologies.

On the other hand, in Table 2.8 and Fig. 2.13 according to Startup Genome (2017), there are more ecosystems of innovation and entrepreneurship around the world, which are in the process of creation and others in development and consolidation. However, the need to improve and link these ecosystems. From the above, there are challenges and opportunities for improvement that can be developed and take advantage of the experience between them to enhance the capacities and natural resources of each region.

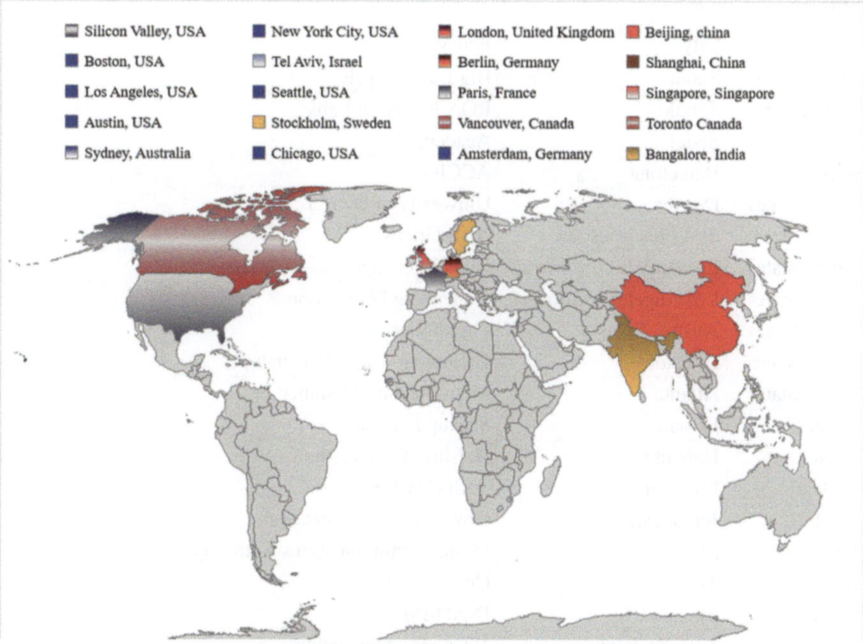

Source: Author (2021), taking as reference

Fig. 2.12 Geographical location of the top 20 innovation and entrepreneurship ecosystems worldwide. Source: Author (2021), taking as reference Table 2.7.

Table 2.8 Rest of innovation and entrepreneurship ecosystems worldwide

Country[a]	City	Ecosystem
Germany	Amsterdam	Startup Delta
Germany	Frankfort	TechQuartier
Australia	Sydney	University of Technology Sydney
Australia	Bryce York	StartupAUS
Australia	Sydney	Tech Sydney
Australia	Sydney	Committee for Sydney
Australia	Victoria	LaunchVIC
Brazil	Sao Paolo	Endeavor Brazil
Canada	Vancouver	Vancouver Economics Commission
Canada	Toronto	MARS Discovery District
Canada	Quebec	Quebec International
Canada	Montreal	City of Montreal
Canada	Montreal	Real Investments and Osmo Foundation
Canada	Montreal	ETS Montreal
Canada	Ottawa	Investment Ottawa
Canada	Ontario	Communitech
Chile	Santiago de Chile	CORFO

(continued)

Table 2.8 (continued)

Country[a]	City	Ecosystem
South Korea	Seoul	Big Bang Angels
South Korea	Seoul	ROA Invention Labs
South Korea	Seoul	Academy X
Spain	Barcelona	ACCIO
United States	Denver	University of Denver
United States	St. Louis Missouri	Arch Grants
United States	Los Angeles California	Bixel Exchange Cross Campus
United States	Los Angeles California	Annenberg Foundation
United States	Austin, Texas	Capital Factory
United States	Houston	Greater Houston Partnership
United States	Atlanta	Metro Atlanta Chamber
Estonia	Estonia	Startup Estonia
Finland	Helsinki	Helsinki Business hub
England	England	Tech City UK
Israel	Jerusalem	Government of Jerusalem
Italy	Malta	Malta Communications Authority
Italy	Turin	City of Turin
Mexico	Mexico City	INADEM
New Zealand	New Zealand	NZ Angel Association
Portugal	Lisbon	City of Lisbon
Singapore	Singapore	Spring Singapore
Singapore	Singapore	Magic
Siri Lanka	Mawatha, Colombo	*Information Communication Technologies (ICT)* Agency of Sri Lanka
South Africa	South Africa	Simodisa The Business Place
South Africa	South Africa	Allan Gray Orbis
Sweden	Stockholm	Stockholm Chamber of Commerce

Source: Author (2021), taken from the report of entrepreneurship ecosystems (Startup Genome, 2017)

[a]Rest of the ecosystems of the Startup Genome network. The relationship is ordered by alphabet

Moreover to taking advantage of the local talent that requires conditions to shape their ideas and creativity, which materialize in startups and once established, accelerate their growth and development.

On the other hand, worldwide, according to Klaus (2019) in the global competitiveness report of the World Economic Forum, there are various advances in the construction and strengthening of innovation and entrepreneurship ecosystems in each country in addition to generating strategic links between regions to accelerate these ecosystems. In this sense, to measure the degree of progress in these ecosystems, Block 4 *innovation ecosystems (IE)* and its pillars 11, business dynamism, and 12, innovation capacity of the report, were considered. In these pillars, progress is measured in different areas by country. The detailed indicators and the country(s) with the best performance are shown in Table 2.9.

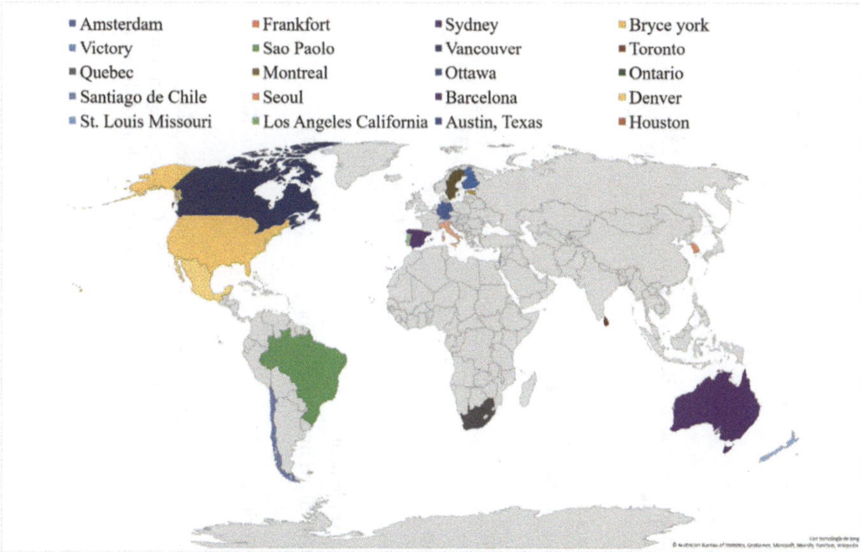

Fig. 2.13 Countries with innovation and entrepreneurship ecosystems. Source: Author (2021), taken from the report of entrepreneurship ecosystems (Startup Genome, 2017). *For reasons of space in Fig. 2.13, the first 20 ecosystems are shown in their description

According to Table 2.9, the countries of the United States, Japan, Israel, Singapore, and Luxembourg come out. However, other countries and regions have become increasingly involved in the creation, development, and growth of innovation and entrepreneurship ecosystems, given the multidimensional economic and social sustainable benefits, in addition to taking advantage of the intellectual capital they possess in their population. From the above, it is important that countries recognize and work on the construction of said ecosystems in a comprehensive manner, creating at the same time an ideal framework in which institutions, infrastructure, *ICT* adoption, macroeconomic stability, and human capital are involved (health and skills), enabling the competitive market (labor market, product market, financial system), adjustments to the regulatory framework that allows freedom of creation and innovation, open government that encourages the adoption, and creation of distributive innovation, as well as fostering the interaction between actors.

To locate the advances and efforts that each country makes to guarantee the creation and progressive development of innovation ecosystems, Table 2.10 shows the position of each country according to its business dynamism and capacity for innovation.

As can be seen in Table 2.10, each country makes efforts to create, develop, and evolve its innovation ecosystems. However, some prioritize business dynamism over innovation capacity. Since both pillars must be developed in parallel to have a better result. On the other hand, although this work focuses on innovation ecosystems, it is important to point out that ecosystems must be accompanied by other factors that shield and ensure their permanent development as much as possible. Hence, comparing the ranking of innovation ecosystems with the Global

Table 2.9 Countries with the best performance in the development of innovation and entrepreneurship ecosystems in 2019

Pillar	Better performance	General indicator	Better performance	Detailed indicator	Better performance
Business dynamism	United States	Administrative requirements	United States	1. Cost to start a business	Multiple (1)
				2. Time to start a business	New Zealand
				3. Recovery rate	Japan
				4. Regulatory framework	Multiple (2)
		Business culture	Israel	1. Better attitudes to face business risk	Israel
				2. Skills to delegate authority	Denmark
				3. Growth of innovative companies	Israel
				4. Companies with better adoptions of disruptive ideas	Israel
Innovation capacity	Germany	Interaction and diversity	Singapore	1. Workforce diversity	Singapore
				2. Cluster status and development	Italy
				3. International co-inventions	Multiple (3)
				4. Multi-stakeholder collaboration	Israel
		Research and development	Japan	1. Scientific publications	Multiple (4)
				2. Number of patents	Multiple (5)
				3. Expenditure on research and development	Multiple (6)
				4. Better educational institutions involved in the innovation cycle	Multiple (7)
		Marketing	Luxembourg	1. Sophistication in the buyer experience	Republic of Korea
				2. Trademark creation	Multiple (8)

Source: Author (2021), taken from the global competitiveness report of the World Economic Forum (Klaus, 2019). Multiple (1): United States, New Zealand, and Japan; Multiple (2): United States and Japan; Multiple (3): Singapore and Israel; Multiple (4): Germany and Japan; Multiple (5): Germany, Japan, United States, Canada; Multiple (6): China, Germany, and the United States; Multiple (7): Switzerland, Sweden, Germany, Israel, and the United States; Multiple (8): Luxembourg, Germany, Israel, Sweden, and the United States

Table 2.10 Ranking of innovation and entrepreneurship ecosystems by country worldwide 2019

Ranking – innovation ecosystems (EI)					
ID	Country	Business dynamism	Innovation capacity	Ranking of EI[a]	Global Competitiveness Index
1	United States of America	1	2	1.50	2
2	Germany	5	1	3.00	7
3	Sweden	6	5	5.50	8
4	Netherlands	2	10	6.00	4
5	Denmark	3	11	7.00	10
6	United Kingdom	9	8	8.50	9
7	Finland	7	12	9.50	11
8	Israel	4	15	9.50	20
9	Japan	17	7	12.00	6
10	Taiwan, China	20	4	12.00	12
11	Switzerland	22	3	12.50	5
12	Singapore	14	13	13.50	1
13	Canada	12	16	14.00	14
14	Iceland	8	23	15.50	26
15	Ireland	10	21	15.50	24
16	Korea	25	6	15.50	13
17	Norway	11	20	15.50	17
18	France	24	9	16.50	15
19	Australia	16	18	17.00	16
20	Belgium	19	17	18.00	22
21	New Zealand	13	27	20.00	19
22	Hong Kong	15	26	20.50	3
23	Austria	30	14	22.00	21
24	Malaysia	18	30	24.00	27
25	Slovenia	26	28	27.00	35
26	Portugal	28	31	29.50	34
27	Spain	34	25	29.50	23
28	China	36	24	30.00	28
29	Czech Republic	32	29	30.50	32
30	Estonia	27	34	30.50	31
31	Luxembourg	42	19	30.50	18
32	United Arab Emirates	31	33	32.00	25
33	Italy	43	22	32.50	30
34	Thailand	21	50	35.50	40
35	Qatar	39	38	38.50	29
36	Cyprus	37	43	40.00	44
37	Russian Federation	53	32	42.50	43

(continued)

Table 2.10 (continued)

Ranking – innovation ecosystems (EI)					
ID	Country	Business dynamism	Innovation capacity	Ranking of EI[a]	Global Competitiveness Index
38	Lithuania	45	42	43.50	39
39	Azerbaijan	23	68	45.50	58
40	Mexico	41	52	46.50	48
41	Latvia	40	54	47.00	41
42	Poland	59	39	49.00	37
43	Slovak Republic	55	44	49.50	42
44	Chile	47	53	50.00	33
45	Indonesia	29	74	51.50	50
46	India	69	35	52.00	68
47	South Africa	60	46	53.00	60
48	Brazil	67	40	53.50	71
49	Mauritius	38	70	54.00	52
50	Bulgaria	61	48	54.50	49
51	Seychelles	64	45	54.50	76
52	Malta	73	37	55.00	38
53	Bahrain	48	65	56.50	45
54	Brunei Darussalam	62	51	56.50	56
55	Oman	56	57	56.50	53
56	Serbia	54	59	56.50	72
57	Jamaica	33	83	58.00	80
58	Philippines	44	72	58.00	64
59	Armenia	57	62	59.50	69
60	Montenegro	50	69	59.50	73
61	Greece	76	47	61.50	59
62	Hungary	83	41	62.00	47
63	Turkey	75	49	62.00	61
64	Colombia	49	77	63.00	57
65	Romania	72	55	63.50	51
66	Barbados	66	63	64.50	77
67	Kenya	51	78	64.50	95
68	Kazakhstan	35	95	65.00	55
69	Pakistan	52	79	65.50	110
70	Argentina	80	56	68.00	83
71	Jordan	88	54	71.00	70
72	Saudi Arabia	109	36	72.50	36
73	Ukraine	85	60	72.50	85
74	Rwanda	46	100	73.00	100
75	Georgia	58	91	74.50	74

(continued)

Table 2.10 (continued)

Ranking – innovation ecosystems (EI)					
ID	Country	Business dynamism	Innovation capacity	Ranking of EI[a]	Global Competitiveness Index
76	Uruguay	82	67	74.50	54
77	Costa Rica	92	58	75.00	62
78	Morocco	71	81	76.00	75
79	Panama	77	75	76.00	66
80	Sri Lanka	70	84	77.00	84
81	Egypt	95	61	78.00	93
82	North Macedonia	65	97	81.00	82
83	Guinea	81	82	81.50	122
84	Vietnam	89	76	82.50	67
85	Tunisia	74	92	83.00	87
86	Dominican Republic	86	85	85.50	78
87	Albania	63	110	86.50	81
88	Nigeria	79	94	86.50	116
89	Croatia	101	73	87.00	63
90	Trinidad and Tobago	87	87	87.00	79
91	Lebanon	110	66	88.00	88
92	Moldova	68	109	88.50	86
93	Joy	93	86	89.50	89
94	Paraguay	97	90	93.50	65
95	Ivory Coast	84	104	94.00	118
96	Ghana	102	89	95.50	111
97	Guatemala	96	98	97.00	98
98	Senegal	99	96	97.50	114
99	Namibia	116	80	98.00	94
100	Mongolia	108	93	100.50	102
101	Kuwait	94	108	101.00	46
102	Uganda	91	111	101.00	115
103	Botswana	104	99	101.50	91
104	Iran	132	71	101.50	99
105	Zambia	90	115	102.50	120
106	Kyrgyz Republic	78	129	103.50	96
107	Honduras	103	106	104.50	101
108	Nepal	98	112	105.00	108
109	Cameroon	112	103	107.50	123
110	Ecuador	130	88	109.00	90
111	Tajikistan	100	120	110.00	104

(continued)

Table 2.10 (continued)

Ranking – innovation ecosystems (EI)					
ID	Country	Business dynamism	Innovation capacity	Ranking of EI[a]	Global Competitiveness Index
112	Benin	105	116	110.50	125
113	Gambia	118	107	112.50	124
114	Bangladesh	121	105	113.00	105
115	Mali	113	113	113.00	129
116	Cambodia	127	102	114.50	106
117	Tanzania	107	123	115.00	117
118	El Salvador	111	121	116.00	103
119	Bosnia and Herzegovina	117	117	117.00	92
120	Burundi	106	135	120.50	135
121	Venezuela	140	101	120.50	133
122	Gabon	128	114	121.00	119
123	Madagascar	114	131	122.50	132
124	Nicaragua	123	122	122.50	109
125	Ethiopia	131	118	124.50	126
126	Bolivia	126	124	125.00	107
127	Mozambique	125	125	125.00	137
128	Malawi	124	127	125.50	128
129	Paraguay	115	137	126.00	97
130	Eswatini	119	134	126.50	121
131	Burkina Faso	122	133	127.50	130
132	Zimbabwe	129	126	127.50	127
133	Lao People's Democratic Republic	137	119	128.00	113
134	Lesotho	120	138	129.00	131
135	Mauritania	135	128	131.50	134
136	Cape Verde	133	132	132.50	112
137	Yemen	136	130	133.00	140
138	Chad	139	136	137.50	141
139	Congo, Democratic Representative	134	141	137.50	139
140	Angola	138	140	139.00	136
141	Haiti	141	139	140.00	138

Source: Author (2021), based on the global competitiveness report 2019 (Klaus, The Global Competitiveness Report, 2019), which includes a total of 141 countries

[a]The calculation of the ranking of innovation ecosystems presented in Table 2.8. was generated from the percentage of representation that according to the report was considered for the pillars of business dynamism and innovation capacity. Scale from 0 to 141, where 1 is the highest ranking and 141 the worst ranking

Competitiveness Index, it is more than 50% different, and this is due to the fact that some countries accompany the development of ecosystems with the development and improvement of other pillars such as infrastructure, adoption of *ICT*, macroeconomic stability, capital skills human, health, institutions, and security, among other areas, in order to support and monitor their evolution. For example, the case of Switzerland, Singapore, and Hong Kong where their *Global Competitiveness Index (GCI)* is much better than the EI ranking, opposite to the case of Israel and Iceland, where they have a better ranking of EI in comparison with the IGC. Even so, these countries occupy positions within the top ten of both indicators, and this suggests that the rest of the countries should work on *IE* in a comprehensive manner. This can be seen in Table 2.10 and Fig. 2.14, where the disparity is considerable in some countries between the ranking and the GCI.

According to Table 2.10 and Fig. 2.15, a sample of countries is presented where it can be identified that they give higher priority to one of the two pillars, be it business dynamism or innovation capacity. There are cases such as Saudi Arabia, Iran, and Lebanon where they give higher priority to the development of innovation capacity over business dynamism. On the other hand, the case of Jamaica, the Kyrgyz Republic, Rwanda, and Kazakhstan gives priority to business dynamism over innovation capacity. In this sense, it is suggested that countries try to balance the development of both pillars for a better result.

As mentioned in previous sections, countries are becoming linked and making agreements among themselves, to promote and accelerate the growth, development, and evolution of innovation and entrepreneurship ecosystems, where they take advantage of research, results, and technology transfers, and they share their experiences, information, and innovation processes, which in the medium and long term results in the development of their ecosystems in an international context. However, at the national level, they develop one pillar more than another.

Fig. 2.14 EI vs GCI Ranking Comparison 2019. Source: Author (2021), taken from Table 2.10

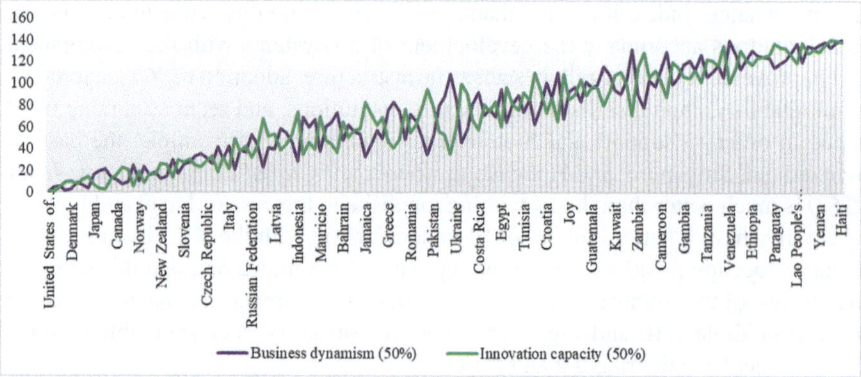

Fig. 2.15 Comparison of business dynamism vs innovation capacity 2019. (Source: Author (2021), from Table 2.10)

Table 2.11 Regional ranking of innovation ecosystems 2019

Region	Business dynamism	Capacity for innovation	Ranking[a]
Europe and North America	68.3	58.1	63.2
East Asia and the Pacific	66.1	54	60.05
East and North Africa	58.2	41.3	49.75
Euro Asia	61.9	35.5	48.70
South Asia	57.8	36.3	47.05
Latin America and the Caribbean	53.8	34.3	44.05
Sub-Saharan Africa	51.8	29.4	40.60

Source: Author (2021), taken from the global competitiveness report (2019), which includes seven regions

[a]The calculation of the ranking of innovation ecosystems presented in Table 2.9 was generated from the percentage of representation according to the report. It was considered for the pillars of business dynamism and innovation capacity. Scale of 0–100, where 100 is the highest ranking and 0 the worst ranking

This can be seen in Table 2.11 and Fig. 2.16 where the seven study regions develop entrepreneurial dynamism with greater impetus than innovation capacity. You can see regions marked as Euro Asia, South Asia, Latin America-the Caribbean, and South Sahara Africa where there is an important difference between business dynamism and innovation capacity, and on the other hand, Europe-North America and East of Asia Pacific, while developing more business dynamism, try to balance the capacity for innovation.

Finally, making a retrospective analysis of the progress of each region from 2016 to 2019 (see Figs. 2.17 and 2.18) on business dynamism, it can be observed that the

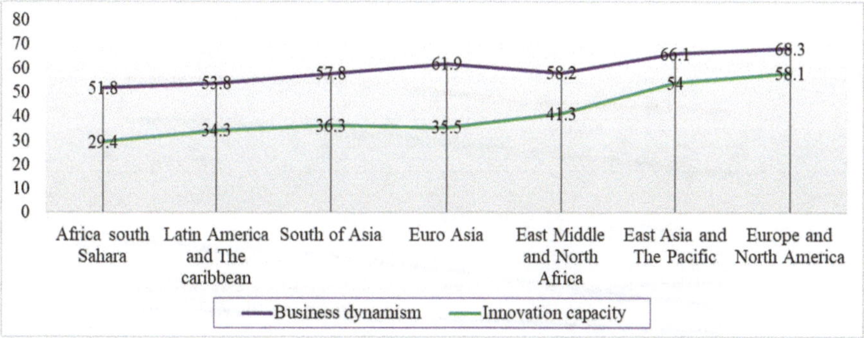

Fig. 2.16 Regional comparison of business dynamism vs innovation capacity. Source: Author (2021), taken from Table 2.11

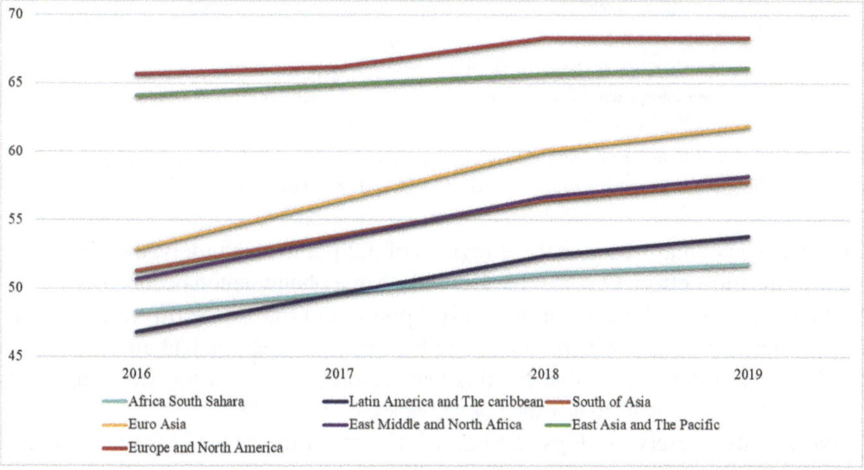

Fig. 2.17 Regional behavior of the business dynamism of 2016–2019. Source: Author (2021), taken from the global competitiveness reports of 2016–2019 (Klaus, 2016, 2017, 2018, 2019)

regions with the best scores are progressing more and more than the leading regions, for example, Euro Asia advanced 9 points, Latin America-Caribbean advanced 8 points, Middle East-North Africa 8 points, South Asia 7 points, and South Africa-Sahara 5 points, representing an average advance of 7.4 points. While the leading regions have advanced an average of 2.5 points, the case of East Asia-Pacific advanced 2 points and Europe-North America advanced approximately 3 points. We certainly see that the lagging regions have made little more than twice as much progress as the leading regions.

On the other hand, in relation to innovation capacity (a pillar that all regions develop less in relation to business dynamism), several situations are observed. The region that had a decline was South Asia with minus 2 points, while the Middle East-North Africa advanced 8 points and South Africa-Sahara advanced 5 points. Finally, Euro Asia advanced 3 points and Latin America-the Caribbean 2 points.

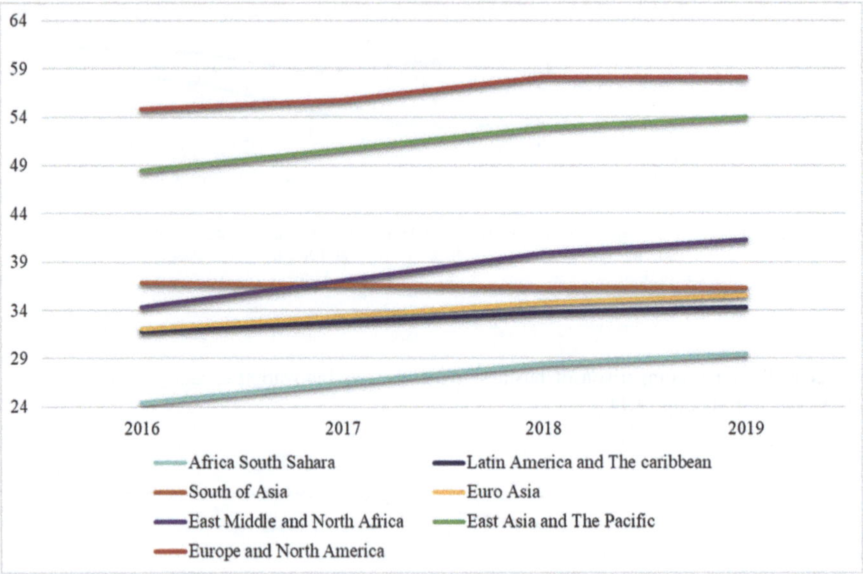

Fig. 2.18 Regional behavior of innovation capacity from 2016 to 2019. Source: Author (2021), taken from the global competitiveness reports of 2016–2019 (Klaus, 2016, 2017, 2018, 2019)

The advance is on average for these regions of 3.2 points. Definitely, the pillar that requires the most effort. On the other hand, the same phenomenon occurs in the East Asia Pacific region whose advance is only 2 points and Europe-North America with an advance of 3 points, which on average for these two regions had an advance of 2.5. It is important to note that for this last region (Europe-North America) from 2018 to 2019, there was no advance or setback (see Fig. 2.18).

We can also observe in Figs. 2.17 and 2.18 that in the capacity for innovation, there is an important gap between the leading regions and the rest of the regions, where they continue to maintain an average of just over 15 points of difference. Another important factor to consider is that in both pillars (business dynamism and innovation capacity) in some regions, they are below 40 points and others below 60 and 70. Although an effort is observed in all regions, it is still necessary to continue improving, building, generating alliances, and strengthening the ecosystems of innovation and entrepreneurship, having better results when they are developed in an integral way.

2.4 Past, Present, and Future of Innovation and Entrepreneurship Ecosystems

Innovation ecosystems have their origin in the *Massachusetts Institute of Technology (MIT)* where Jay Forrester (1958), who perceived that business and the economy throughout the world are all cyclical feedback systems that can be modeled and understood as analogs or electrical diagrams with feedback loops.

The dynamics of the systems was used by Meadows et al. (1972) in the book *The Limits of Growth* to show why without restrictions or rules (rules of the game), global economic growth cannot be sustained. Sterman (2007) shows how competitive firms can be successfully modeled as a cyclical interdependent feedback system. Countries are companies too, and the innovation aspects of the national company system can also be successfully modeled using system dynamics.

On the other hand, the *OECD* (1997) in its report on "national innovation ecosystems" indicates that the approach of national innovation systems highlights that the flows of technology and information between people, enterprises, and institutions are key to the innovation process. Innovation and technological development are the result of a complex set of relationships between the actors in the system, which includes enterprises, universities, and research institutes. This report shows the point made to those responsible for formulating policies as a core part of the proper functioning of said innovation ecosystem, to improve the understanding of the national innovation system, and the said policies can collaborate in identifying points of influence to improve innovative performance and overall competitiveness. From the above, the policies seek to improve work and ensure order, collaboration, and equitable results where ecosystem actors and institutions intervene and that aim to improve the innovative capacity of enterprises, in particular their ability to identify and absorb technologies.

About to the *present of ecosystems*, today, innovation is part of government strategies, which form the basis for building a strengthened economy. In the case of the European Union, it proposes transforming the member countries, based on the knowledge economy. To do this, they have created areas of knowledge for this purpose, following the idea of clusters, technology parks, and poles of competitiveness. The same case is presented by France when it is part of the European Union. However, there is a risk of decentralizing knowledge, which generates knowledge losses and a change of leadership toward the countries, which they often imitate without having the knowledge. Faced with these difficulties, many companies have reduced or stopped their investments in the research and development sector.

The rest of the world has not been left behind. In the case of the United States, Finland, Ireland, Sweden, and Switzerland, being the leading countries according to the *World Intellectual Property Organization (WIPO)* (2020), they continue to make important efforts for the construction of competitiveness pillars, in which they integrate innovation as indicated in Table 2.12.

According to Table 2.12, the contribution of innovation to economic development depends on the pillar of business evolution (competitiveness), infrastructure, and institutions to protect the intellectual property of the market. Under these pillars, the United States attributes business innovation to university systems and the joint work they do together. In this sense, education is essential, as well as its main actors (students and teachers) who mobilize learning toward innovation and accelerate technology transfer and competitiveness, promoting creativity, the culture of entrepreneurship, having access to *ICT* and *artificial intelligence (AI)* (Mercier-Laurent, 2015).

Table 2.12 Pillars of competitiveness

Pillars	Key factors
Basic requirements: Institutions Infrastructure Macroeconomic environment Health and primary education	Boosting the economy
Efficiency enhancers Higher education and training Efficiency in the goods market Efficiency in the labor market Development in the money market Technological preparation Market size	Efficiency-driven economies
Innovation and sophisticated factors (creativity) Business sophistication Innovation	Innovation-driven economics

Source: Author (2021), taken from the 12 competitiveness pillars (Mercier-Laurent, 2015)

In the case of Japan, another leading country in innovation ecosystems is located among the first countries at the forefront according to the *OECD* (2021) and the World Intellectual property organization (2020). It has rebuilt its economy based on innovation applied to nanotechnology and computing, notably translating into the domain of computer science worldwide. It emphasizes the expansion of education and its collaboration with culture, and it also includes the coordination between public and private research to encourage competitiveness, which allows creating balanced policies to make innovation grow. The above is not simple, since it requires according to Mercier-Laurent (2015) to reformulate the meaning of technological renewal and reorganization in management. The said reformulation includes the adoption and creation of new technologies and different ways of thinking, to create technology that contribute to development. Japan emphasizes innovation as a strategy for the future, which is why they have prioritized innovation in medicine, science and *IT*, environmental science, nanoscience, nanotechnology, energy, social infrastructure, space science, and the study of oceans.

The case of Switzerland is one of the most important countries in innovation ecosystems behind Sweden according to the *World Intellectual Property Organization* (*WIPO*) (2020), the *Organization for Economic Cooperation and Development* (*OECD*) (2021), and the *European Innovation Scoreboard (EIS)* (2021). For these organizations, the role of public and private higher-level research institutions is of utmost importance.

The following stand out as a strength of the Swiss innovation ecosystem:

- Industrial structure and innovation
- The growth of large enterprises
- Gradual increase in the innovation capacity of small enterprises
- Globally recognized academic research
- Professional education focused on its application and on the intercultural environment

It is worth highlighting the development of financing programs to promote the culture of innovation, as well as its promotion. This coupled with the regulatory adjustment to facilitate said impulse and prepare young people for entrepreneurship, taking education and training as pillars, combined with laws that favor not only the creation of businesses but also guarantee sustainability.

Regarding the *future of innovation ecosystems*, they are in continuous development, growth, and evolution, seeking with greater emphasis that innovation and sustainable development collaborate with the environment, to the extent of creating eco-innovation programs by the European Union (European Commission, 2020), whereas core points are creativity and innovation, to dynamize the actors in a systematic way, adding up the research to make a real impact on the economy. However, there are challenges ahead to be able to dynamically transition from an invention (new product, improvements, methods, and concepts) developed by scientists to an applied innovation that can be placed on the market. On the other hand, with a view to the future of ecosystems, the issue of entrepreneurship requires taking risks, where the role of the government is paramount with initiatives that encourage researchers to create their own enterprises. However, unfortunately most prefer to continue their research in laboratories or classrooms.

An opportunity for improvement in education, found in universities, is in the lack of initiatives or programs to encourage students to be entrepreneurs and researchers as a significant activity, with the aim of obtaining results that transform products. It was possible to transfer technology to the enterprises. To get from an invention, patent, or copyright to the market, it is complicated since generally 20 years pass between the generation of the invention and its application. To improve this time, capital and knowledge are required. This is through the leap of researchers to materialize their inventions in a company, but it is required to accelerate and increase the degree of success, through collaboration between universities-researchers and universities-private initiative. An example is what they do in American enterprises, where their inventions are not exploited immediately. They first pass the knowledge and make collaboration agreements with specialized research institutions, to enhance and improve the invention, as well as discover new products/services and methodologies derived. This link promotes the acceleration of inventions and their commercialization (Mercier-Laurent, 2015).

On the other hand, the European Commission (2020) in the 2019–2020 report on robust innovation ecosystems for the future of Europe presents the results of the consultation carried out with representatives of innovation ecosystems, investors, corporations, universities-*research and technology organizations (RTO)*, cities, agencies, and national innovation ministries. The objective was to collect information to build the future of innovation and entrepreneurship ecosystems, funding programs for research and innovation, considering greater inclusiveness, diversity, and better connection channels.

The results are presented in Table 2.13 where the following recommendations are made.

Finally, continuing with the future of innovation ecosystems, in the case of Canada, it created a program called superclusters accompanied by regional innovation ecosystems. Superclusters are areas of frequent business activity formed by enterprises, universities, and civil society organizations whose main objective is to promote innovation and growth in the industry, something like Silicon Valley (Government of Canada, 2021a, b). Each supercluster worldwide is unique, and in these, the following actors interact:

- Small and large enterprises
- Researchers and academics
- Nonprofit civil organizations
- Accelerators and incubators

The Canadian-designed supercluster encourages entrepreneurs, small- and medium-sized businesses, and commercial institutions to collaborate on large-scale projects, to accelerate growth in some of the most promising industries such as:

- Digital technologies
- Vegetable proteins
- Advanced manufacturing
- Improved use of artificial intelligence in supply chains
- Oceans

It is important to note that as these industries grow and their ecosystems strengthen, they become global companies, resulting in the development and growth of the Canadian economy by creating jobs and attracting investment and talent to Canada. Alternatively, the said supercluster helps in (Government of Canada, 2018):

1. Connectivity to hundreds of collaborators to solve industry challenges, as well as develop strong supply chains or properly manage data
2. Attraction of talent, research, capital, and new companies helping to establish themselves in Canada
3. Innovation in the global market with new products and processes
4. Growth of more productive industries, healthier ecosystems, more jobs, and success for companies in all industries
5. Empowerment of small- and medium-sized enterprises to accelerate their growth, and take advantage of their experience, facilitate the search for new markets and access to intellectual property.

Alternately and aligned with superclusters, the *regional innovation ecosystems (RIE)* cross-cutting program aims to create, grow, and nurture Canada's regional ecosystems that support business needs throughout the innovation and innovation

Table 2.13 Recommendations on robust innovation and entrepreneurship ecosystems

Section	Recommendations	Challenges
Connectivity	1. Support a structure and coordinate the network to encourage expansion.	Lack of organization to support European expansion Lack of aggregate stakeholder maps in each region Need to increase knowledge on how to internationalize inside and outside the European Union Increase cooperation between startups and universities
	2. Improve connectivity between corporations, universities, and *RTO*.	Lack of cooperation between industry and academia Lack of marketing-oriented research
	3. Improve connectivity between universities, *RTO*, startups, and accelerators.	Weak links between startups and academic
	4. Improve connectivity between startups and investors.	The fluid connection between startups and investments has not yet been achieved, as well as the lack of increasing their responsibilities within the ecosystem.
	5. Encourage and expand the functions and acquisitions of *Initial Public Offerings (IPO)* among startups and corporations.	Increase partnerships between corporate and startups. Increase the activity of functions and acquisitions. Increase the size of the offer of corporate and existing investments.
	6. Improve connectivity between cities and regions.	Improve collaborations and connectivity between cities, regions, cities, and transnationals. Improve the quality of existing cooperation programs and instruments.
	7. Improve connectivity between local public entities and local innovation stakeholders.	Strengthen connectivity among local actors to provide support for a comprehensive innovation ecosystem.
	8. Increase commitment to citizenship.	Citizens are the least involved in the innovation process in their locality. Increase inclusivity in innovation and entrepreneurship ecosystems.
	9. Empower national innovation agencies.	Lack of a unified and coordinated network of national innovation agencies Lack of standards for the creation and operation of national innovation agencies Weak flow of information on innovation and best practices from all regions Lack of trends on innovation globally
	10. Development of a European forum to improve coordination between all actors	Lack of coordination between cities, regions, and entities of the European Union Lack of cooperation between innovation actors Undocumented changes of various actors Lack of effective interactions on improved solutions

(continued)

Table 2.13 (continued)

Section	Recommendations	Challenges
Competence	1. Promote the culture of entrepreneurship in universities and research centers (*RTO*).	Lack of connectivity between academia and startups Little production of disruptive startups
	2. Increase social responsibility and diversity and advanced inclusive ethics and disruptive innovations.	Increase social responsibility. Prevent and minimize inequality and discrimination. Increase diversity and inclusion with a vision of innovation. Improve data on the impact of diversity on innovation ecosystems.
	3. Needs for better actionable information on all fronts	There is no monitoring of each actor's critical innovation indicators. There are no centralized databases that allow the monitoring of all innovation agents across Europe. There is no centralization and updating of information on the key indicators of each innovation ecosystem. There are no data for the diversity of key actors or instruments of the European Union.
	4. Lack of innovation capacities in public actors.	Public procedures not designed and thought from the perspective of innovation Low levels of innovation capabilities within the public administration
Capital	1. Maintain support from seed funds and accelerators in early stages.	Prevent seed capital crises and detection of innovation systems. Ensure the steady flow of potential investments that may include expansions in technologies related to space specializations. Sustain accelerators that can expand business training to all actors, not just startups.
	2. Reduce risk investment in innovative enterprises.	Reduce the risk of investments in experimental and disruptive innovations. Encourage frontier investments and development of cutting-edge enterprises.
	3. Increase the identification of partnerships between corporations and startups.	Reduce friction/complications between corporations and startups. There is the misalignment of goals between corporations and startups. Lack of activity in procurement.
	4. Lack of funding in critical areas of innovation.	Some actors lack financial support to drive innovative activities.
	5. Increase knowledge and startup in startups to improve expansion or scaling procedures.	Weak knowledge of closing processes. Low number of progressive increases in international European startups. Reduced number of escalations even internationally.

Section	Recommendations	Challenges
Cross-cutting actions	1. Reduce the regulatory burden.	Conflict of access to *EU* instruments Lack of synergy between the instruments Increase or attract talent to innovation ecosystems.
	2. Controlled environment of European regulations	Lack of information about the use and impact of controlled regulatory environments Lack of a regulatory framework that allows experimentation with experimental technological innovations
	3. Stimulate the hiring of public servants for innovation	Few public procurements designed for innovation actors Lack of knowledge on how to design public procurement of innovation Fragmented, restricted, and incomplete information on public procurement of innovation

Source: Author (2021), taken from the report 2019–2020 of the European Commission (2020)

process and foster a business environment conducive to innovation, growth, and competitiveness. The *RIE* pursues the following objectives (Government of Canada, 2021a, b):

1. Support the growth of strategic clusters to take advantage of regional strengths and help enterprises to market products, technologies, and services.
2. Improve the development and reach of business accelerators and incubators and other organizations that support entrepreneurs, startups, and companies with high growth potential.
3. Support projects led by innovation-oriented organizations to increase and promote business productivity and global competitiveness, investment, and talent attraction.
4. Improve the capacity of ecosystems to support different groups of actors without distinction of gender, indigenous peoples, and young entrepreneurs.

The projects supported and funded by the *RIE* are:

5. Technological commercialization, growth, and business development
6. Improved productivity
7. Strengthening the capacity of innovation ecosystems
8. Business incubation and acceleration

2.5 Entities That Operate the Ecosystem of Innovation and Entrepreneurship

In an innovation ecosystem-entrepreneurship, different actors intervene; however, there is one that takes the leadership role and is in charge of operating the ecosystem (in this work, it is called *EOE*). In collaboration with this, all actors carry out activities entrusted to them, seen as a system in which each actor is part of a subsystem with a particular objective, which together fulfill the main objective and where the lack of weakness of a subsystem complicates or delays the scope of the main objective (Bertalanffy, 1969), hence the importance of each actor within the ecosystem to carry out their work satisfactorily.

In this sense, according to Komorowski (2019), the existence of leading entities within the ecosystem that oversee operating it in coordination and collaboration with the rest of the actors is observed. He also points out the diversity of these actors, where their intervention may be very broad or limited, depending on the degree of maturity, specialization and evolution of each ecosystem, and the way it is organized.

A clear example is the following *EOE*:

- Government entities
- Universities through technology parks, or innovation parks
- Private enterprises whose role is binding and/or manager
- Social associations/nonprofit social organizations
- Networks and communities
- Accelerators
- Among others

In this way, we have various *EOE* with different roles such as managing agents, operatives, intermediaries, stakeholders, trainers, mentors, commercial agents, and strategic agents, among others.

To exemplify the roles of some *EOE*, Table 2.14 is presented.

Now, to know the role that the *EOE* will play in each ecosystem, it depends to a large extent on:

Table 2.14 Entities that operate ecosystems of innovation and entrepreneurship

Country	*EOE* name	Role
United States	Oxford University Innovation (Oxford University, 2021)	Manages capital through investments Provides access to consulting services Support in the generation of new entrepreneurships
New Zealand	Twente Technology Fund (University of Twente, 2021)	Capitalization for startups with technological developments Commercial support on products and technologies in the clean energy, nanotechnology, *ICT*, and biomedical technology sectors It specializes in startups in early stages, which go through a commercial phase. Assessment of academic products with entrepreneurial potential
United States	Technological innovation center (Deshpande Center for Technological Innovation, 2021)	Provides assistance and mentoring to academic members (teachers, students, researchers) whose work is feasible to create a startup with the potential to benefit society, transform markets and industries, and improve people's quality of life
Switzerland	ETH Zurich (ETH Zurich, 2021)	Promotes the development of results derived from research Commercially develop the products derived from the ecosystem, through the creation of a new company They seek that the enterprises that are established have a social relevance. Offers mentoring and advisory services to entrepreneurs

(continued)

Table 2.14 (continued)

Country	*EOE* name	Role
Japan	Strategic organization of open innovation (University of Tsukuba, 2021).	Promotes an interprofessional research system and expands collaborative research Interacts with faculties and research groups of the university in the search for innovation, collaboration, and entrepreneurial ideas originated in the classrooms Collaborates in guiding projects that promote social change and long-term care of the environment They integrate nine fields of specialties aligned to the university's programs. Collaborate with projects with industry and the university Collaborates with international projects between universities and productive sectors
Australia	AplusB Scale-up in Austria (Austria Wirtschaftsservice Gesellschaft mbH (aws), 2021)	Works in conjunction with six incubators to support new entrepreneurship projects from their academic environment to the pre-seed stage and initial stages of operation Collaborates with enterprises and academic institutions in the region Provides funding support to new companies during the preparation of the venture Collaborates with the linking of teams and networks of experts to collaborate with entrepreneurship projects before and after the startup begins Works in conjunction with the Australian Federal Ministry to enrich and support the ecosystem
Israel	T3 Technion Entrepreneur (Technion University, 2020)	Introduces businessmen and entrepreneurs to a research environment Works in conjunction with the technology transfer office to identify promising technologies when starting startups He spends several months on entrepreneurship programs to discover business ideas and start startups. For this, he interacts with various expert areas, students, and citizens of the region that participates. Provides support to enrich your marketing processes Develop programs to provide support to entrepreneurs for three months to develop their ideas and business strategies to refine the business concept
European Union	EIC Accelerator (European Commission, 2021)	Supports projects from their pilot phase to their market launch It funds projects based on combined financing between public and private initiative with the aim of accelerating the growth of innovative European companies.
Canada	MaRS Discovery District (MaRS, 2021)	Offers infrastructure services and services oriented to new enterprises, including networking and consulting with experts depending on the sector Offers physical spaces for enterprises to carry out research in conjunction with other companies and universities in the region

(continued)

Table 2.14 (continued)

Country	*EOE* name	Role
Canada	Tecconnect, RINSA, and WESTEM (Tecconnect Entrepreneur Program, 2021), (WESTEM, 2021)	Tecconnect: Ecosystem that encourages and supports entrepreneurs in the region to start and grow their business within an innovative and supportive environment. It is a space and a community that encourages the development of new ideas that transform industries and shape the future. RINSA: It is an association belonging to Lethbridge College, Economic Development Lethbridge, Blood Tribe Economic Development, and the University of Lethbridge, with the support of Community Futures Lethbridge Region, South Grow Regional Initiative, Alberta Southwest Regional Alliance, and The *National Research Council of Canada Industrial Research Assistance Program (NRC-IRAP).* Collaborates with the development of support programs for innovation, technology transfer, and commercialization Offer marketing, business development, training, and export development services Assists in developing business incubation, matchmaking, and networking opportunities Manages and links enterprises for financing in various stages (angel investment, venture capital) Manages financing through Community Futures loan services for startup and/or expansion WESTEM: The Women Entrepreneurs-in-STEM (WESTEM) program supports and empowers all women entrepreneurs in southern Alberta. She specializes in working with professional women and supports them to incorporate emerging technologies into their businesses. Through this program, training, networking, mentoring, and access to current and emerging technologies are offered. The Women Entrepreneurs-in-STEM (WESTEM) program focuses on promoting gender, rural-urban, and racial equality in entrepreneurship. This is accomplished by supporting underrepresented women in rural and remote regions of southern Alberta and creating a highly collaborative and streamlined female-based community and network. Specific support is offered to WESTEM participants on the needs of women entrepreneurs through partnerships with women entrepreneurs, business advisers, business leaders, mentors, business organizations, and postsecondary institutions.

(continued)

Table 2.14 (continued)

Country	*EOE* name	Role
Denmark	DTU Tech Transfer (DTU-dk, 2021)	Specialized in providing financing in all stages of entrepreneurship, from its ideation to the search for growth and development. It offers a wide portfolio of financing programs depending on the startup, amount, performance, and age of the enterprise.
Ireland	Enterprise Ireland (Enterprise Ireland, 2021)	*EOE* specialized in collaborating with increasing the digital capabilities of enterprises in the region to grow to international markets Links and manages resources and experts to achieve the digital modernization of startups Offers collaborative support to encourage the creation of new startups Manages and links new companies with direct clients Support in the commercialization of the product, as well as research services aimed at the growth of the enterprises and the generation of patents and improvements to the products or services of said company Offer funding to enterprises that want to grow in the market

Source: Author (2021), taken as reference to Kulicke (2020)

- Form of organization of the ecosystem
- Maturity level
- Scale of operation/size (local, regional, national, or international)
- Number of actors
- Volume of ventures
- Startups within the ecosystem in its different stages of growth and development
- Sectors of specialization
- Among others

However, it is important that all stakeholders are aware and have identified the objective, goals, and strategies, since as the ecosystem grows and develops, its operation will be more complex. This will allow adjustments in its attributions to allow the evolution of the ecosystem. On the other hand, after the experience of *EOE*, those whose origin and leadership is from a university, it brings with it different benefits such as (Kulicke, 2020):

- Encourages the culture of entrepreneurship and commercialization
- It encourages the financing of new enterprises and gives certainty and viability to entrepreneurship projects.
- Ensures support through its infrastructure
- Exponentially increases knowledge and its appropriation
- Significantly increase the quality of investigations
- Increases technology transfer and continues with the production of quality labor and improves entrepreneurship opportunities
- Creates new skills for the actors involved and improves their institutional infrastructure

- Increase the creation of business units through technology transfer
- Universities are the source for creating entrepreneurship skills.
- Supports the birth of new paradigms
- Collaborates with the development of the regional social environment

Finally, it is important to note that regardless of the *EOE* that assumes leadership and operates the ecosystem, it must consider its scope and limitations, to distribute activities with the rest of the ecosystem actors.

2.6 The Role of Universities in Innovation and Entrepreneurship Ecosystems

Since this work focuses on innovation and entrepreneurship ecosystems, one of the central actors are universities, which are multifunctional for the ecosystem, which facilitates its development, growth, and evolution. According to the study carried out in nine universities in Europe by Sybille (2019), Aalto University, Finland; Masaryk University, Czech Republic; Sorbonne University, France; TU/e-Eindhoven University of Technology, The Netherlands; *Technical University of Munich (TUM)*, Germany; University of Manchester, *United Kingdom (UK)*; University of Minho, Portugal; University of Warsaw, Poland; *University Polytechnic of Catalonia (UPC)*, Spain, it showed, among other results, that the roles and expectations of the actors in the ecosystem have been transformed in recent years, which are summarized in seven changes, including paradigm shifts in the conception and organization of innovation. These changes are:

1. From linear to repetitive innovation: Universities and enterprises already view innovation as a process that goes from basic to applied research and is about to be commercialized. They also recognize and engage in innovation as an iterative process in which basic, applied research, and prototype development can be stimulated and improved on each other and multiple times in a cooperative process.
2. From closed to open innovation: Open innovation enhances the role of universities. Given the increasing complexity of technological development and innovation acceleration cycles, enterprises have adopted new models of open innovation that include external partners.
3. From technological innovation to challenge-driven systemic: Innovation approaches are growing to include technological, social, and economic innovation on a common agenda, where universities play a central role in the breadth and depth of research and education.
4. From individual to collaborative and interdisciplinary innovation: With increasing specialization, digitization, and hybrid technologies, collaborative interdisciplinary research and development become a necessity where stakeholders find the most important in the role of university in innovation and its ability to "incubate interdisciplinary research" and to educate interdisciplinary thinking and its competencies.

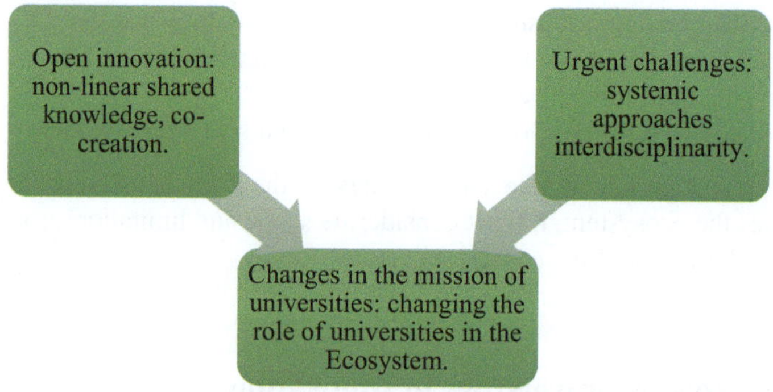

Fig. 2.19 Innovation and the change of role in universities within ecosystems. Source: Author (2021), taken from the role of universities in innovation ecosystems (Sybille, 2019)

5. From spontaneous to systematic innovation: All the actors of the triple helix (university, government, and companies) develop innovation in a systematic and strategic way. Government agencies are engaging universities, enterprises, and stakeholders in structured dialogues to identify, analyze, and exploit regional strengths and potentials, facilitating strategic specialization.
6. From innovation based on exchange to co-creation in innovation spaces: Innovation can evolve from exchange between independent actors. Now innovation becomes an interdependent co-creation between actors from different sectors and institutions. Researchers, innovators, and leaders of universities, enterprises, or public agencies are developing strengths, increasing their skills, and identifying regional challenges.
7. From innovation projects to common innovation cultures: In favor of co-creation through universities, intermediary agencies such as clusters or science parks and commercial partners guide relevant events to turn spaces into cultural poles of innovation, where innovation becomes a cultural practice.

As seen in Fig. 2.19, open innovation and urgent challenges guide the role changes in universities within innovation ecosystems. In this way, the university assumes and recognizes two roles: as an actor in the production of knowledge for competitiveness and as an entity that encourages the culture of innovation to facilitate interaction between the actors involved. To successfully achieve these roles, there are challenges, processes, and elements that contribute to universities. These elements are (Goldstein & Drucker, 2006):

- Culture of the ecosystem and human capital (intellectual capital)
- Knowledge production and support structures (financing, services, and infrastructures)
- Institutional and regional strategic processes
- Network communication channels and formats

To accompany and collaborate with the change of role in universities, two more actors are involved: the role of the government and the role of companies, which,

Table 2.15 Roles of universities to implement innovation and entrepreneurship ecosystems

A. Role of universities	B. The role of governments	C. The role of companies
Education: Provide human capital for innovation Research: Knowledge and coproduction for the creation of public and private value Knowledge exchange for innovation systems Strategic transformation: innovation implemented	Strategic Regulatory Financing Facilitator of innovation	Training School-work integration Integration to research projects

Source: Author (2021), taken from the change of roles and key factors in innovation ecosystems (Sybille, 2019)

according to Table 2.15, are on the way to facilitating innovation with the university role.

According to Table 2.15, there are three central roles: universities, government, and companies. To understand their performance a little more, they are detailed in the following topics. It is worth noting the existence of the fourth and fifth helix, which according to Carayannis and Campbell (2019) are the social economy and the protection of the environment that guide innovation, sustainable development, and economic growth. The integration of these propellers will give an opportunity to the production of knowledge and innovation, provided that the objectives are defined in the medium and long term, supported by the fifth propeller. For the purposes of this work, these propellers are included in the following chapters as indicators.

2.6.1 *Universities as the First Helix*

The role of universities as creators of knowledge in the postindustrial economies and societies of the twentieth century has built and endowed universities with a fundamental role in society. However, over time, this role as a natural center for the generation of knowledge has changed. Now the university is designed to direct, manage, link, and create innovation networks of multiple actors, accompanied by four dimensions (Adner, 2017; Sybille, 2019):

1. Education, Providing human capital for innovation. The central challenges are related to the quantity and relevant quality of "human capital/intellectual capital," the appropriate skills and competencies, to be able to identify the challenges and means to face them satisfactorily (see Fig. 2.20 and Table 2.16).

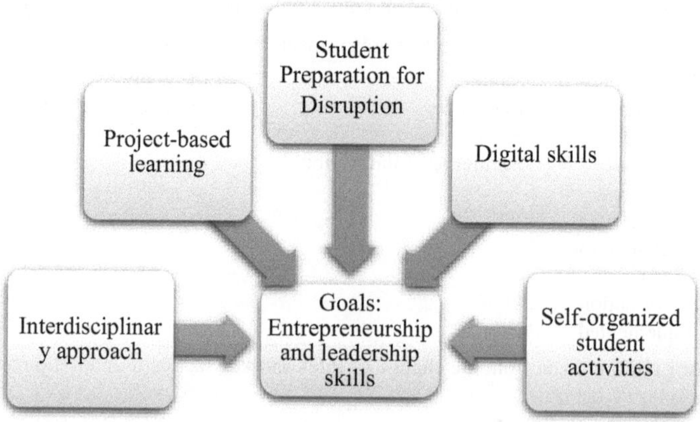

Fig. 2.20 Means and objectives for learning and education. Source: Author (2021), taken from the role of universities in regional innovation ecosystems (Sybille, 2019)

Table 2.16 Learning and teaching: needs, responses, and conditions of the framework

New needs related to the role of universities in innovation	Institutional responses from universities	Necessary conditions for the framework
Qualitative objectives	Teacher reforms	Regulation
Prepare and train for disruptive innovation. Promote systemic understanding and competencies. Create changes to the rules. Expand the research-related competencies that students do. Promote digital skills. Foster mindset and entrepreneurial skills.	Expand project-based interdisciplinary learning. Support students' self-organization. Improve teaching innovation services and resources. Expand coverage in tutoring, even by the stakeholders. Provide entrepreneurial modules, as an extra offer or integrated into the curriculum, grid, or programs of the academic offer. Develop digital skills modules. Encourage and support startups.	Autonomy of universities to introduce new study programs and design their content Sufficient academic autonomy of universities for the selection of students Sustainable financing to support student demand, enabling project-based learning, guidance on various learning paths, and mentoring

(continued)

Table 2.16 (continued)

New needs related to the role of universities in innovation	Institutional responses from universities	Necessary conditions for the framework
Qualitative objectives	Teacher reforms	Regulation
Quantitative objectives:	Diffusion	Regulator:
Broaden the competency base for localities, regions, and nations. Increase engagement in the academic area, particularly when it comes to digital knowledge. Increase continuous professional development for employers. Continuous training and improvement of competencies related to innovation	Work collaboratively with schools to promote entrepreneurial mindset and digital skills. Work with schools to update and develop teaching skills. Expand the offer of continuous professional development and act as points of contact to facilitate the access of enterprises to universities.	Sufficient financial autonomy of universities to finance professional development, through alternative funding flows Provide sufficient resources so that staff can provide the necessary support, and even generate their own resources. Provide financial incentives for continued professional development, in areas of need for innovation.

Source: Author (2021), taken from the role of universities in regional innovation ecosystems (Sybille, 2019)

Although education is a primary factor for innovation ecosystems and the quality of higher education, what competencies need to be optimized to enhance innovation? To determine these competencies according to Sybille (2019), the following is needed:

- Integrate multidisciplinary approaches into curricula and teaching methods.
- Prepare students to face the disruptive social, technological, and economic challenges of the future.
- Emphasis on project-based learning as a key ingredient of teaching methodologies and curricula with that which links theoretical learning with the solution of real problems in companies in the locality or region.
- Promote entrepreneurial skills and mindset, through additional modules, projects, or tutorials. Consider student self-organization ideas, team collaboration, and project-based learning.
- Consider the integration and expansion of digital skills in the study plans.
- Promotion of leadership skills and social responsibility of students
- Ensuring enough qualified graduates means that universities can provide the right to the development of the competencies, skills, and mentality of students.
- Carry out reforms that allow addressing innovation challenges where the alignment of learning and teaching should be the starting point.

2. Research, coproduction of knowledge for the creation of public and private value

   In this second dimension, the universities collaborate with the impulse of innovation, which consists of coproducing relevant knowledge. This is achieved by the university, which permanently seeks a balance between international, national, regional, and local research. Universities in their search for internationally competitive research that is also relevant to stakeholders and universities emphasize five important developments:

Table 2.17 Research: needs, responses, and framework conditions

New needs related to the role of universities in innovation	Institutional responses from universities	Necessary conditions for the framework
Produce relevant knowledge:	Support curiosity-driven research with long-term perspectives. Adapt the recruitment policy to combine excellence in research and impact criteria. Strategic partnerships with few companies and organizations, including the forecasting function Research contracted for specific solutions Research support service and business facilitation as a point of contact for enterprises Promote interdisciplinary networks. Create and moderate thematic groups that bring together various disciplines and institutions.	Regulation
In the short term: concrete solutions to current innovation problems In the long term: horizon of exploration of scientific and technological developments Co-create knowledge by connecting different actors to address the challenge of innovation in the various areas of knowledge.		Sufficient organizational and academic autonomy of universities to allow flexible interdisciplinary functions Support curiosity-driven research with sufficient funding sources. Support plans for university-business collaboration. Provide competitive medium-term support for the development of thematic groups.
Access to research infrastructures:	Strategic investment in public-private research infrastructures Provide long-term technical staff to support the infrastructure. Establish co-creation spaces and access to research facilities for outsiders.	Finance
Share state-of-the-art infrastructure. Access to technical facilities and equipment with technical support staff		Provide sufficient institutional financing for investment in infrastructure and technical personnel. Provide special competitive funding for large-scale research infrastructures.

Source: Author (2021), taken from the role of universities in regional innovation ecosystems (Sybille, 2019)

- Promote interdisciplinary collaboration in research to address the main challenges of innovation.
- Specialization on the different challenges
- Pursue innovation including social innovation.
- Significantly increase revenue for external research including industry research.
- Finding the balance between curiosity-driven research and usage-driven research.

To address this second dimension, Table 2.17 is presented, where the needs and solutions are appreciated.

3. Knowledge exchange for innovation systems: from technology transfer to multi-actor and co-creator.

To enhance knowledge sharing, universities should focus on six activities listed below (Sybille, 2019):

- Technology transfer, value creation, and intellectual property from university research
- Facilitate business innovation by facilitating the use of university research.
- Carry out collaborative research with enterprises.
- Build long-term strategic partnerships with enterprises.
- Support for the creation of companies (where the enterprises are derived from students and research).
- Offer multidisciplinary continuous training/professional development innovation courses for external stakeholders.

According to Table 2.18, it is possible to observe the needs that it is suggested to cover by the universities to progressively achieve the exchange and transfer of knowledge.

Table 2.18 Knowledge exchange and transfer: needs, responses, and conditions of the framework

Needs related to the role of universities in innovation	Institutional responses from universities	Necessary conditions for the framework
Facilitate joint innovation between universities, enterprises, and public organizations.	Create incentives to reward academic staff to participate in cooperation on external social impact. Create infrastructure in conjunction with external partners. Establish and use experts for the development of common agendas. Expand support services for research and entrepreneurship.	Regulation: Facilitate public-private partnerships to minimize regulatory hurdles and reduce the economic burden. Finance: Provide competitive support plans for research and creation of research structures. Provide sufficient funding for universities to be equal partners.
Create and protect intellectual property. Create new businesses with potential for innovation and growth.	Develop technology transfer and intellectual property services. Develop support services for startups and spaces for students and researchers. Link with external factors, such as startup services, science, and technology parks and funding agencies.	Regulatory and financial: Provide financial support for business creation and growth. Establish or support the establishment of venture capital.
Promote social innovation, including citizen participation.	Reward commitment to social innovation.	Create financial incentives to reward research and teaching commitment to social innovation.

Source: Author (2021), taken from the role of universities in regional innovation ecosystems (Sybille, 2019)

4. Strategic transformation and innovation implemented

In its constant evolution, innovation should be linked to an agenda of progressive transformation of development; hence, among the central institutional processes, universities seek links between research developments with high potential and the innovation priorities of each country. This serves as a guide so that universities are aware of the importance that the development of their infrastructure can play in fostering the dynamics of innovation. Such infrastructure development includes investments in state-of-the-art research facilities that attract innovators, as well as infrastructures that allow the construction of co-creation nuclei between a. researchers-enterprises, b. university entrepreneurs-researchers-enterprises, and c. university entrepreneurs-researchers. In this sense, the development of knowledge co-creation spaces generates networks and platforms where creativity and knowledge creation can flourish to the point of becoming an increasingly important dimension of university development and of the innovation ecosystem itself, entrepreneurship. Examples that derive from university development as a search for co-creation spaces are entrepreneurship ecosystems, research enterprises, technology parks, innovation, and incubators. Hence, entrepreneurship ecosystems are perhaps the most successful and comprehensive ecosystem with the possibility of evolving, given the actors and conditions they present. With all this, these spaces acquire a crucial role in promoting innovation dynamics. In addition, these spaces and infrastructures collaborate in the redesign of cultural and social integration (Sybille, 2019). Normally, the entrepreneur (with the advice of the ecosystem) explores and discovers opportunities for circular innovation in business models, for the creation of new products or social enterprises.

2.6.2 *The Role of Governments as a Second Helix*

According to Sybille (2019), Sun et al. (2017), Adner (2017), and Fromhold-Eisebith (2018) for the development of successful innovation systems, governments and authorities play a crucial role at all levels, local, regional, and national, to create conditions that are established in the regulatory framework that favor innovation. This role acts as a central regulator and funder, infrastructure developer, as well as a moderator and facilitator of strategies, and some other functions, as indicated below:

- The strategic role of the government. One of the main strategic roles is to safeguard regional attractiveness for innovation by ensuring local, regional, national, and international accessibility to strengthen infrastructure, digital connectivity, state-of-the-art communications infrastructure, and the quality of life of intellectual capital.
- The regulatory function of the government. The regulatory framework is an important factor to collaborate significantly in the innovation capacity of actors such as universities, enterprises, and the system. The above is shown in various aspects such as:

  - The regulatory framework of universities determines the level of autonomy they have about organizational issues, university governance structures, legal frameworks for collaboration with private organizations, and the use of intellectual property, also financial matters such as academic and personnel matters.
  - Government regulations must also include tax conditions for knowledge-intensive enterprises.
  - Generate sectoral regulations that impact innovation.
  - Include in the regulations the access and mobility of researchers, experts, and the influx of talent.

- The financing function of the government. Governments should be the main funders of universities (in this sense, the case of Europe is an example of success), as this allows universities to guarantee and significantly increase quality teaching and research activities, as well as investment in its infrastructures to direct innovation and entrepreneurship ecosystems.
- As a facilitator of innovation. This boils down to allowing the inclusion of support schemes and services for business creation, knowledge transfer, collaboration, and co-creation between the university-business, university-entrepreneur, and university-business-entrepreneur.

2.6.3 The Role of Companies as a Third Helix

With the boom in the openness of innovation and its increasingly close relationship between universities and enterprises, their relationship has changed at an accelerated rate where the development and complexity of innovation and enterprises have learned not to depend solely on their internal research and development processes but must externally focus and absorb knowledge from a wide variety of disciplinary areas, sectors, and institutions (Chesbrough, 2003). An example is long-term strategic partnerships which help a multinational enterprise to expose itself to different global innovation environments, to face the challenges of the constant and increasingly advanced technological generation (Sybille, 2019). To appreciate the dynamics of innovation in enterprises, Table 2.19 is presented, where business interaction, universities, and students are observed.

On the other hand, according to the study presented by Sybille (2019), the networks and interaction channels produced by the triple helix are:

- Connective leadership
- Connective cultural norms and assumptions
- Strategy development
- Connectivity infrastructures: intermediate platforms and co-creation centers
- Connective spaces: infrastructures for co-creation and implementation of innovation

Table 2.19 Instruments of cooperation and interaction in universities and enterprises

Instrument of cooperation – interaction	Function for companies, universities, and students[a]
Support bachelor's or master's theses, based on the interaction between the university/external stakeholder, the academic advisor, and the student.	Support students to expose themselves to real work environments and train their problem-solving skills. It helps companies solve concrete short-term problems that require technical knowledge and time to develop research.
Provide internships for students in enterprises.	Support graduates to be more successful in the job market. Collaborate with enterprises to find and test potential future employees.
Courses and trainings taught by professionals, from laboratories on specific topics to conferences or seminars that are included in the university curriculum	Provide students with information about real professional challenges and solutions.
Integrate in conferences and university seminars the real cases and challenges of the business world.	Support students to develop interdisciplinary problem-solving skills. Increase relevance and improve curricula.
Generate and take advantage of successful entrepreneurs as mentors for new enterprises or entrepreneurs as a model to follow in business training.	It helps students to consider the opportunities and challenges of starting their own business and to reduce the risk of failure and instead becoming successful entrepreneurs.
Joint research projects	Collaborates with the generation of ideas for the solution of research problems It brings together industry-based researchers and academics to collaborate with understanding the interests and challenges together.
Private investigation	Helps enterprises solve specific problems and innovation challenges in particular It provides funding to university researchers, in addition to solving the research problem presented by the company. These funds can be freely used for other research, infrastructure, or maintenance purposes.
Funding of research laboratories at the university (sponsorship of space to graduate students participating in research)	It develops specific technological solutions and prototypes for enterprises. It improves the innovative capacity of the company in the long term. It provides an expensive research infrastructure for university researchers.
Sponsoring chairs, with a competitive salary in the international context, including startup funds and for the improvement of research infrastructures	Reinforce the key competence area of a company. Collaborates in the internationalization of the university
Opening of part-time positions for industry researchers at the university and vice versa (cross-work)	Collaborates with mutual knowledge of needs and challenges, understanding methods, concepts, and attitudes
Laboratories or coworking spaces collaborate in addressing long-term challenges that are of mutual interest to academia and industry.	Supports state-of-the-art infrastructure and thus improves international competitiveness Cofinancing (companies/public funds) alleviates public budgetary pressures.

(continued)

Table 2.19 (continued)

Instrument of cooperation – interaction	Function for companies, universities, and students[a]
Long-term agreements within the framework of university-business collaboration	Reduce transaction costs for individual cooperation projects. Create transparency and reliability regarding intellectual property agreements. Justify long-term investments in research infrastructure for enterprises and universities.
Strategic partnerships	Collaborates with companies to address their long-term goals, giving them access to scientific and technological frontiers Analyzes technologies, problems, and opportunities for improvement that may require immediate action It collaborates with universities to develop long-term research areas with a high demand from stakeholders.

Source: Author (2021), taken from the role of universities in regional innovation ecosystems (Sybille, 2019)

[a]Although some of these points are made in some universities, an important challenge is to measure the results in relation to the objectives set

Finally, according to Sybille (2019), European Commission (2020), and Dedehayir et al. (2018), stakeholders also represent a factor to consider in the integration of the ecosystem, and their way of contributing lies in the interaction of the triple helix (university, companies, and government) in order to collaborate with the co-creation structure. This can be seen in Table 2.20.

2.7 Success Factors and Criteria in Innovation Ecosystems

Although the creation of innovation ecosystems brings with it the birth of startups from entrepreneurships, innovation in products, services or methods, linkage, knowledge, and economic and social growth, among others, these must have a minimum of infrastructure, actors, and conditions that favor their growth, development, and circular evolution. In this sense, it is important to identify and consider the success factors of the innovation ecosystems of some countries that are within the top ten worldwide. These factors are (swissnex India, 2018):

- High level of competitiveness and internationalization
- Well-trained workforce and excellent academic institutions
- Fully developed infrastructure
- Various financing possibilities
- Freedom for creative thinking
- A solid network of actors and startups
- High expenses in research + development
- Involvement of the public, private, social, and academic sectors

As can be seen, these factors collaborate to create the virtuous circle of innovation ecosystems. However, if they do not have the conditions and success factors, it

Table 2.20 Stakeholders' contribution for co-creation

Co-creation structure	University contribution	Business contribution	Government contribution
Strategic networks	Creation of emerging research fields and technological developments	Prospective emerging markets and technological developments	Regional or local development and investment planning
Thematic research groups	Different disciplinary competences on the development of research Access to partners in international research Creativity and ideas for new research Link graduates with researchers	Experience in the evolution and potential of the market Applied experience in research and development Access to global business partners Knowledge of global economic developments	Specific funding for research staff and research support staff Funding for research for priority areas of regional partners (cluster) Funds for the implementation of priority thematic areas
Services for innovation	Students and researchers with business ideas Community building between students and researchers Marketing and communication of events	Mentors Project evaluator members Venture capital Partners for startups	Funding for service personnel Financing and regulatory framework Startup grants
Transfer and innovation services	Funding and training staff Encourage marketing as an activity	Mentoring and financial support for intellectual property	Creation of funds Services. Provided by a government agency
Joint basic facilities	Technical and personal knowledge to ensure maintenance and support	Infrastructure financing	Infrastructure financing
Macro shared research infrastructures	Research and technical expertise to ensure state of the art and develop methodologies	Financing of infrastructures and technological experience	Infrastructure financing
University research centers with an impact mission	University research with international visibility, which attracts national and international funds and talent to the regions	Companies and public stakeholders adapt research for development and collaborate to tackle challenges together.	Competitive financing to face social and economic challenges Adapt regulations to meet challenges.
Joint research and innovation laboratories and centers	Provide researchers and facilities for applied research and prototype development. Generate research experience. Researchers (master's, doctoral, postdoctoral students)	Financing and expertise for intellectual property and commercialization Funding for doctorates Financing of research infrastructures	Funding for research centers Infrastructure Regulations for public-private partnerships
Joint campuses and science parks	Openness to external partners, public-private partnerships, in research and education to create dynamic campus environments	Investments in infrastructure Public-private partnerships with a long-term perspective	Urban planning and zoning laws that allow mixed use between research and society Negotiation for obtaining national and international funds Investments in infrastructure

Source: Author (2021), taken from the role of universities in regional innovation ecosystems (Sybille, 2019).

is suggested that the actors immersed in the innovation ecosystem promote the minimum conditions in the area that concern them to be able to host the ecosystem. On the other hand, in this virtuous circle of innovation, it is worth highlighting the scenarios that startups play and the support system in innovation ecosystems, as indicated in Fig. 2.21.

On the other hand, according to Komorowski (2019), the success factors and criteria in innovation ecosystems in Europe are based on those that have been influenced by the management of ecosystems whose characteristics that suggest success are:

(a) The first criterion that indicates success is the scale of operation, which, according to Fig. 2.22, more than 69% of the successful ecosystems are national, followed by international and regional ecosystems.

Fig. 2.21 Startup support system. Source: Author (2021), taken from Swiss Innovation Ecosystem (swissnex India, 2018)

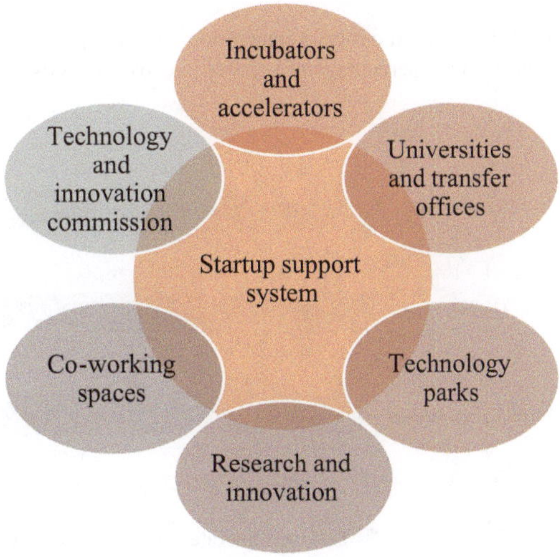

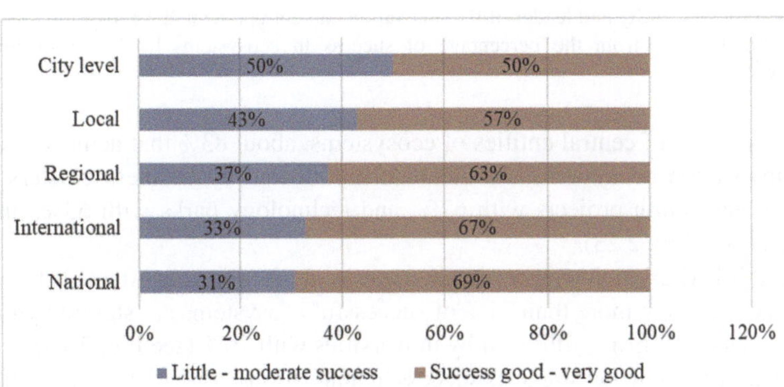

Fig. 2.22 Scale of operation. Source: Author (2021), taken from the percentage of success in ecosystems by scale of operation (Komorowski, 2019)

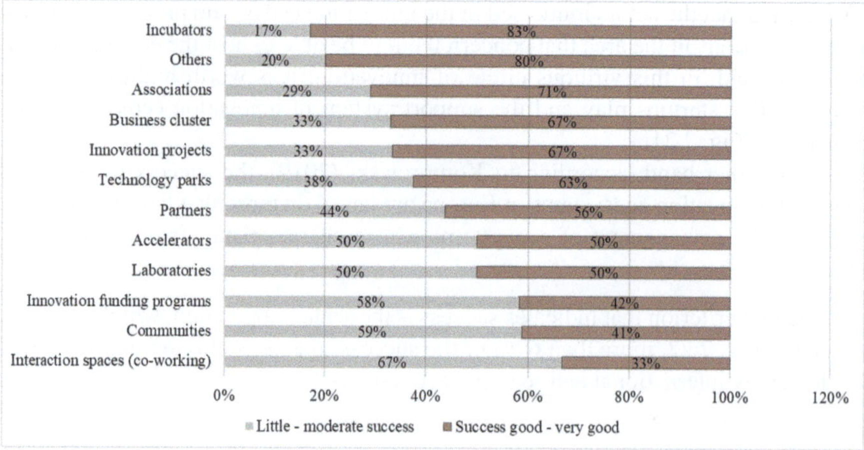

Fig. 2.23 Central entity in innovation and entrepreneurship ecosystems. Source: Author (2021), taken from the percentage of success in ecosystems by central entity (Komorowski, 2019)

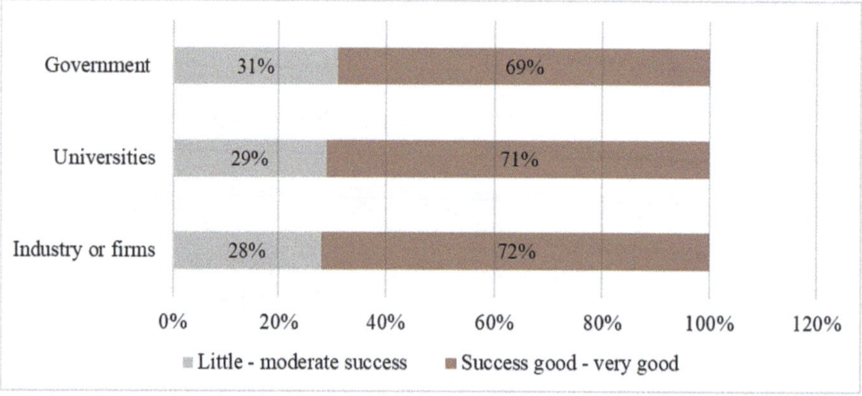

Fig. 2.24 Principal entity and leader of the innovation and entrepreneurship ecosystems. Source: Author (2021), taken from the percentage of success in ecosystems by leader or initiator (Komorowski, 2019)

(b) The criterion of central entities of ecosystems, about 83% that achieve success in innovation ecosystems are incubators, followed by business clusters with 67%, innovation projects with 67%, and technology parks with 63%, among others (see Fig. 2.23).

(c) The third criterion that represents success in innovation ecosystems is the leading actor, where more than 71% of successful ecosystems are started by industry or business firms, followed by universities with 70% (see Fig. 2.24).

(d) The last criterion that suggests success in innovation ecosystems with the objectives or actions. According to Fig. 2.25, more than 63% of successful ecosystems are aimed at technological development and the creation of innovation, followed by the creation of firms and the growth of the industry with 62%. In this

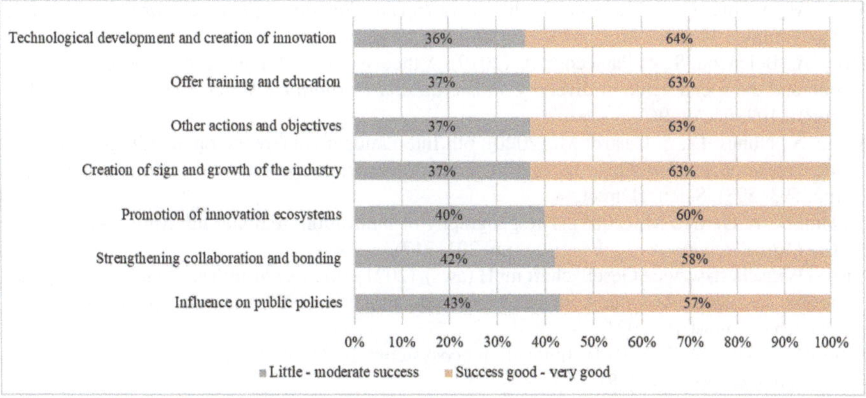

Fig. 2.25 Goal and/or actions. Source: Author (2021), taken from the percentage of success in ecosystems by actions and/or objectives (Komorowski, 2019)

criterion, those ecosystems where their objective or actions are oriented to training and education stand out with 63%.

On the other hand, according to Asefia et al. (2020), there are success factors that collaborate with the growth and evolution of innovation and entrepreneurship ecosystems, with the commercial and social benefits of the regions. However, success depends largely on the conditions that are designed and implemented for the birth of the ecosystem, and such factors are presented below:

- Diversity of actors: small and large entities in addition to the intermediation of mentors, trainers, entrepreneurs, researchers, etc.
- Interaction between the actors: exchange of knowledge and collaboration between the triple helix and generate relationships in common
- Comparative factors between regions: sustained flow values, openness to innovation capacities, obtaining and accessibility to resources, adoption of strategies for innovation, and adequate regulatory instruments
- Minimum structure: material, ecosystem services, and for the ecosystem, culture, and social aspects of adoption of the innovation
- Public policies: regional policies and strategies such as:
  - Diversification and instruments of local, regional, and national public policy
  - Government support with policies and strategies related to incentives

References

Aarikka-Stenroos, L., & Ritala, P. (2017). *Network management in the era of ecosystems*. Obtenido de https://doi.org/10.1016/j.indma, recovered July 20, 2021.

Adner, R. (2017). Ecosystem as structure: An actionable construct for strategy. *Journal of Management*, 39–58.

Arena, M., Azzone, G., & Piantoni, G. (2018). *System building for resilient innovation ecosystems*. Stockholm.

Arora, A., Belenzon, S., & Patacconi, A. (2019). A theory of the US innovation ecosystem: evolution and the social value of diversity. *Industrial and Corporate Change*, 289–307. https://doi.org/10.1093/icc/dty067

Asefia, S., Nunes, D., & Castro, M. (2020). 6th International conference on energy and environment research. In *Modeling a successful innovation ecosystem toward a sustainable community* (pp. 593–598). ScienceDirect.

Asheim, B., & Gertler, M. (2005). The geography of innovation: regional innovation systems. In *The Oxford handbook of innovation* (pp. 291–317).

Austria Wirtschaftsservice Gesellschaft mbH (aws). (2021). *Support by university-associated incubators: AplusB Scale-up in Austria*. Obtenido de https://www.aws.at/en/aws-aplusb-scale-up/, recovered August 10, 2021.

Autio, E., & Thomas, L. (2014). Innovation ecosystems. In *The Oxford handbook of innovation management* (pp. 204–288).

Bertalanffy, L. (1969). *General system theory; Foundations, development, applications*. George Braziller.

Bogers, M., Zobel, A., & Afuah, A. (2017). The open innovation research landscape: Established perspectives and emerging themes across different levels of analysis. *Industry and Innovation*, 8–40.

Breschi, S., & Malerba, F. (1997). Sectoral innovation systems: Technological regimes, Schumpeterian dynamics, and spatial boundaries. In *Systems of innovation: Technologies, institutions and organizations* (pp. 130–156).

Carayannis, E., & Campbell, D. (2009). *Mode 3 and Quadruple Helix*. Obtenido de https://doi.org/10.1504/ijtm.2009.023374, recovered January 17, 2021.

Carayannis, E., & Campbell, D. (2019). *Smart quintuple helix innovation systems. How social ecology and environmental protection are driving innovation, sustainable development and economic growth*. Springer.

Carayannis, E., Battista, G., Alvarez, S., & Faraci, R. (2018). *Entrepreneurial ecosystems and the diffusion of startups*. Edward Elgar.

Chesbrough, H. (2003). *Open innovation: The new imperative for creating and profiting from technology*. Boston.

Colombelli, A., Paolucci, E., & Ughetto, E. (2019). Hierarchical and relational governance and the life cycle of entrepreneurial ecosystems. *Small Business Economics, 52*, 505–521.

Constantinides, P., Henfridsson, O., & Parker, G. (2018). Introduction – Platforms and infrastructures in the digital age. *Information Systems Research, 29*, 381–400.

Dattee, B., Alexy, O., & Autio, E. (2018). Maneuvering in poor visibility: How firms play the ecosystem game when uncertainty is high. *Academy of Management Journal, 61*, 466–498.

Dedehayir, O., Mäkinen, S., & Ortt, J. (2018). Roles during innovation ecosystem genesis: A literature review. *Technological Forecasting and Social Change, 136*, 18–29.

Deshpande Center for Technological Innovation. (2021). *The mission of the MIT Deshpande Center for Technological Innovation can be summed up in one word: Impact*. Obtenido de https://deshpande.mit.edu/about, recovered May 23, 2021.

Ding, L., & Wu, J. (2018). *Sustainability, 39*.

DTU-dk. (2021). *Start-up*. Obtenido de https://tt.dtu.dk/, recovered May 28, 2021.

Durst, S., & Poutanen, P. (2013). Success factors of innovation ecosystems – Initial insights from a literature review. In *The boundary-crossing conference on co-design in innovatio*n (pp. 27–38).

Edquist, C. (1997). Systems of innovation approaches: Their emergence and characteristics. In *Systems of innovation: Technologies* (pp. 1–35). Edward Elgar.

Enterprise Ireland. (2021). *Start your digital enterprise*. Obtenido de https://www.enterprise-ireland.com/en/, recovered May 28, 2021.

ETH Zurich. (2021). *ETH pioneer fellowships*. Obtenido de https://ethz.ch/en/industry/entrepreneurs/entrepreneurship/pioneer-fellowships.html, recovered February 02, 2021.

European Commission. (2020). *Eco – innovación: At the heart of European policies*. Obtenido de A Robust Innovation ecosystem for the future of Europe: https://ec.europa.eu/environment/ecoap/frontpage_en, recovered June 15, 2021.

European Commission. (2021). *EASME – Executive agency for SMEs*. Obtenido de https://wayback.archive-it.org/12090/20210412123959/https://ec.europa.eu/easme/en/, recovered March 4, 2021.

European Innovation Scoreboard. (2021). *Internal market, industry, entrepreneurship and SMEs*. Obtenido de https://ec.europa.eu/growth/industry/policy/innovation/scoreboards_en, recovered June 17, 2021.

Ferasso, M., Takahashi, A., & Gimenez, F. (2018). Innovation ecosystems: A meta-synthesis ecosystems. *International Journal of Innovation Sciences*. https://doi.org/10.1108/IJIS-07-2017-0059

Forrester, J. (1958). Industrial dynamics: A major breakthrough for decision makers. *Harvard Business Review, 36*, 37–66.

Fromhold-Eisebith, M. (2018). Bridging scales in innovation policies: How to link regional, national and international innovation systems. *European Planning Studies, 15*, 217–233.

Galdino de Barros, J., & Almeida, A. (2020). Comparative study of innovation ecosystems inducing success of startups in the world. *International Journal for Innovation Education and Research, 8*, 647–658.

Goldstein, H., & Drucker, J. (2006). The economic development impact of universities on regions: Do size and distance matter? *Economic Development Quarterly, 20*, 22–43.

Gomes, L., Figueiredo, L., Salerno, S., & Rodrigo, I. (2018). Unpacking the innovation ecosystem construct: Evolution, gaps and trends. *Technological Forecasting and Social Change, 136*, 30–48.

Government of Canada. (2018). *Canada's superclusters*. Obtenido de https://www.ic.gc.ca/eic/site/093.nsf/eng/home, recovered July 07, 2021.

Government of Canada. (2021a). *About Canada's innovation superclusters initiative*. Obtenido de https://www.ic.gc.ca/eic/site/093.nsf/eng/00016.html, recovered July 06, 2021.

Government of Canada. (2021b). *Regional innovation ecosystems*. Obtenido de https://www.wd-deo.gc.ca/eng/19775.asp, recovered July 03, 2021.

Granstrand, O. (2000). Corporate innovation systems: A comparative study of multi-technology corporations in Japan, Sweden and the USA. In: *Dynacom series* (p. 13). Chalmers University of Technology.

Granstranda, O., & Holgersson, M. (2020). Innovation ecosystems: A conceptual review and a new definition. *Technovation*, 1–12.

Hannah, D., & Eisenhardt, K. (2018). How firms navigate cooperation and competition in nascent ecosystems. *Strategic Management Journal*, 3163–3192.

Iyer, B., & Davenport, T. (2008). Reverse engineering Google's innovation machine. *Harvard Business Review*, 1–12.

Jacobides, M., Sundararajan, A., & Van Alstyne, M. (2019). *Platforms and ecosystems: Enabling the digital economy* (Briefing paper). World Economic Forum.

Järvi, K., Almpanopoulou, A., & Ritala, P. (2018). Organization of knowledge ecosystems: Prefigurative and partial forms. *Research Policy, 47*, 1523–1537.

Jucevicius, G., Juceviciene, R., Gaidelys, V., & Kalman, A. (2016). The emerging innovation ecosystems and "valley of death": Towards the combination of entrepreneurial and institutional approaches. *Engineering Economics, 27*, 430–438. https://doi.org/10.5755/j01.ee.27.4.14403

Kapoor, R., & Lee, J. (2013). Coordinating and competing in ecosystems: How organizational forms shape new technology investments. *Strategic Management Journal*, 274–296.

Klaus, S. (2016). *The global competitiveness report*. World Economic Forum.

Klaus, S. (2017). *The global competitiveness report*. World Economic Forum.

Klaus, S. (2018). *The global competitiveness report*. World Economic Forum.

Klaus, S. (2019). *The global competitiveness report*. World Economic Forum.

Klimas, P., & Czakon, W. (2020). Species in the wild: A typology of innovation ecosystem. *Review of Managerial Science*, 1–34.

Komorowski, M. (2019). *Innovation ecosystems in Europe: First outline of an innovation ecosystem index*. Mec – SMIT – VUB, 4.

Kulicke, M. (2020). *Fostering innovative startups in the pre seed phase*. Scientific Analysis Fraunhofer.

Launonen, M., & Viitanen, J. (2011). *The global best practice for managing innovation ecosystems and hubs*. Hubconcepts.

Llewellyn, T., & Erkko, A. (2019). Ecosistemas de innovación. *Electronic Journal*, 1–38.

Lundvall, B.-Å. (1992). *National systems of innovation: Towards a theory of innovation and interactive learning* (p. 12). Pinter Publishers.

Luo, J. (2018). Architecture and evolvability of innovation ecosystems. *Technological Forecasting and Social Change*, 132–144. https://doi.org/10.1016/j.techfore.2017.06.033

MaRS. (2021). *We help high-impact Canadian tech ventures grow and succeed*. Obtenido de https://www.marsdd.com/startup-services/, recovered August 21, 2021.

Mazzucato, M., & Robinson, D. (2018). Co-creating and directing innovation ecosystems? NASA's changing approach to public-private partnerships in low-earth orbit. *Technological Forecasting and Social Change*, 166–177. https://doi.org/10.1016/j.techfore.2017.03.034

McIntyre, D., & Srinivasan, A. (2018). Networks, platforms, and strategy: Emerging views and next steps. *Strategic Management Journal, 38*, 141–160.

Meadows, D., Meadows, J., Randers, W., & Behrens. (1972). *The limits to growth*. Universe Books.

Menzel, M.-P., Henn, S., & Fornahl, D. (2010). Emerging clusters: A conceptual overview. In *Theoretical, empirical and political perspectives on the initial stage of cluster* (pp. 1–13). Edward Elgar.

Mercier-Laurent, E. (2015). *Innovation ecosystems*. Wiley.

Nambisan, S., & Baron, R. (2013). *Entrepreneurship in innovation ecosystems*: Obtenido de https://doi.org/10.1111/j.1540-6520.2012.00519.x, recovered January 13, 2021.

OECD. (2021). *OECD science, technology and innovation Outlook 2021: Times of crisis and opportunity*. Obtenido de https://doi.org/10.1787/75f79015-en, recovered June 17, 2021.

Oh, D., Phillips, F., Park, S., & Lee, E. (2016). Innovation ecosystems: A critical examination. *Technovation*, 1–6. https://doi.org/10.1016/j.technovation.2016.02.004

Oxford University. (2021). *We help Oxford ideas come to life*. Obtenido de https://innovation.ox.ac.uk/, recovered August 24, 2021.

Phillips, M., & Srai, J. (2018). Exploring emerging ecosystem boundaries: defining 'the game'. *International Journal of Innovation Management*, 8–9.

Planko, J., Chappin, M., Cramer, J., & Hekkert, M. (2017). Managing strategic system-building networks in emerging business fields: A case study of the Dutch smart grid sector. *Industrial Marketing Management*, 37–51. https://doi.org/10.1016/j.indmarman.2017.06.010.

Pombo-Juárez, L., Könnölä, T., Miles, I., Saritas, O., Schartinger, D., & Giesecke, S. (2017). Technological forecasting & social change wiring up multiple layers of innovation ecosystems: Contemplations from personal health systems foresight. *Technological Forecasting and Social Change*, 278–288. https://doi.org/10.1016/j.techfore.2016.04.018

Rabelo, R., & Bernus, P. (2015). A holistic model of building innovation ecosystems. *IFAC-PapersOnLine*, 2250–2257. https://doi.org/10.1016/j.ifacol.2015.06.423

Radziwon, A. (2018). *Managing inter-organizational collaboration of SMEs in a regional ecosystem*. In ISPIM conference 2018.

Reynolds, E., & Uygun, Y. (2018). Strengthening advanced manufacturing innovation ecosystems: The case of Massachusetts. *Technological Forecasting and Social Change*, 178–191. https://doi.org/10.1016/j.techfore.2017.06.003

Rocha, C., Mamédio, D., & Quandt, C. (2019). Startups and the innovation ecosystem in Industry 4.0. *Technology Analysis and Strategic Management*, 1–14. https://doi.org/10.1080/09537325.2019.1628938

Rong, K., Hu, G., Lin, Y., Shi, Y., & Guo, L. (2015). Understanding business ecosystem using a 6C framework in Internet-of-Things-based sectors. *International Journal of Production Economics, 159*.

Russell, M., & Smorodinskaya, N. (2018). Leveraging complexity for ecosystemic innovation. *Technological Forecasting and Social Change*, 114–131. https://doi.org/10.1016/j.techfore.2017.11.024

Schroth, F., Häußermann, J., & Schraudner, M. (2018). *Strategies for cooperation between companies and research organisations in innovation ecosystems – A case study of the German microelectronics and photonics industries*. In ISPIM innovation symposium, (pp. 1–13).

Smart Social City. (2014). *Nuevos modelos de desarrollo sustentable: Centro de Innovación Social*. Obtenido de http://www.spainbusiness.com/icex/cma/contentTypes/common/records/mostrarDocumento/?doc=4767581, recovered January 15, 2021.

Sölvell, Ö., Lindqvist, G., & Ketels, C. (2008). *The cluster initiative greenbook: Scotland's digital media and creative industries CI, the U.K.* Obtenido de https://www.hhs.se/contentassets/f51b706e1d644e9fa6c4d232abd09e63/greenbooksep03.pdf, recovered July 19, 2021.

Spelmeyer, M., & Lingens, B. (2018). *How young entrepreneurial companies orchestrate business ecosystems Bernhard Lingens*. In Proceedings of the XXIX ISPIM innovation conference.

Spigel, B. (2017). The relational organization of entrepreneurial ecosystems. *Entrepreneurship: Theory and Practice*, 49–72.

Startup Genome. (2017). *The urgency of ecosystem investments. Global startup ecosystem: Report 2017*. Obtenido de https://cdn.startupgenome.com/sites/, recovered April 18, 2020.

Sterman, J. (2007). Exploring the next frontier: System dynamics at 50. *System Dynamics Review*, 2–3.

Su, Y., Zheng, Z., & Chen, J. (2018). A multi-platform collaboration innovation ecosystem: The case of China. *Management Decision*, 125–142. https://doi.org/10.1108/MD-04-2017-0386

Sun, S., Chen, V., Sunny, S., & Chen, J. (2017). *Venture capital as an ecosystem engineer for regional innovation in an emerging market*. In 2017 IEEE technology and engineering management society conference, (pp. 13–18). https://doi.org/10.1109/TEMSCON.2017.7998347.

swissnex India. (2018). *Swiss innovation ecosystem*. Obtenido de https://www.swissnexindia.org/about/public-diplomacy-initiatives/yosi/swiss-innovation-ecosystem/, recovered November 01, 2018.

Sybille, R. (2019). *Asociación Europea de Universidades: El rol de las universidades en los ecosistemas de innovación regionales*. The hangue.

Tecconnect Entrepreneur Program. (2021). *A bright Choice for entrepreneurs*. Obtenido de https://entrepreneur.chooselethbridge.ca/, recovered August 2, 2021.

Technion University. (2020). *The T3 Technion entrepreneur in residence program at Technion University in Haifa*. Obtenido de https://ver2015.presidentsreport.technion.ac.il/technion-entrepreneur-in-residence-program-eir/, recovered March 3, 2021.

Teece, D. (2018). Profiting from innovation in the digital economy: Enabling technologies, standards, and licensing models in the wireless world. *Research Policy*, 1367–1387.

Thomas, L., & Tee, R. (2019). Generativity: A systematic review and integrative model. *Electronic Journal*, 1–23.

University of Tsukuba. (2021). *Organizational chart*. Obtenido de https://oiso.tsukuba.ac.jp/en/chart/, recovered July 11, 2021.

University of Twente. (2021). *The fund focuses on seed and early stage companies*. Obtenido de http://www.twentefund.nl/, recovered August 20, 2021.

Vargas, M., Pertuz, J., & Guerra, J. (2018). *Descripción del estado actual del ecosistema de innovación en Colombia* (p. 38). Universidad cooperativa de Colombia.

Walrave, B., Talmar, M., Podoynitsyna, K., Romme, A., & Verbong, G. (2018). A multi-level perspective on innovation ecosystems for path-breaking innovation. *Technological Forecasting and Social Change*, 103–113. https://doi.org/10.1016/j.techfore.2017.04.011

WESTEM. (2021). *Women Entrepreneurs-in-STEM (WESTEM) program*. Obtenido de https://westem.ca/, recovered August 2, 2021.

Witte, P., Slack, B., Keesman, M., Jeanne-Hélène, J., & Wiegmans, B. (2018). *Facilitating startups in port-city innovation ecosystems: A case study of*. Obtenido de https://doi.org/10.1016/jtrangeo, recovered January 20, 2021.

World Intellectual Property Organization. (2020). *Global innovation index 2020.* SC Johnson College of Business.

Xu, G., Wu, Y., Minshall, T., & Zhou, Y. (2018). Exploring innovation ecosystems across science, technology, and business: a case of 3D printing in China. *Technological Forecasting and Social Change*, 208–221. https://doi.org/10.1016/j.techfore.2017.06.030

Yaghmaie, P., & Vanhaverbeke, W. (2019). Identifying and describing constituents of innovation ecosystems: a systematic review of the literature. *EuroMed Journal of Business*, 1–32. https://doi.org/10.1108/EMJB-03-2019-0042

Zavala, F. (2015). *Centros de innovación, lugares para potenciar al talento.* Obtenido de http://fernandozavala.pe/centros-de-innovacion-lugares-para-potenciar-al-talento/, recovered January 10, 2021.

Ziyaad, A. (2018). *London's lost innovators; Understanding Brexit's effect on venture capital and startup investing in the UK.* The University of Texas at Austin.

Chapter 3
Phase 1. Birth of the Innovation and Entrepreneurship Ecosystem

3.1 Stage I. Planning

In this first stage, it is suggested that the university develop activities indicated in Fig. 3.2 (non-limiting) through its own specialized area/department, related to innovation and entrepreneurship ecosystems.

As can be seen in Fig. 3.2, it is suggested to develop seven activities to support the creation or enablement of the innovation and entrepreneurship ecosystem.

3.1.1 Define the Mission and Vision of the Entity That Will Operate the Ecosystem (EOE)

To define the mission and vision, it is recommended to align with local, regional, national, and international frameworks so as not to disperse the objectives of the ecosystem (see Fig. 3.3).

According to Fig. 3.3, to correctly define the mission and vision of the ecosystem, it is suggested to align them with the sustainable development objectives, the development/strategic plans of the national, regional, and local governments, then make a link with the mission and vision regional and national ecosystems (since at some point, they will be linked and interact), as well as linking the framework of the university where the ecosystem will be born, since although it is an "independent" entity, it must be aligned with its mission and vision.

I. Patiño-Galván, *Innovation and Entrepreneurship Ecosystems*, Innovation, Technology, and Knowledge Management,
https://doi.org/10.1007/978-3-031-24517-6_3

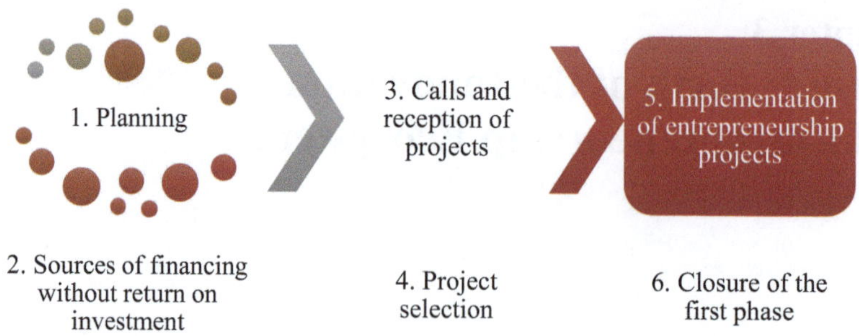

Fig. 3.1 Stages of phase 1 of the innovation and entrepreneurship ecosystem. (Source: Author, 2021)

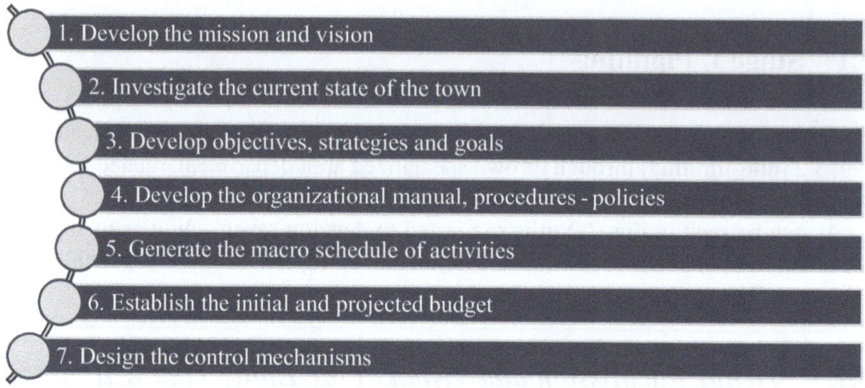

Fig. 3.2 Activities to be developed in the planning stage. (Source: Author, 2021)

Fig. 3.3 Definition of the mission and vision of the ecosystem. (Source: Author, 2021)

3.1.2 Research of the Current State of the Town

This section is of vital importance for the construction of the innovation and entrepreneurship ecosystem, since the results will become inputs and foundations for the design of the ecosystem. In this sense, it is suggested to collect, analyze, and interpret the information stated in Fig. 3.4 (non-limiting):

In relation to Fig. 3.4, the following tasks are generally suggested:

- Present and future local and regional capacities. In this area, it is suggested to collect the following information:
  - List with their characteristics the local natural and/or artificial resources that are available and could potentially have the ecosystem in the future.
  - Determine the size of the city and carry out projections for 10, 20, and 30 years.
  - Detail and integrate the characteristics of the locality.
  - List and detail the sectors of specialization of the locality.
  - Identify the proximity with localities in the region, according to the mission, objectives, and strategies of the ecosystem.
  - Obtain and analyze socioeconomic indicators and their characteristics.
- Business capabilities. In this section, it is suggested to identify the type of enterprises in the locality, in addition to the technology they use in their processes and the life cycle of the product; the type of labor they consume, specialties, or disciplines; and their potential market, as well as characteristics associated with the logistics of your operation, without putting confidential or strategic information at risk.

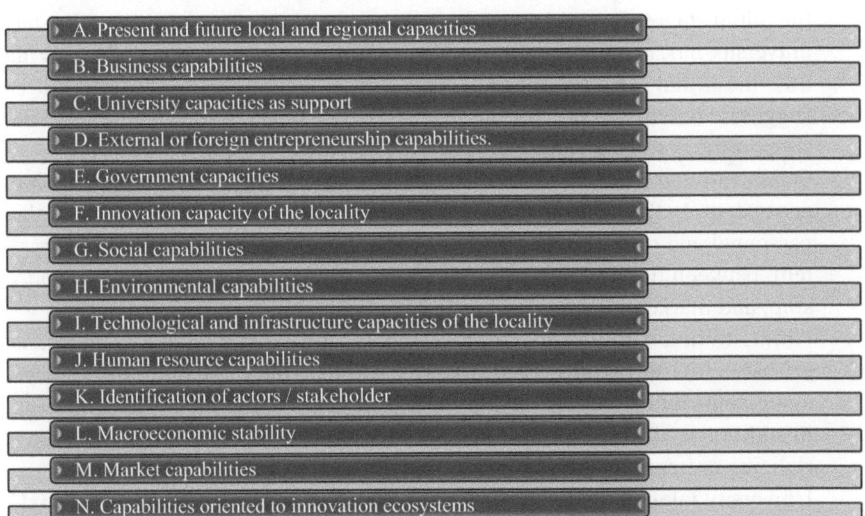

Fig. 3.4 Topics to consider in the investigation of the current state of the town. (Source: Author, 2021)

- Capacities of the university. This is an area of vital importance, since it will be the one that will support the ecosystem, and as such its initial operation. From the above, it is suggested to deburr the information:
  - Laboratories and equipment for the development of initial projects. Normally, they are the same as those used for the teaching of practical classes in academic undergraduate and graduate programs offered by the university and training centers, among others.
  - Information and communication technologies. Carry out an inventory of the communication technologies that the university has, as well as their characteristics, same case for information technologies.
  - Infrastructure for research. To have postgraduate programs oriented toward research and professionalization, lines of research congruent with the programs and needs of the region, mission, and vision of the institution, as well as a staff of researchers with the appropriate profile. Have research projects related to the business, government, social, and academic sectors.
  - Teachers. Have professors with the appropriate profile who support the programs offered by the university and who comply with the profile to collaborate with the support of entrepreneurship projects, all of them aligned to the objectives, goals, and strategies as a whole.
  - Experts. Have expert staff either as a teacher, administrative, technical, or researcher, in the various training disciplines of the university, in the same way to collaborate in supporting entrepreneurship projects.
  - Economic resources. Gather the accounting and financial information that demonstrates the solvency of the university to provide initial support to the innovation and entrepreneurship ecosystem. For this, various studies must be prepared to identify the resources that the ecosystem must have. Normally, in the initial stages, it is suggested that you consume the same resources that the university has, personnel, laboratories, and infrastructure, among others. With this, the initial operation of the ecosystem is guaranteed. Additionally, it is suggested to have an item for the specialized administrative structure that will support the ecosystem (*EOE*).
  - Organizational structure that will support the innovation and entrepreneurship ecosystem. In this section, it is suggested to carry out a careful analysis of the personnel and resources that will be required for the operation of the ecosystem, between linking, financing, technology transfer, research, entrepreneurship, and marketing, among others.
  - Ability to link with universities, researchers, and experts related to the enterprises/sectors to be prioritized. Identify whether there are currently linkage agreements with other universities or stakeholders of the university's interest, in addition to the type of linkage since these will be used at the time of materializing entrepreneurship projects.
  - University talent to undertake and its leadership. Identify entrepreneurial talent through programs/subjects and through the identification of university students who have had contact with the university about undertakings or innovations, university students with real and active undertakings, among others.

- Academic programs oriented to entrepreneurship. Identify the programs whose entry and exit objective is the training of human resources aimed at the creation of enterprises or innovations in any sector. In case of not having a related program, it is suggested to carry out the analysis and study of relevance for the creation of a program or adaptation of an existing one that meets the corresponding requirements without jeopardizing the objective of the program.
- Agenda associated with entrepreneurship and innovation. In this area, it is suggested to identify for each program which subjects/topics are associated with entrepreneurship and innovation.
- Generation of entrepreneurship projects. Collect information on the projects of each semester/subject of the last 3 years and, as far as possible, classify them as appropriate to undertakings, practices, or specializations.
- Generation of own resources. Generate a justified list of services and products that can be offered in the innovation ecosystem to generate its own resources.
- Creation and dissemination of events. It is suggested to make a list of the events related to the undertakings carried out by the university and/or the locality or, failing that, to generate a proposal. As far as possible, it is suggested to carry out this activity in interinstitutional collaboration of local upper and higher levels, to encourage the culture of entrepreneurship.
- List or create events to address business risk and failure. This section of events is directed to stop stigmatizing business failure and risks as something negative that marks entrepreneurs, the above to focus these events to improve attitudes and face business risk and guide it as an advantage not only for the entrepreneur but for the collective of entrepreneurs.
- Identify and encourage the creation of enterprises with disruptive innovations. In this activity, it is important to make continuous dynamics that promote this type of innovations. For this, it will be possible to carry out coworking sessions, brainstorming, and other techniques to be able to identify them and give them the corresponding follow-up to materialize them.
- Identify the services that you will provide to entrepreneurs. In this section, it is suggested to make a list of services that will be provided specifically to entrepreneurs. In this initial stage, it is recommended to minimize costs to give the entrepreneur the opportunity to focus his resources on the venture.
- Innovation capacity of the university. This section refers to those elements that the company must support and promote innovation and cover the largest possible percentage with its own resources. Among the capacities suggested are 1. interaction and diversity (diversify the workforce), 2. seek local co-inventions, 3. research and development, and 4. marketing (sophistication in the experience of the buyers of each enterprise and creation of trademarks and copyrights).
- External or foreign entrepreneurship capabilities. In this activity, it is suggested to collect as much as possible the local or foreign talent that remains in the town, the personal investment that the entrepreneur has available for the venture and from this list of ventures which are disruptive.

- Government capacities. Make an analysis of the services oriented to the creation, monitoring, development, and growth with which the local, regional, or federal government contributes, such as:
  - Business dynamism. Administrative requirements:
    Cost to start a business.
    Time to open business.
    Corresponding regulatory framework.
- Innovation capacity of the locality. This section is oriented to the locality. It is suggested to collect information from the following items:
  - Interaction and diversity.
    Diversity in the workforce.
    Development of alliances and linkages (between local, regional, national, and international ecosystems).
    Collaboration of multiple actors in the ecosystem.
  - Research and development.
    Scientific publications.
    Patents applied.
    Institutions dedicated to research.
  - Commercialization.
    Sophistication in the user experience and in the purchase of the product or service.
    Trademark applications.
- Social skills. In this area and to integrate the social helix, it is suggested to collect and/or collaborate in the creation of *civil society organizations (CSO)* oriented toward entrepreneurship. The above to join efforts in:
  - Adoption of business culture.
  - Existence of *CSO* oriented toward entrepreneurship.
    Integrate them strategically in the process chain of the innovation and entrepreneurship ecosystem.
  - Collaboration in the dissemination of corporate culture.
- Environmental capabilities. While it is true that much of the success or failure of the venture depends on the entrepreneur and his ecosystem, there are external factors that will have to be documented, analyzed, and, where appropriate, managed to favor success. These capacities refer to:
  - Social security.
  - Available share capital.
  - Regulation and application of standards to the public and private sector.
  - Transparency in processes.
  - Optimization of processes in obtaining copyrights.
  - Corporate, open, and electronic governance.
  - Government oriented to the construction, collaboration, and facilitator in the medium and long term of the ecosystem.

- Technological and infrastructure capacities of the locality. In this section, it is suggested to collect information on the capacities that the locality has in this regard, such as:
  - Internet connectivity.
  - Infrastructure quality.
  - Efficiency of interdependent services.
  - Media connectivity (transport).
  - Technology services support.
  - Access to electricity and means for its generation of a renewable nature.
  - Quality basic services.
- Human resource capabilities. These capabilities focus on human resources, on the one hand, to guarantee or build available qualified, creative, and entrepreneurial human resources. Suggested blondes to collect are:
  - Life expectancy; age averages.
  - Abilities; academic training.
  - Training; quality in teaching and research.
  - Educational expectations of the new generations (ensure HR).
  - List of experts by sector.
- Identification of actors/stakeholders. In this section, it is suggested to take prior information as a reference and generate the list of strategic actors that can be strategically and gradually integrated into the ecosystem. It is possible to profile each actor based on his experience, regardless of whether at the time and after meetings the stakeholder gives an opinion on his profile, either to modify or confirm it.
- Macroeconomic stability. In this section, it is suggested to collect information on the stability of the locality/region/country from the following indicators (not limiting): 1. inflation, 2. interest rates, 3. *gross domestic product (GDP)*, and 4. income per capita, among others. It is important to mention that such information should be from at least 10 previous years, to give opportunity for analysis and apply statistical methods or intelligent systems for future prediction or projections.
- Macroeconomic stability. In this section, it is suggested to collect information on the stability of the locality/region/country from the following indicators (not limiting): 1. inflation, 2. interest rates, 3. *GDP*, and 4. income per capita, among others. It is important to mention that such information should be from at least 10 previous years, to give opportunity for analysis and apply statistical methods or intelligent systems for future prediction or projections.
  - Local, regional, national, and international competition.
  - Market opening; cooperation or creation of market cluster.
  - Orientation of the financial system for accessible domestic credits.
  - Financing for businesses and *Micro, Small, Medium, and Large enterprises* (*MSML*).

  - Investment in ventures.
  - Bank diversification (bank offering).
  - Regulation of banks with respect to the credits of the undertakings.
  - Existing products and services in the local market.
  - Import and export products and services.
- Capabilities oriented to innovation ecosystems. In this section, it is suggested to collect information on the following items:
  - Cyclical stages of development projected for the ecosystem.
  - Operation scale.
  - Actor who will serve as the leadership.
  - Identify innovation ecosystems – similar ventures in the local, regional, national, and international context.
  - Initial investment and projections of at least 3 years.

Finally, it is suggested that the collection of information be accompanied by digital methodological instruments, which favor the systematization, documentation, transparency, and evidence of the activity, which at the time of being analyzed and interpreted allows the correlation and association of the information for taking the decision-making.

3.1.3 Develop the Objectives, Goals, Strategies, and Indicators

Once the mission and vision of the *Ecosystem of Innovation and Local Entrepreneurship (EIEL)* have been identified and developed, and after the analysis of the current state, it is suggested to develop the objectives, goals, and strategies, all of them aligned and in congruence to collaborate with the scope of the objectives.

According to Fig. 3.5 and starting from the mission as the general objective, the objectives, the goals, and finally the strategies will emerge. It is important to point out that all goals and/or strategies are measurable and quantifiable, as this will make it possible to identify deviations and establish corrective measures to reduce the risks that hinder the achievement of the objectives.

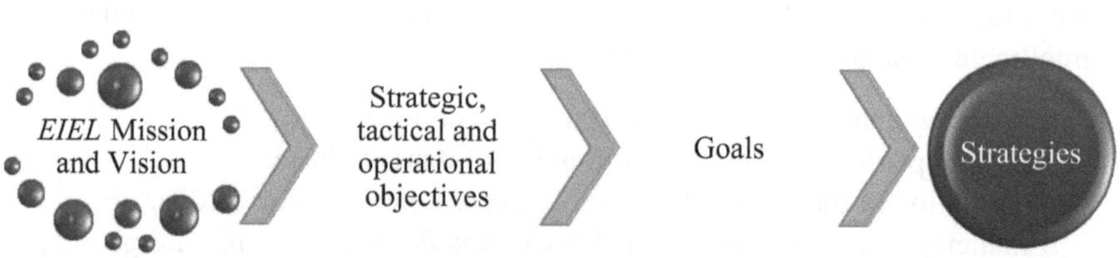

Fig. 3.5 Development of objectives, strategies, and goals. (Source: Author, 2021)

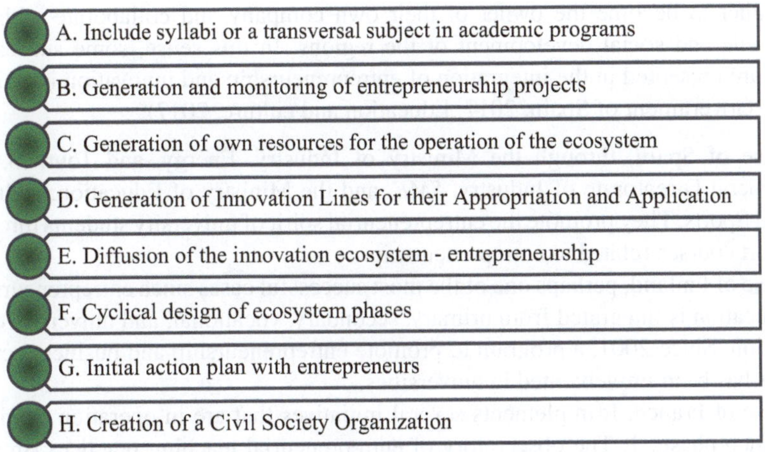

Fig. 3.6 Sample of strategies (non-limiting). (Source: Author, 2021)

3.1.3.1 Suggestion of Non-limiting Strategies

Although it is true that the objectives, goals, and strategies should be developed for the local ecosystem, and since it is suggested to start the proposal with the prioritization of the students' undertakings (without leaving aside the undertakings of other actors), they are presented in Fig. 3.6, some strategies (non-limiting) that can be linked to the objectives and goals as appropriate.

As seen in Fig. 3.6, it is suggested to apply the strategies and align them accordingly. It is important to reiterate that the strategies, goals, and objectives must obey and/or align as mentioned in previous sections. On the other hand, to detail the suggested strategies, they are presented below:

(a) Include courses or a transversal subject in academic programs.

Taking into consideration the author's teaching experience, more than 40% of the subjects in any university program and more in postgraduate degrees have in their evaluation indicators the development of a project, not necessarily of entrepreneurship or innovation. However, it only applies in some semesters and subjects. Later (in most cases), that project is lost because it has already met the objective for the subject. In this sense and to give continuity and improvement to the project, it is suggested to incorporate a transversal and serial subject in all semesters, whose objective is to polish and follow up on this project and more on those that are disruptive. To put this suggestion in context, a bit of the state of the art on the subject is attached. In the international context, it has been identified that the university academic disciplines that implement subjects on entrepreneurship and innovation are primarily those whose profile is business. However, they put aside the rest of the disciplines that also have the possibility of undertaking business from their areas of specialty. This could become in the long term an option for the working life of students, where they would not only be at the expense of a company and/or employer but rather to become the owner of their own company and collaborate with the economic and social development of the regions. In this sense, some successful cases are presented in the integration of entrepreneurship and innovation in universities (Government of Spain, 2017; Education and culture, 2017):

- Case of Spain, through the Ministry of Industry, Energy, and Tourism, the General Directorate of Industry, *SME*, and the Ministry of Education, Culture, and Sports. They promote the entrepreneurial spirit of university students through short courses related to entrepreneurship.
- Case of Finland, perhaps one of the most successful cases since entrepreneurship education is integrated from primary, secondary, vocational, and university education. Since 2001, a program to promote entrepreneurship and business activities has been implemented in universities.
- Case of France. It implements several initiatives that are in operation or in the launch phase: 1. The observatory of entrepreneurial teaching practices (in secondary and vocational and higher education). 2. Academic programs are visualized, and awareness campaigns are carried out with the teaching institutions in that field of study. The aim is to disseminate practices and information on business education.
- Case of Norway. The strategy consists of generating collaboration between the Ministry of Research and Education, the Ministry of Local Government and Regional Development, and finally the Ministry of Commerce and Industry. The purpose is to motivate and inspire educational institutions and local municipalities to plan and establish entrepreneurship education, in collaboration with industry and other relevant actors at the local level. Something to highlight is that the responsibility for the implementation of the strategic plan for entrepreneurship in education rests with educational institutions. Responsibility for coordination is absorbed by the Ministry of Education and Research.
- Case of the Netherlands. Entrepreneurship education originates from business clusters and is brought into academia through entrepreneurship courses, modules, and programs available at higher education institutions. In this, they emphasize the transversal introduction of entrepreneurial skills and competencies along with the provision of academic studies.

It is suggested that the university from which the ecosystem is born gradually integrates into the academic programs, a cross-cutting subject related to "entrepreneurship and innovation" in all semesters and careers (at the beginning, it is proposed to do pilot tests with an academic program), which help students in the natural process of innovative development and entrepreneurship. In these subjects, it is suggested that the following topics (non-limiting) be integrated into their content:

- Know the social, cultural, economic, and political context that may lead to the identification of opportunities or needs in which they can contribute from their training and professional action.
- Obtain tools and methods for the ideation process.
- Have bases that allow the development of business models of the proposed ideas.

- Know tools that allow to validate the ideas generated, which help to enhance the chances of success of ideas and projects.
- Obtain bases and tools to help develop prototypes or initial versions of the proposed solution, product, or service.
- Include research methodologies in the production process of the initiatives.
- Development of skills to present projects to potential investors or funders, as well as to review possible sources of financing that could be seed capital to start your project.
- Develop plans that contemplate all the actions necessary for the startup of the project, foreseeing the important activities, the possible risks, and the actions that will be essential for the business to be maintained and/or grow.

It is important to note that the implementation of this initiative is not a simple task. It must be gradual, so it is suggested that the academic directorates or coordinators assess the proposal to measure its implications and scope, or, failing that, propose different alternatives, as long as they do not deviate from the mission of the university and the objective of the academic program. This proposal can be seen in Fig. 3.7.

(b) Generation and monitoring of entrepreneurship projects.

Generate a list of projects from recent years generated by students, which are aligned with the ecosystem (not limiting), with the aim of supporting the orientation of entrepreneurship projects, without this meaning limiting the creativity of entrepreneurs; therefore, that project integration should be left open.

Based on the opportunities for improvement that he has observed in different areas of knowledge in universities, as well as external forums on the need to give continuity to student projects, it has been suggested to look for mechanisms that allow to give continuity to the projects of students with implementation potential and more those whose potential is disruptive, which otherwise at the end of a period or semester are truncated.

Reflecting in a general way about this area, higher education trains human resources to be integrated into the productive and social sector, but what happens if the human resources generated in the universities do not manage to insert themselves into these sectors? According to National Association of Universities and Institutions of Higher Education (*ANUIES)* (2019) in the Higher Education Yearbook 2018–2019, only 28% have graduated from the higher level, and of those graduates, less than 50% managed to join the productive and social sector, that is, just under 20% of graduates have achieved or obtain a formal or even informal job. What happens to the rest of the graduates? They will probably join gradually, manage to find a job other than the one they prepared for, start a company, and migrate

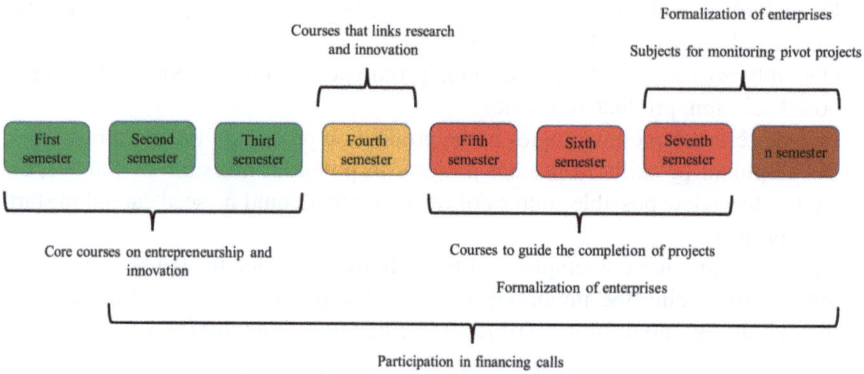

Fig. 3.7 Implementation process of entrepreneurship and transversal innovation material. (Source: Author, 2021)

to other cities or countries, among other alternatives. What results would be obtained if the students in their university life refined their entrepreneurship project, taking advantage of the infrastructure offered by the university in their training stage, and at the end of their degree, they had the possibility of starting their company derived from the entrepreneurship project?

(c) *Generation of own resources for the operation of the ecosystem.*

It is suggested that the *EOE* can generate its own resources, at least to guarantee its operation and collaborate with the initial funding of entrepreneurships. From the above, according to Table 3.1, it is proposed to offer the following non-limiting services derived from the abilities and capacities of the resources available to the ecosystem (some services can be offered free and others with a cost to generate the resources).

(d) Generation of innovation and entrepreneurship lines for their appropriation and application.

It is suggested to develop *Lines of Innovation and Entrepreneurship (LIE)* or thematic axes that are oriented to those that the university pursues and which in turn are linked to the mission and vision of the ecosystem. The foregoing, to take advantage of the potential that the locality and region have with their natural, technological, human, and infrastructure resources, which will allow in the long term to develop specialized clusters within the ecosystem and as such identify the potential in certain disciplines. Derived from the above, the design and alignment of the *LIE* is outlined in Fig. 3.8.

(e) Diffusion of the innovation ecosystem – entrepreneurship.

It is suggested to develop a dissemination plan which defines the actions to achieve effective communication inside and outside the ecosystem. For the above, the following actions are presented (see Fig. 3.9):

1. Segment the target population:

- Students from the university where the ecosystem was born.
- Administrative, operational person, teachers, and researchers.
- Businessmen, government.
- Civil society organizations and institutions of higher education of the locality.

2. What instruments can be applied for dissemination:

   - Local digital media and local newspapers and radio.
   - Events (conferences, academic fairs, congresses) and social networks.

3. Plan of dissemination activities:

   - Develop a plan to identify, among other things, the activities to be carried out for its dissemination. To collaborate with this section, Fig. 3.9 presents a general example for its temporal scope in each segment, specifying the objective, instruments, and frequency.

   (f) Cyclical design of ecosystem phases.

Table 3.1 Services of the entity that will operate the ecosystem (*EOE*)

Service	Description
1. Workshops	Disruptive ventures Techniques/methodologies for the generation of business ideas Preparation of business plans
2. Management of financing resources/ fundraising	Depending on the project and sector, services aimed at obtaining resources to fund projects may be offered.
3. Consulting	Accountant/financial Fiscal, legal Marketing: Branding Management and monetization of social networks Patent development Patent and copyright registration Design, creation, management, and linkage with social organizations Technology transfer
4. Courses	Entrepreneurship Startup and spinoff Project incubation Oriented to programs as enterprise specialties
5. Conferences	Project incubation Business plan development Networking with other entrepreneurs
6. Feasibility/feasibility studies (operational/ financial/technical)	Feasibility/feasibility studies Risk analysis Cost-benefit analysis Financial analysis of the project aimed at savings or obtaining profits

(continued)

Table 3.1 (continued)

Service	Description	
7. Rental of facilities (depending on the infrastructure)	Administrative offices	Offices available 24 h a day, for a certain number of employees: Executive desks Executive chairs Worktable/meetings High-speed internet Video conferencing/video calls Cafeteria service Computers/laptops Recreational area Boardroom Video projector
	Virtual offices Customizable	Virtual office available 24 h a day, for a certain number of employees (up to a limit allowed by the infrastructure): High-speed internet Video conferencing/video calls
	Training offices	Offices available to train personnel of the entities (companies/government/*CSO*): Workspace High-speed internet Video conferencing/video calls Cafeteria service Computers/laptops Recreational area Video projector
	Business simulation areas	Areas intended to generate a work environment like fieldwork, with the aim of testing the functionality of some product or service/method/process
8. Business acceleration	Expert support to accelerate the growth of enterprises	
9. Congresses and conferences (academic, social business, and government)	Related to ventures Early stimulation of science and technology Early stimulation of innovation Creation of enterprises Capitalize on business failure Project incubation Business plan development Networking with other entrepreneurs	

Source: Author (2021)

Derived from the above, the following design is proposed according to Fig. 3.10 given that it is expected to receive new entrepreneurships on a continuous basis. The stages and phases must be cyclical to meet said demand for services. With this, it will be possible to attend as far as possible those undertakings that are favored with integration into the ecosystem.

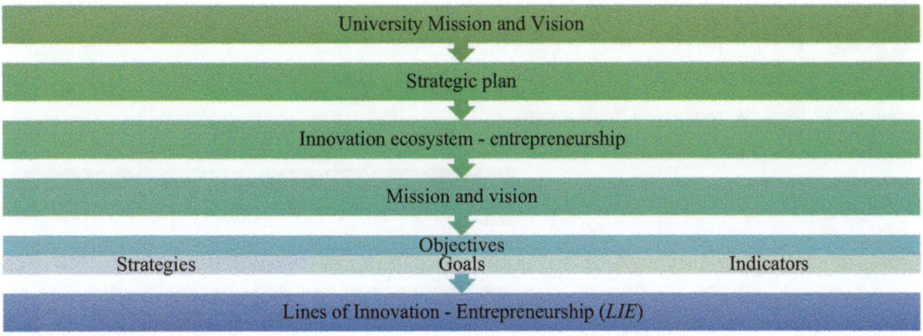

Fig. 3.8 Design of the Innovation and Entrepreneurship Lines of the Ecosystem. (Source: Author, 2021)

(g) Initial action plan with entrepreneurs.

Aware of the capacity and intellectual wealth, creativity, and ideas of all people regardless of age, efforts should be made to guide or refine said capacity, through programs, courses, and education, in addition to shielding their adequate development. In this sense, educational institutions are a natural source to refine this capacity and serve as an input for the ecosystem. However, it is suggested to generate various actions to collaborate with the monitoring, shielding of the entrepreneur and his entrepreneurship ideas, as well as correctly orient said talent. Therefore, in this activity, it is suggested to develop action plans to attend the initiatives of

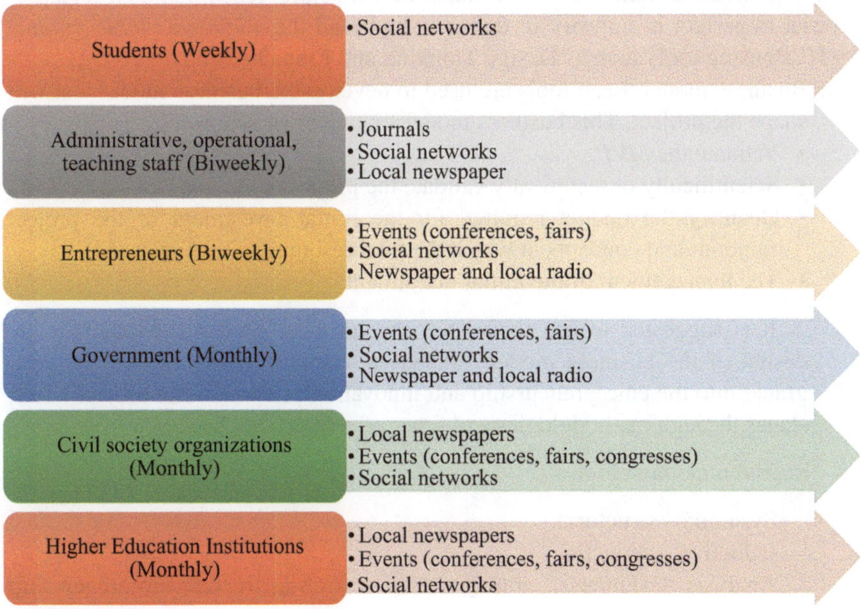

Fig. 3.9 Suggested spread by segment – instrument. (Source: Author, 2021)

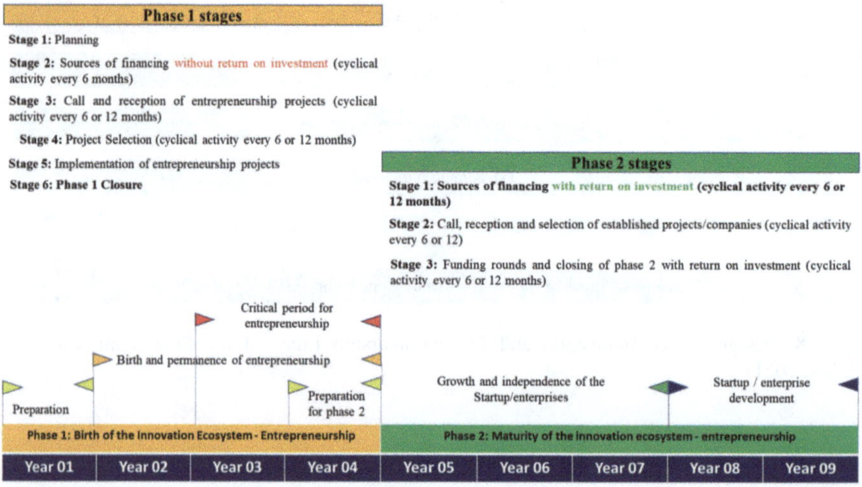

Fig. 3.10 Phases and stages proposed for the innovation and entrepreneurship ecosystem. (Source: Author, 2021)

entrepreneurs (see Fig. 3.13). One of these actions is presented in Fig. 3.11, which refers to the development of a work map for entrepreneurship projects and initiatives, which is suggested by the *EOE*.

The steps of the suggested process map suggested in Fig. 3.11 are detailed below:

1. Entrepreneurs and the idea. We collaborate with entrepreneurs in their idea proposal to perfect it, improve it, define it, and land the *minimum viable product (MVP)* using tools such as Design Thinking and Empathy Map.
   a. Business model. Lean tools are used to develop the business model that will shape the project. This business model should allow us to:
      - Validate the *MVP*.
      - Scientifically or technically validate the proposal.
      - Quantify the budget required for the initial investment of the project (amount and concepts in which the total resource will be invested).
      - The management of the initial investment.

      It is suggested to use tools such as Canvas or Business Model for the design of the business model. Likewise, scientific validation will be integrated into the entrepreneurship and innovation process in the project's start stages through methodologies and types of research such as:

   – Research methodologies.

      Systemic – structural.
      Inductive – deductive.
      Analysis – synthesis, among others according to the entrepreneurship project.

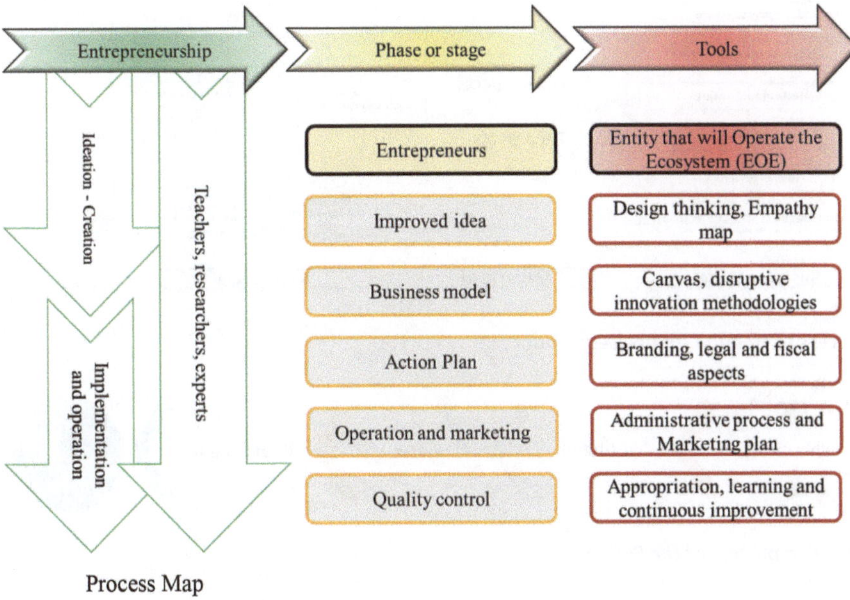

Fig. 3.11 Process map. (Source: Author, 2021)

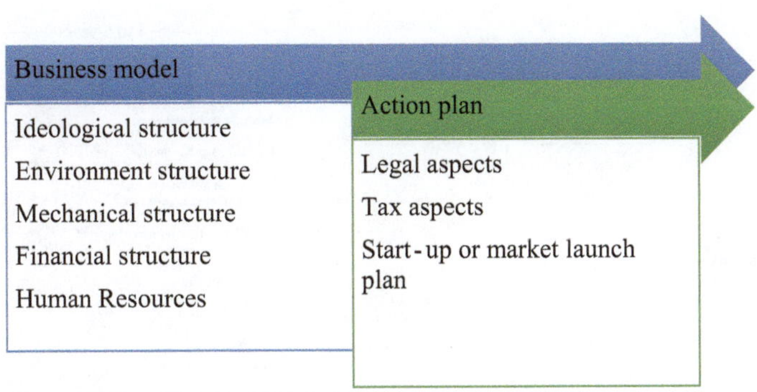

Fig. 3.12 Planning stage. (Source: Author, 2021)

– Type of research (non-limiting).

  Mixed (documentary and field). On the other hand, scientific and technological validation will also be included in the project's production process stage through methodologies that technically correspond to the project to ensure the process and validate the originality and operation of the project.

b. Action plan. It includes the detail of the activities that must be carried out to implement the project. This will allow to visualize all the actions as well as

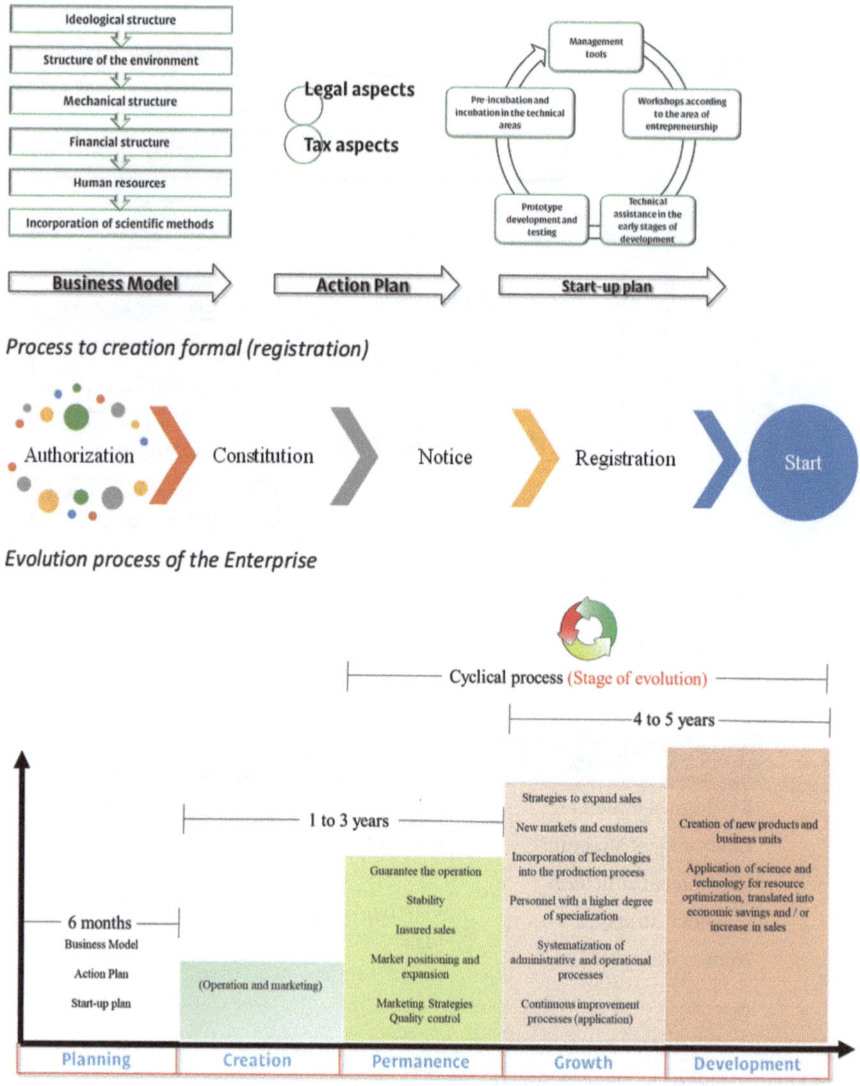

Fig. 3.13 Steps to open the business. (Source: Author, 2021)

assign responsible people, resources, and times to execute the project. Actions such as:

- Legal aspects.
- Tax aspects and startup or market launch plan.

c. Operation and marketing. The enterprise is operated to exchange products/services with customers. All the activities of the administrative and marketing process are included.

d. Quality control – continuous improvement process. The enterprise will require the start, and that will allow to have an apprenticeship where the plans are deployed in real situations. Assumptions will be adjusted or validated under operating and market conditions.

2. General responsibilities of each entity.

   a. Participant/student. The student or participant is the main person interested in their project moving forward; therefore, they concentrate the responsibilities of attending and monitoring their activities. Suggested general responsibilities are:

      - Propose the initial idea with which you want to participate in the entrepreneurship process.
      - Request professional advice in the university, the academic area, and the *EOE*.
      - Develop the project within the scope defined by the process (initial idea, *MVP*, plan or business model, demo or prototype, product, company).
      - Attend the work sessions that are scheduled.
      - Make corrections or improvements that are indicated in the different stages of the process.
      - Be aware of notifications.
      - Attend the forums and workshops indicated by the ecosystem operator and that are relevant to the objectives of your project.
      - Participate in the management of resources that the project requires.

3. Entity that will operate the ecosystem (suggested). It promotes the initiative of entrepreneurs; therefore, its role focuses in this process on the following key activities:

   - Summon periodically to present entrepreneurship and innovation projects.
   - Explain the process in detail to those interested in participating.
   - Provide guidance on the approach of ideas.
   - Provide support in the definition of the business model for the proposed projects.
   - Support in the development of the startup plan.
   - Provide guidance on legal or fiscal aspects that the participant needs to attend to.
   - Give support or support in the management of resources that are necessary for the participant's project.
   - Serve as a manager or link as the various actors involved or who need to be included in the entrepreneurship project/process.
   - Follow up on the maturation process of the companies that are created because of the support given to the entrepreneurs.
   - Provide the necessary support to ensure the success of the company created.

With the above, it seeks to collaborate in the creation of new enterprise that include elements of innovation focused on those that are disruptive and provides a flexible methodology that enterprise entrepreneurs throughout the process, where at each stage there is a progressively maturing product. The entrepreneur sets the standard in the speed of the process and is the main stakeholder, while the *EOE* seeks to create the optimal conditions that allow the materialization of the undertaking.

In the same way in Fig. 3.11 in the tools section, the *EOE* has the task of accompanying the entrepreneur throughout the process of creating and *Small, Medium, and Large (SML)* or startup, from his idea to its materialization and permanence (during the first 3 months), either advising or even participating/collaborating in the implementation of each stage together with the entrepreneur. However, the entrepreneur is the one who ultimately decides at what stage they want the ecosystem to intervene, leaving open the possibility of seeking alternative solutions. For this, the *EOE* is suggested to implement and disseminate the following methodology in its planning stage for all the initiatives received (see Fig. 3.12).

- Planning stage. In the planning stage, it is intended to identify those minimum aspects that are essential for the idea to become an *SML* project, defining in detail the business model and the action plan to avoid as much as possible the failure of the project. This, although it is complicated since according to organizations such as the defunct National Entrepreneur Institute (*INADEM*) (2018), the *OECD* (2021), and the European Commission (2021a, b), indicates that more than 90% of the newly created *SML* fail among the first 3 years of existence, hence the importance of accompanying entrepreneurship projects with infrastructure and advice, which will previously go through methodological processes to seek their fine-tuning and optimization.

- Business model. Taking into account the methodologies of lean (Ries, 2013), design thinking (Brown, 2009; Brown & Wyatt, 2010), as well as good entrepreneur practices (Entrepreneur, 2018), the points that are suggested for entrepreneurs are the following (non-limiting):
- Ideological structure. Includes the name of the company, mission, vision, values, and a description of the competitive advantages of the business.
  - Name of the company and mission and vision.
  - Values, commitment, and competences.
- Structure of the environment. It is based on an analysis of the strengths and weaknesses of the company, as well as the behavior of the sector in which it operates, market trends, competition, and potential customers.
  - Minimum viable product.
  - SWOT Analysis (Strengths, Weaknesses, Opportunities, Threats).
  - Describe the target audience. Research market demographics.
  - Know how often your product and/or service is purchased.
  - Study your competitors and competitive advantages.
- Mechanical structure. Distribution, sales, marketing, and advertising strategies are listed.

- Price of your product and/or service and strategic planning.
- Payment plans and sales force and distribution channels.
- Communication channels and logo and brand.

• Financial structure. This point suggests the calculation and projections of scenarios, the viability of the idea in economic terms, and whether it will generate an attractive profit margin.

  - Pro forma income statement projected for 3 years.
  - Pro forma balance sheet projected for 3 years.
  - Pro forma cash flow projected over 3 years.
  - Balance point analysis.
  - Scenario analysis and sources of financing (own and external income).

• Human resources. It helps to define each of the essential jobs and determines the rights and obligations of each of the members that make up the organization.

  - Organization chart.
  - Certificate of positions and determine the cost of the template.

• Action plan. It includes a detail of the activities that must be carried out to implement the project. This allows to visualize all the actions, as well as to assign responsible people, resources, and times in which it is suggested to execute the project (Fig. 3.13).

(h) Creation of a civil society organization.

The creation of the civil society organization directly linked to the *EOE* will give the opportunity to be directly linked with other *CSO*, share strategic information, seek to integrate society into the processes as appropriate, and above all seek financing channels exclusively for entrepreneurships, through donations. This will relieve the *EOE* of certain responsibilities.

It is suggested that said *CSO* be created with an international scope, which will allow participation in calls for financing external entrepreneurship, as well as experiences from abroad that benefit, on the one hand, the absorption of knowledge for the *CSO* and *EOE*, as well as links that favor construction of startups or companies derived from the entrepreneurships.

3.1.3.2 Creation of Indicators

In this area, it is suggested, on the one hand, to design and create indicators for the *EOE* and, on the other hand, indicators to measure the progress of phases 1 and 2 of the ecosystem, both groups of complementary indicators since they are sequential. From the above, according to Fig. 3.14, the design of the indicators (non-limiting) is presented.

According to Fig. 3.14, to design the indicators, they start from the design of the objectives, goals, and strategies, where it is suggested that these be measurable and quantifiable so that they are considered naturally by the indicators.

According to Fig. 3.15, the indicators must be aligned with the goals, which must be in congruence with the strategies. This will allow to measure what is committed to the objectives.

On the other hand, to collaborate in the design of the indicators, three suggestions for innovation indicators are presented:

A. The first proposal is made up of five groups of indicators.
B. The second proposal is presented in two pillar groups of indicators.
C. The third proposal is presented in three groups of indicators.

First Proposal

It is made up of five groups of indicators, as can be seen in Table 3.2.

According to Table 3.2, the first group of related factors/indicators are (Dziallasa & Blinda, 2019):

1. Category and specific dimensions.
   - Culture of innovation. This factor mentions the importance of culture, which is a means to achieve success and foster innovation capacities. Some enterprises beliefs and values influence its tolerance for risk and innovation activities and its motivation to develop and implement new ideas.
   - Strategy. A company's strategy defines long-term activities and is the basis for defining specific innovation objectives. The strategy translates into the number of new innovations.
   - Competence and knowledge. This area is a crucial source for generating new ideas and innovation projects. Individual competence is the ability to implement knowledge and in turn actions to define objectives.
   - Organizational structure. The organizational structure regulates, controls, and coordinates the rules, hierarchies, and responsibilities. This makes it possible to identify the relationship between the size of the company in relation to the innovation that it manages to manage and implement.

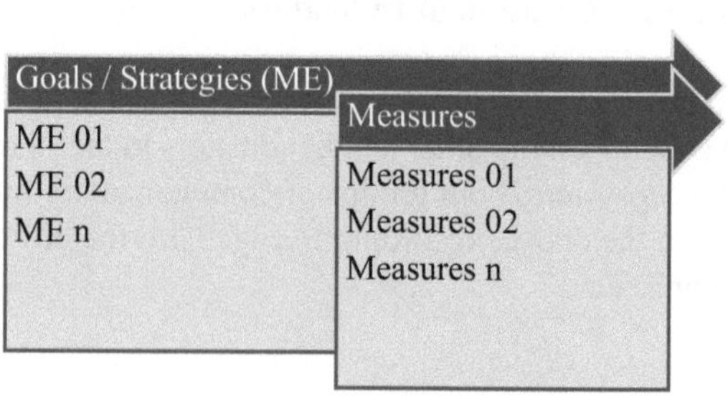

Fig. 3.14 Design and creation of indicators for the *EOE*. (Source: Author, 2021)

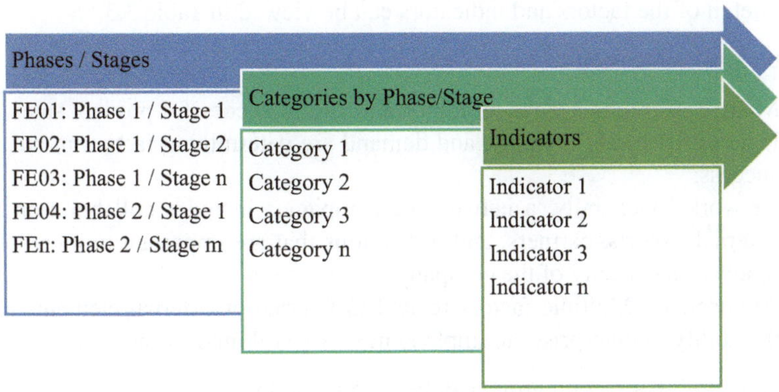

Fig. 3.15 Design and creation of indicators associated with the phases of the ecosystem. (Source: Author, 2021)

Table 3.2 Innovation and entrepreneurship indicators

Description	Category	Percentage (%)	Tables
By category and specific dimensions	Culture of innovation	10	Table 3.3
	Strategy	4	
	Competence and knowledge	9	
	Organizational structure	10	
	Innovation and development activities	11	
	Innovation performance	7	
Contextual dimensions	Market	13	Table 3.4
	Networks	4	
	Environment	5	
Innovation products	–	17	Table 3.5
Innovation processes	–	5	Table 3.6
Innovation project management	–	5	Table 3.7
Total		100	–

Source: Author (2021), taken from the framework of dimensions to generate the innovation indicators (Dziallasa & Blinda, 2019)

- Innovation and development activities. Research and development activities and inputs are related to the financial situation of the enterprise, as well as the availability of resources, which are used in human resources, machinery, tools, and materials and which are dedicated to the development of innovations.
- Performance of innovation. Performance is defined as the profits of a business through the sales of innovative products, methods, and services supported by marketing.

The detail of the factors and indicators can be viewed in Table 3.3.

2. Contextual dimensions.

   - Market. Marketing plays an important role in successful product sales. The level of the market, supply, and demand are determining factors in business success.
   - Networks. Generally, a network of companies includes collaboration with external experts, partners, and institutions that are important to increase the innovation capacity of the company.
   - Atmosphere. Multiple factors related to internal or external elements affect the ability of enterprises to implement successful innovations.

   The detail of this second group can be seen in Table 3.4.

In relation to innovation products and processes, these share five indicators and factors, which have the following function (Dziallasa & Blinda, 2019; Kline & Rosenberg, 1986; Lester, 1998):

- Product definition. The product is defined together with the market requirements that are identified and known by consumers and viewers. Ideas for product innovation are generated and evaluated.
- Product concept. The product concept is created based on the definition of the product to coordinate it and initiate the validation and production phases. The potential cost and required sources are considered according to the business case calculation of the innovative idea. Product development begins.
- Validation phase. Prototypes are developed and tested to meet various requirements.
- Production phase. When the innovation is produced on a small scale and the processes are approved, mass production begins.
- Launch to the market. The innovations start by being produced in series. The final product is introduced to the market with the communication and marketing strategy to guarantee sales.

To identify the indicators and factors of the innovation products and processes, Tables 3.5 and 3.6 are presented.

3. Innovation products.

According to Torrisi et al. (2016) and Dewangan and Godse (2014), the relevant factors of innovation products are essentially to increase product performance. This implies that the advantages that a product could have must be visible and intuitive to the consumer, as well as its demonstrable functionality. In this sense, standardization is a good alternative to improve the technological performance of the product. On the other hand, the importance of the innovation product lies in the number of product ideas materialized, as well as their duration and the number of projects defined or completed. In this sense, indicators play an important role in defining products before starting their mass and scale development. These indicators can be viewed according to Table 3.5.

Table 3.3 Indicators by category and specific dimensions

Category	Factor	Indicator
Culture of innovation[1]	Creativity	Percentage of leaders trained in creativity techniques
	Innovation-oriented companies	Time spent by administrators with innovations compared to normal tasks
	Opening companies toward change and innovation	Number of external ideas/ideas generated by consumers
Strategy[2]	Resistance to change, innovation strategies, and new product strategy	Number of newly created innovations
Competence and knowledge[3]	Innovation-oriented learning	Number of managers trained with innovation methods and tools
	Openness to knowledge, internal knowledge, external, by experiences	Use of external knowledge and native information
Organizational structure[4]	Business data, organizational factors	Company size, geographical location, age of the company, internal and external growth, formal structure
	Flexibility and rapid adaptation of customers; internal communication	Leader with strengths, satisfaction of the work team, dedicated activities and with transversal and multidisciplinary interaction
Innovation and development activities[5]	Investment in innovation, research, and development; willingness to carry out new research projects; financial resources dedicated to innovation	Expenditure/investment in *research and development (R&D)* Average expenditure per idea or venture financed Percentage of sales generated by new products Company budget for innovation expenditure
Innovation performance[6]	–	Return on investment in innovation; profit margin in *R&D*; new markets and businesses; percentage of innovations that benefit

Source: Author (2021), taken from the category of indicators by specific dimensions (1980–2015). Dziallasa and Blinda (2019)[1]; Bayarçelik and Taşel (2012), Slater et al. (2014), Yang et al. (2015)[2]; Dewangan and Godse (2014), Hittmar et al. (2015)[3]; Hittmar et al. (2015), Kato et al. (2015)[4]; Kim (2014), Avdar and Aydin (2015)[5]; Tsai (2001), Tseng and Wu (2007)[6]; Caird et al. (2013), Kim (2014)

4. Innovation processes.

The innovation process is commonly complex; therefore, to assess the relevance of the indicators in said process, the results of the indicators must be analyzed before and afterward. The innovation process is divided into different stages based on different phases indicated in Table 3.6. It is important to point out the dynamics and feedback of the innovation process and product indicators (Dodgson & Hinze, 2000; Cooper, 1990; Hart et al., 2003).

Table 3.4 Indicators by category according to their contextual dimensions

Category	Factors	Indicator
Market[1]	Market demand	Growth in demand in the industry and duration of demand
	Maintenance and expansion of the shared market	Market share and position
	Analysis and monitoring of the competition	Introduction of new products vs competition
	Consumer satisfaction	Customer complaints; response time to customer requests; reliability and speed of delivery; customer retention rate
Networks[2]	Internal and external collaboration	*R&D*&I alliances; activities of transfer of knowledge and technology
Environment[3]	Innovation environment	Number of innovation businesses; new ventures
	Stakeholders; policies and support for specific innovation programs	–

Source: Author (2021), taken from the contextual dimensions (1980–2015) (Dziallasa & Blinda, 2019). Considering[1]: Palmberg (2006), Mendes Luz et al. (2015), Ivanova and Avasilcăi (2014), De Felice and Petrillo (2013), Dewangan and Godse (2014)[2]; Belitz, et al. (2011), Oyelaran-Oyeyinka and Adebowale (2012), Caird et al. (2013), De Medeiros et al. (2014)[3]; Pervan et al. (2015), Bloch and Bugge (2013), Al-Mubaraki et al. (2015)

5. Management of innovation processes.

This group of indicators are important for the proper interaction between the indicators of the innovation processes and products since they are involved in the planning, supervision, and control of both groups. Management in the innovation process is essential because it affects success or failure and consequently affects the innovation product, so the follow-up, dialogue, and decisions that are made derived from the management indicators will be essential for its success; the indicators of this group are presented in Table 3.7 (Cooper, 1999).

Second Proposal

This second proposal is made up of 2 pillars, 5 categories, and 18 indicators as shown in Table 3.8.

To understand a little more the indicators in Table 3.8, the following concepts are presented (Klaus, 2019)*:*

- Pillar: business dynamism.
  - Cost of starting a business. Costs include official fees and professional fees.
  - Time that elapses to start a business from the idea to its implementation and operation. This indicator refers to the average time it takes for the company to be legally created, from the beginning of the registration of the idea.

Table 3.5 Indicators of innovation and entrepreneurship products

Indicators and factors		l/p	i/d
Product definition[1]	Number of ideas or suggestions for new products	p	d
	Percentage of viable ideas for commercialization	p	d
	Precise definition of new, stable products before their development begins	l	i
	Potential for synergy vs dependence on other products	l	i
	Balance of the innovation portfolio	l	i
	What's new in enterprises vs new products	l	d
	Projected product life	l	d
Product concept[2]	Intellectual property rights, patents, citations, applications, and licenses	p	i
	Distribution of patents with the support of laws	l	i
	Technological significance	l	i
	Technical standards and standardization degrees	p	i
	Number of projects with their implementation in business and marketing	p	d
Validation phase[3] Production phase[3] Market launch[3]	New product performance/new product success rate	p	d
	Number of new or improved products/number of products launched on the market	p	d
	Cost of introducing a new product, introducing technological innovation to the market	p	d
	Successful implementation of new ideas transformed into shared products or ideas	p	d
	Identification of innovation by business managers	l	d
	Expert assessments	l	d
	Perceived value	l	d
	Taxation	p	d
	Openness or reality/consumer familiarization with innovation and specialization	l	d
	Product advantages	l	d
	Degree of innovation	l	d
	Appearance	l	d
	Content of the innovation	l	d
	Product quality and profitability	p	d
	Functionality comparisons	l	i
	Compatibility, corrections, or adaptations	l	i
	Complexity of innovation	l	i
	Social benefits	l	i
	Advantages of opportunity	l	i
	Launch quality and quantity	p	d
	Product life cycle length	p	d
	Sustainability and eco-efficiency of the product	l	d
	Extension of innovative products offered	p	i
	Ranking of innovative products	p	i
	Percentage of sales protected by patents	p	i
	Use of licensed technologies	p	i
	Trademarks	l	d

l = light-easy (qualitative indicator); p = heavy-complex (quantitative indicator)

(continued)

Table 3.5 (continued)

i = indirect influence on the success of innovations; d = direct influence on the success of innovations

Source: Author (2021), taken from the indicators of innovation products and factors identified in the innovation process (Dziallasa & Blinda, 2019). Considering[1]: Dewangan and Godse (2014), Cooper (1999), Astebro and Michaela (2005), Griffin and Page (1993)[2]; Dewangan and Godse (2014), Basberg (1987), Veugelers and Cassiman (1999), Buesa et al. (2010), Cavdar and Aydin (2015), Raja and Wei (2015)[3]; Griffin and Page (1993), Dewangan and Godse (2014), Hittmar et al. (2015), Fleuren et al. (2014), Cooper (1999), Astebro and Michaela (2005), Tipping et al. (1995)

Table 3.6 Indicators of innovation and entrepreneurship processes

Indicators and factors		l/p	i/d
Product definition[1]	Time for next-generation development	p	d
	Diversity in the idea generation process	l	i
	Time for idea generation	p	i
	Management for the accumulation of ideas	l	d
	Generation of ideas and management of these	l	d
	Motivational factors in the work environment for the generation of ideas	l	d
	Product development planning and processes	l	i
	Business planning	l	i
	Participation of successful products/effective projects	p	i
Product concept[2]	Number of ongoing innovations	p	d
	Innovation activity	l	d
	Explicit selection of projects	l	i
	Number of designs made by the company	p	i
	Business cases	l	i
Validation phase[3]	Innovative projects	l	i
	Detailed tactical project planning	l	i
	Formal ratification by management	l	i
	Implementation of innovation activities	l	i
	Motivational factors in the work environment for the implementation of ideas	l	d
	Gap between planned and executed	l	d
Production phase[4]	Cost of production/development of new products	p	i
	Ease of manufacture	l	i
	Manufacturing efficiency and productivity	p	d
	Increased production capacity and flexibility	l	d
	Deadline for the execution of internal processes	p	i
	Number of optimized production processes the company uses for products	p	i
	Use of new technology to produce new products	l	i
	Planning and implementation systems	l	i
	Re-evaluation efforts: Updating and reoriented project plans and aligning team elements to obtain it	l	i
	Innovation implementation time	p	i
	Processing time	p	d

(continued)

Table 3.6 (continued)

Indicators and factors		l/p	i/d
Market launch[5]	Time for the identification of needs of a consumer product until its commercialization	p	d
	Time for marketing	p	d
	Construction of the delivery time	p	i
	Labor productivity	p	i
	Number of improved processes	p	i
	Decrease in the percentage in the cost of processes and innovation products	p	d
	Percentage of project milestones achieved	p	i
	Duration of product introduction	p	d
	Achieving the purpose of innovation	l	i
	Launch planning and execution	l	d
	Facilities for the implementation of innovation	l	i
	Total cost of project marketing vs number of successfully marketed projects.	p	d

l = light-easy (qualitative indicator); p = heavy-complex (quantitative indicator)
i = indirect influence on the success of innovations; d = direct influence on the success of innovations
Source: Author (2021), taken from the indicators of innovation products and factors identified in the innovation process (Dziallasa & Blinda, 2019). Considering[1]: Ivanova and Avasilcăi (2014), Kim (2014), Koc (2007)[2]; Hittmar et al. (2015), Therrien and Mohnen (2003)[3]; Fleuren et al. (2014), Lester (1998), Astebro and Michaela (2005)[4]; Tipping et al. (1995), Sawang (2011)[5]; Astebro and Michaela (2005), Tohidi and Jabbari (2012), Lester (1998)

- Insolvency recovery rate. Registered with a monetary value that refers to the beginning of the procedure as a new company integrating the lost value because of the time of the value of the money that is lost or immobilized in an insolvency proceeding.
- Insolvency regulatory framework. This index is calculated by assigning scores of the procedures and negotiations with the interested parties.
- Actions and attitudes to face business risk. These indicators refer to items related to reducing business risk.

    Delegation of authority. This item refers to the leadership capacity and the quality of human resources to decentralize decision-making.
    Growth of innovative enterprises. It refers to the total of ideas that have managed to mature, until they become legal enterprises.
    Enterprises that adopt disruptive ideas. This indicator refers to the identification of disruptive ideas that are identified and materialized in an enterprise that creates disruptive products or services.
    Diversity of the workforce. It refers to the diversity of human resources with which the work groups are integrated in the ecosystem without being discriminatory based on gender, religion, or ethnicity.

Table 3.7 Management indicators of innovation and entrepreneurship processes

Indicators and factors		l/p	i/d
Innovation process management[1]	Efficiency of projects in relation to their cost and time	p	d
	Project delay	p	d
	Pass rate	p	i
	Quality of execution of the activities committed in the innovation process	p	d
	Quality process in new products	l	i
	Efficient processes/wrong decision points	l	i
	New product development processes/own process management	l	i
	Complex project management	l	i
	Percentage of projects in the total projects defined by the management system through milestones	l	i
	Clear objectives and aligned indicators	p	i
	Percentage of targets completed on target date	l	i
	Planning and monitoring of innovation processes	p	i
	Alternative pathways for the development of new product processes	l	i
	Understanding of the processes for new product development	l	i
	Clarity in procedures	l	i
	Own projects	l	d
	Flexibility and agility, decentralization in decision-making	l	i
	Effects of feedback between innovation decisions	l	i
	Responsibility	l	i
	Project leaders	l	i
	Replacement for departing staff	l	i
	Monitoring of innovation processes with special attention to technological flaws	l	i
	Skills for the performance of technological flaws	l	i
	Number of meetings	p	i

l = light-easy (qualitative indicator); p = heavy-complex (quantitative indicator)
i = indirect influence on the success of innovations; d = direct influence on the success of innovations
Source: Author (2021), taken from the indicators of innovation products and factors identified in the innovation process (Dziallasa & Blinda, 2019). Considering[1]: Fleuren et al. (2014), Lester (1998), De Felice and Petrillo (2013)

Cluster development status. It refers to the work groups that are managed to integrate in the same locality, such as enterprises, suppliers, experts, specialists, and social organizations, which participate directly in the creation of enterprises derived from the ecosystem.

International co-inventions. It refers to the direct interventions of experts, entrepreneurs, or international actors, who intervene directly in materialized companies that are created in the ecosystem, measured by international patents.

Table 3.8 Pillars and indicators of an innovation and entrepreneurship ecosystem

Pillar	Category	Indicator	Percentage (%)
Business dynamism	Administrative requirements	Cost of starting a business	6
		Time that elapses to start a business from the idea to its implementation and operation	6
		Insolvency recovery rate	6
		Insolvency regulatory framework	6
	Business culture	Actions and attitudes to face business risk	6
		Delegation of authority	6
		Growth of innovative companies	6
		Companies embracing disruptive ideas	6
Capacity for innovation	Diversity and collaboration	Workforce diversity	5
		Cluster development status	5
		Co-international investments	5
		Multi-stakeholder collaboration	5
	Research and development	Scientific publications	5
		Patent application	5
		Expenditure on *R&D*	5
		Index of research programs	5
	Marketing	Buyer sophistication	5
		Trademark enforcement	5
Total			100

Source: Author (2021), adapted from the methodology and technical notes of the global competitiveness index 4.0 (Klaus, 2019)

Multi-stakeholder collaboration. In this area, the number of collaborators and/or entities that share ideas based on the initial entrepreneur's ideas are considered, which in turn are formalized with the creation of enterprises derived from the innovation and entrepreneurship ecosystem.

Scientific publications. This indicator measures the number of published articles cited in other works with at least an h-index, considering publication of articles, reviews, and lectures at conferences.

Patent application. The sum of patent applications per million inhabitants is considered in this indicator.

Expenditure for *R&D*. It refers to the research and development expenses allocated by the ecosystem that are used and implemented directly to the ventures created derived from particularly disruptive innovations.

Index of programs dedicated to research and innovation. This item refers to academic programs that aim to train future entrepreneurs, those who have materialized their innovations, and ideas in legal enterprises.

Sophistication of the buyer. It refers to the application of field instruments to know the bases on which consumers make their purchasing decisions.

Application of trademarks. It refers to the number of international applications per million inhabitants, which are directly destined for the enterprises created in the ecosystem.

Third Proposal

This proposal is made up of three groups of indicators as observed in Tables 3.9, 3.10, and 3.11. The first of them integrates nine pillars which it is suggested to apply in the two phases of the ecosystem. This first group aims to measure the activities that directly affect the ecosystem in its process of birth, growth, development, and maturity.

According to Table 3.9, nine pillars are proposed in this first group of indicators, which are described below:

- Culture of innovation. These indicators refer to incentivize, promote, and share the vision and mission of the ecosystem focused on innovation so that this is shared with all internal and external factors involved in the ecosystem with a long-term view and its inclusion as natural, diverse, and collaborative, as well as disseminating the products, services, or methods created by the entrepreneurs and/or materialized entrepreneurships.
- Business. In these indicators, it is suggested to measure the creativity of entrepreneurs, as well as the materialization of their ideas in enterprises. In the same way, it monitors the ventures created from creativity and ideas, in particular those disruptive ones that manage to transform into startups.
- Investment in innovation. These indicators are those aimed at collaboration as sources of financing for entrepreneurships, in addition to monitoring and recovery of investments and financing depending on each phase vs entrepreneurships. In addition, it identifies the spectrum of new financing opportunities for local innovations.
- Strategic. They are oriented to the optimization of administrative processes and requirements to accelerate the creation of startups, in addition to allowing their transparency. On the other hand, it also makes it possible to measure the business culture of entrepreneurs translated into skills, actions, growth, and the adoption of disruptive ideas.
- Competence and knowledge. Directed to measure the capacities, tools, and methods of administrators or actors involved in decision-making, in addition to measuring the knowledge of the external context and local information projected to the growth of the ecosystem and its local use.
- Organizational structure. It suggests measuring the capacity and abilities of the human resource, as well as the interaction of the work team to achieve the objectives from a multidisciplinary perspective.
- Market. It suggests measuring aspects related to market demand, as well as its interaction and positioning. Finally, it suggests considering aspects related to the consumer and their degree of satisfaction and sophistication.

Table 3.9 Proposal of general indicators

Pillar	Category	Indicator description
Culture of innovation	Events, forums, congresses, etc.	Time dedicated to the event (days)
		Derivative products
		Population served by segment
	Creativity	Time spent on innovations compared to normal tasks
		Identification of innovation by professors, researchers, and experts
		Methods or techniques in the idea generation process
		Number of newly created innovations (disruptive vs nondisruptive)
	Diversity and collaboration	Workforce diversity (categorize)
		Local cluster development status/index
		Number of multi-stakeholder collaborations
		Number of alliances of research + development + innovation
		Knowledge and technology transfer activities
		Policies vs support for specific innovation programs
	Research and development	Number of scientific publications (articles, books, and conferences)
		Index of programs dedicated to innovation and research
		Total patents/total patents accepted
		Intellectual property rights, patents, citations, applications, and licenses
Business	Enterprises	Number of internal/external ideas
		Number of ideas/ideas generated by consumers
		Enterprise's size, geographical location, age of the enterprise, internal and external growth, formal structure
		Entrepreneurship ideas/entrepreneurship materialized in enterprises
		Total ideas materialized/disruptive ideas materialized

(continued)

Table 3.9 (continued)

Pillar	Category	Indicator description
Investment in innovation	Resources for innovation	Expenditure/investment in research + development + innovation
		Average expenditure per idea or venture financed
		Cost of starting a business
		Co-local-international investments
		Rate of return on investment
		Return on investment in innovation
		Profit margin in research + development
		New markets and businesses
		Percentage of innovations that benefits
		Total investment/recovered investment
Strategic	Administrative requirements	Time that elapses to start a business from the idea to its implementation and operation
		Transparent regulatory framework aligned with the ecosystem
	Business culture	Actions and attitudes to face risk and business failure
		Skills to ensure delegation of authority
		Growth of innovative companies
		Companies embracing disruptive ideas
Competence and knowledge	Oriented to innovation	Number of managers trained with innovation methods and tools
		Use of external knowledge and native information
Organizational structure	Organizational structure of the *EOE*	Leader with strengths
		The work team
		Dedicated activities with transversal and multidisciplinary interaction
		Specialized academic training
		Years of experience
		Quality of teaching
		Quality of research
		Experts by sector

(continued)

Table 3.9 (continued)

Pillar	Category	Indicator description
Market	Market demand	Growth in demand in the industry and duration of demand
	Maintenance and expansion of the shared market	Market share and position
	Analysis and monitoring of the competition	Introduction of new products vs competition
		Customer complaints; response time to customer requests; reliability and speed of delivery; customer retention rate
		Buyer sophistication
		Trademark enforcement
Sustainability	Innovation environment	Number of entrepreneurships oriented to the circular economy and social economy
		Sustainability – Care for the environment and eco-efficiency of the product
Entrepreneurship	Efficiency	Total potential entrepreneurs/total of real entrepreneurs
		Total enterprises/total of enterprises derived from entrepreneurship
		Academic programs/programs with entrepreneurship profile
		Total entrepreneurships/total successful resilient entrepreneurships
		Total of materialized entrepreneurships/total of social enterprises
		Total of processes/total of transparent processes
Banking products and services	Banking	Diversification of banks
		Regulation of banks in favor of entrepreneurship
		Import and export products and services
		Existing products and services in the local market

Source: Author (2021), adapted from Dziallasa and Blinda (2019)

- Sustainability. It seeks to measure the degree of sustainable enterprises, considering those oriented to the circular economy. In this block, sustainability indicators are integrated to guide the emergence of enterprises oriented to the social economy, care for the environment, and eco-efficiency of the product (Carayannis & Campbell, 2019).
- Entrepreneurship. This group of indicators is related to the activities of the entrepreneur, as well as the propitious context to increase their efficiency translated into undertakings materialized in startups.
- Banking products and services. This type of indicator suggests the valuation of banking services aimed at promoting entrepreneurship, as well as their accessibility to the ecosystem and to entrepreneurship projects.

The following group of indicators according to Table 3.10 are linked to the innovation process, like those previously presented, with the addition of two categories, continuous improvement and systematization, to accompany the sustainability of the ecosystem, as well as optimization and transparency of processes and information.

According to Tables 3.10 and 3.11 in relation to innovation products and processes, these share five indicators and factors, which have the following function (Dziallasa & Blinda, 2019, Kline & Rosenberg, 1986, Lester, 1998):

- Product definition. The product is defined together with the market requirements that are identified and known by consumers and viewers. Ideas for product innovation are generated and evaluated.
- Product concept. The product concept is created based on the definition of the product to coordinate it and initiate the validation and production phases. The potential cost and required sources are considered according to the business case calculation of the innovative idea. Product development begins.
- Validation phase. Prototypes are developed and tested to meet various requirements.
- Production phase. When the innovation is produced on a small scale and the processes are approved, mass production begins.
- Launch to the market. The innovations start by being produced in series. The final product is introduced to the market with the communication and marketing strategy to guarantee sales.

The following three pillars correspond specifically to the innovation process, which refer to:

- Management. This group of indicators are important for the proper interaction between the indicators of the innovation processes and products, since they are involved in the planning, supervision, and control of both groups. In the same way, these indicators function as dialogue and support the decision-making derived from the indicators (Cooper, 1999).
- Continuous improvement. It suggests the continuous assessment of the processes and their continuous improvement, in addition to establishing evaluation periods in accordance with the regulatory framework to which the ecosystem is sug-

Table 3.10 Indicators oriented to the innovation and entrepreneurship process

Pillar	Category	Indicator description
Innovation process	Product definition	Time for next-generation product development
		Time for idea generation
		Management for the accumulation of ideas
		Motivational factors in the work environment for the generation of ideas
		Product development planning and processes
		Participation of successful products/ effective projects
	Product concept	Number of ongoing innovations
		Innovation activity
		Explicit selection of projects
		Number of designs made by the enterprises
	Validation phase	Innovative projects
		Implementation of innovation activities
		Motivational factors in the work environment for the implementation of ideas
	Production phase	Cost of production/development of new products
		Number of optimized production processes the company uses for products
		Use of new technology to produce new products
		Innovation implementation time
	Market launch	Time for the identification of needs of a consumer product until its commercialization
		Time to market implementation
		Construction of the delivery time
		Decrease in the percentage in the cost of processes and innovation products
		Percentage of project milestones achieved
		Duration of product introduction
		Achieving the purpose of innovation
		Launch planning and execution
		Facilities for the implementation of innovation
		Total cost of project marketing vs number of successfully marketed projects
	Continuous improvement	Total process/number of improved processes
		Periodicity of quality assessments

(continued)

Table 3.10 (continued)

Pillar	Category	Indicator description
	Management	Quality of execution of the activities committed in the innovation process
		New product development processes/own process management
		Planning and monitoring of innovation processes
		Alternative pathways for the development of new product processes
		Understanding of the processes for new product development
		Effects of feedback between innovation decisions
		Monitoring of innovation processes with special attention to technological flaws
	Systematization and use of *information technologies* (*IT*) and *artificial intelligence (AI)*	Skills for the performance of defects related to the use of *IT* and artificial intelligence
		Total process/systematized procedures
		Total procedures/procedures where *AI* intervenes

Source: Author (2021), adapted from Dziallasa and Blinda (2019)

gested, as well as those suggestions and good practices of national and international quality standards.

- Systematization and use of *ICT* and artificial intelligence. This group of indicators suggests the measurement of the processes that have been systematized to systematize the entire flow and process in accordance with the organizational manual and procedures manual determined for the ecosystem, in addition to measuring the capacities of the actors.

In the third and last group of indicators presented in Table 3.11, it is oriented to the innovation product or service, from its definition to its launch. This allows to measure and make decisions about those ventures that manage to stay and grow, focusing on innovation, the core objective of the entrepreneurship.

It is important to mention that the **proposal of the three groups of indicators** is comprehensive. Therefore, it is suggested to carry out correlated analyses of the results of each indicator, since some will be a cause and others a consequence. This will allow to reduce risks and make decisions to avoid deviations in the fulfillment of the objectives.

Table 3.11 Indicators oriented to the innovation product or service

Pillar	Category	Indicator description
Innovation products	Product definition	Number of ideas or suggestions for new products
		Percentage of viable ideas for commercialization
		Precise definition of new, stable products before their development begins
		Balance of the innovation portfolio
	Product concept	Distribution of patents with the support of laws
		Technological significance
		Technical standards, standardization degrees
	Validation phase Production phase Market launch	New product performance/new product success rate
		Number of new or improved products/number of products launched on the market
		Cost of introducing a new product, introducing technological innovation to the market
		Expert assessments
		Openness or reality/consumer familiarization with innovation and specialization
		Product advantages
		Grade of innovation
		Content of the innovation
		Product quality and profitability
		Complexity of innovation
		Product life cycle length
		Extension of innovative products offered
		Ranking of innovative products
		Percentage of sales protected by patents
		Opening of the market
		Trademarks

Source: Author (2021), adapted from Dziallasa and Blinda (2019)

3.1.3.3 Mechanisms to Link and Spread the Innovation Ecosystem – Entrepreneurship

It is suggested to link to the goals and strategies as appropriate. They are the mechanisms to link and disseminate the innovation and entrepreneurship ecosystem, and as such to the entrepreneurs with the stakeholders and interested actors, either to specify their link or serve as dissemination mechanism in the local, regional, national, and international environment. To achieve this, there are different mechanisms of which the following are suggested according to Tables 3.12 and 3.13 (non-limiting).

According to Table 3.12, it is important to mention that these mechanisms are considered within the ecosystem and form part of them as another actor within external ecosystems.

In relation to dissemination strategies, it is suggested to be based on a methodological and technical framework that takes advantage of the information generated

Table 3.12 Linkage mechanisms

Mechanism	Description
Calls	It is an operational linkage mechanism with greater result, not only to obtain funds from the entrepreneurships but to encourage the entrepreneurial culture. From the above, it is suggested to diversify the calls according to the objective. For example (European Innovation Council, 2021; Henríquez, 2020): Internal, external. For the financing of entrepreneurial projects. For prototypes, disruptive innovations. For basic research oriented to entrepreneurship. Open or closed. Oriented to the generation of grounded disruptive ideas. Among others.
Forums and events of entrepreneurship and innovation	Directly linked to the attraction of potential entrepreneurs, stakeholders, and other actors that collaborate with the successful linking of the ecosystem. For example: Business models. Entrepreneurship and innovation. Linking and strategic stakeholders of the locality and region. Entrepreneurship skills. *IT* skills and artificial intelligence as a tool for entrepreneurship. Difference between classical innovation and disruptive innovation. Business risk and failure as a learning process and its resilience. Sources of public, private, and mixed financing. Among others.
Advisory councils	This figure formalizes the collaborative relationship between the strategic stakeholders, which obey the nature and interest of the ecosystem. Among the councils can be the following classification and/or orientation to (Bureau of career – Iowa Department of education, 2020): Standalone. Local, regional, and international. Research and innovation (panel of experts) – Entrepreneurs. Local sustainable economic development. Government – Social – Ecosystem stakeholders. Competitiveness and regulatory improvement. Independence-oriented. Academy – *EOE.*
Seminars, workshops, and courses	These suggest being aligned to focused themes/sectors aimed at traditional and disruptive entrepreneurship opportunities, as well as for the solution of problems, demands, or needs of the local, regional, and international environment.
Volunteer activities for entrepreneurship	These activities suggest the creation of spaces for integral formation, social development, if and only if these are oriented to the innovation ecosystem and its context.

(continued)

Table 3.12 (continued)

Mechanism	Description
Knowledge transfer and innovation	This activity is aimed at sharing and building knowledge and innovation among the actors involved, to accelerate the ventures and innovation processes of a product, service, or method. It is important to mention that this transfer is appropriated by the local ecosystem.
Entrepreneurship-oriented community services	Social activities that include initiatives, projects, and programs through which the ecosystem seeks to give back to society, in addition to collecting information from the local environment that allows linking people and localities, especially to priority social issues.
Creation of agreements	This activity is relevant, since through these you can share infrastructure, human resources, and other resources between ecosystems or actors, for those entrepreneurships that require a complex production process that by itself the local ecosystem cannot afford, without transferring the cost to the entrepreneur.

Source: Author (2021)

from the current and future market, in addition to considering the progressive growth of the ecosystem. Within the diffusion mechanisms, it is suggested to consider what is indicated in Table 3.13.

Finally, according to Table 3.13, it is suggested that the indicated mechanisms be integrated, that is, refer and link between all the mechanisms, to cover the greater coverage of information depending on the type of actor, user, or consumer (Gallardo et al., 2019).

3.1.4 Organizational Manual

The organizational manuals according to the United States International Development Agency (2017) are part of the strategies of every organization for the review and fulfillment of the vision, mission, and adaptation of the strategic objectives to allow the constant review of its compliance, accompanied by indicators, policies, and procedures. Therefore, the organizational manual is designed based on the mission, vision, and objectives, and on the other hand, it is based on context research and medium- and long-term plans to support the operations and strategies of the ecosystem of innovation and entrepreneurship. According to Kramis (1994), Franklin (2009), and Rodríguez (2002), the organization manual facilitates and provides the arguments for the generation of the following documents and activities, such as:

- Documents that emerge from the organization manual:
  - Manual of general and specific procedures.
  - Procedural policy manual.

Table 3.13 Diffusion mechanisms

Mechanism	Description
Social media	It is suggested to develop a marketing plan and, based on it, align the creation of branding, social networks such as Facebook, twitter, Instagram, LinkedIn, and YouTube.
Traditional media	Given the diversity in the technological accessibility of the localities, it is suggested to include traditional media such as magazines, newspapers, radio, and television.
Neuromarketing and artificial intelligence	It is suggested to use these techniques and/or tools to successfully develop the design of marketing strategies and plans (Sánchez et al., 2019).
Development of the ecosystem webpage	Its development is recommended from a formal point of view, where the following items are considered: Home page (introductory items). Shield or logo of the ecosystem (integrating copyright). Slogan (integrating copyright). Ecosystem name (integrating copyright). Organizational structure. Means of contact and linking. Statistics and publications. Events. Gallery of images and videos. Terms and conditions and privacy notices. Links to social networks and blogs. Change/language options. About the ecosystem. Tools for gathering information, continuous improvement, and functionality. Frequently asked questions. Among other characteristics that are required to be disseminated. Secondary pages (details of the main items): In that section, you must include the detail of what is stated on the main page. Finally, it is suggested: Include links with the rest of the media included in the marketing plan. Develop the dynamic page from the user's perspective, that is, encourage and encourage the user experience. Constant updating of content and designs.
Creation of content in blogs oriented to the ecosystem	Create content oriented to entrepreneurship, where stakeholders and entrepreneurs are given the opportunity to publish their experiences and some other related topic.
Scientific dissemination	Another mechanism of academic dissemination and research is scientific dissemination, in which it is suggested, on the one hand, to publish scientific articles on articles on innovation ecosystems – Entrepreneurship, originated in the ecosystem itself and, on the other hand, to create a journal with its editorial staff where they can receive, value, and, where appropriate, publish international articles from other actors.

Source: Author (2021)

Table 3.14 Congruence and alignment to the mission and vision of the university and the *EOE*

Entity	Mission	Vision	Institutional values
University	Mission of the university	Vision of the university	Values of the university
EOE (entity that will operate the innovation-entrepreneurship ecosystem)	Aligned *EOE* mission or objectives	Aligned *EOE* vision or objectives	Aligned *EOE* values

Source: Author (2021)

  - Internal regulations.
  - Among others.

- Activities allowed by the organizational manual:
  - Systematize company information.
  - Know the background and evolution of the enterprise.
  - Know the organizational structure.
  - Assistant in the induction and training of personnel.
  - Standardize the procedures, functions, and activities of the enterprise.
  - Comply with International Organization for Standardization (IOS) certifications and local and international standards.
  - Support the continuous improvement of the organization.

In this sense, the creation of this document for the *EOE* will be crucial to be able to operate the ecosystem. The following proposal for the design of the procedure's manual is presented, as well as the suggestion for its structure. Derived from the previous concepts, and according to Table 3.14, the manual must be aligned with the mission and vision of the *EOE*.

As can be seen in Table 3.14, the mission and vision of the *EOE* are harmonized with its counterpart of the university; therefore, the generation of the corresponding manuals ensures their monitoring, compliance, and constant updating. On the other hand, to have the basis for the design of the *EOE* organizational manual, three suggestions for organization manual structures are presented, indicated in Table 3.15.

3.1.4.1 Organizational Structure to Support the Innovation Ecosystem

Within the organizational manual, the organizational structure of the *EOE* is established, which, for the purposes of this document, several organizational structures (non-limiting) are shown below, which are suggested to start the operations of the innovation and entrepreneurship ecosystem. In the same way, it is recommended to allow the evolution of the ecosystem, and as such its organizational structure. Derived from the above, they are presented in Figs. 3.16, 3.17, 3.18, 3.19, 3.20, 3.21 and 3.22.

According to Fig. 3.16, the departments are grouped into five sections to attend to the following activities:

- Departments: Research, technology transfer, and administration are oriented to support office work.
- The research and development center. It is aimed at promoting projects.
- Direction. In charge of collaborating with large-scale research depending on the industrial field.

In Fig. 3.17 of the *GMCA* is a general organization chart that carries out linking activities and shares responsibilities with ten municipalities and the mayor of the region, which work together with other local services, companies, communities, and partners for the improvement of the city and collaborate with local ecosystems.

According to Fig. 3.18, the board of directors, advisers, and scientific directors are a strategic area for decision-making. The rest of the areas are operational and execution.

As can be seen in Fig. 3.19 from a general co-direction, six directions emerge from which the business, programs, and research direction have a direct link with the areas of academia within the university, while the executive and management direction communications are strategically oriented for planning and decision-making.

According to Fig. 3.20, there are operational areas such as *IT* and digital, finance and project management, and a strategic area of linking with academic experts, research, and entrepreneurs. It is important to note that this last area, together with project management, has complementary functions to integrate work teams.

According to Fig. 3.21, like Fig. 3.16, they share two strategic and complementary areas, where the area of entrepreneurship programs requires the entrepreneurship and management division to obtain human resources, stakeholders, and financing, respectively. On the other hand, it is important to mention that the organizational structures contained in Figs. 3.16, 3.17, 3.18, 3.19, 3.20, 3.21 and 3.22 are general, where each one consumes and/or shares areas of the university itself to

Table 3.15 Structure alternatives for the creation of organizational manuals

Suggestions	Structure
Authors: National Autonomous University of Mexico, Kramis (1994), Franklin (2009), and Rodriguez (2002)	1. Cover or identification 2. Contents 3. Introduction 4. Objective of the manual 5. Historical background 6. Legislation or legal basis 7. Powers 8. Organic structure 9. Organization chart 10. Functions 11. Glossary of terms 12. Directory

(continued)

Table 3.15 (continued)

Suggestions	Structure
Author: Texas A&M University (2019)	1. Governing documents. Constitution and statutes. Constitution and statutes. Mission status. Vision statement. Core values. Medium-term goals and action plans. History of changes in the governing documents and explanation/reason for the changes. 2. Officer information. Job descriptions and responsibilities (specific to the current year). Organization chart. Contact information. Transition procedures. 3. Administrator information. Advisor's letter of agreement and copies of previous years. Expected roles and responsibilities. Contact information. 4. Standard operating procedures. Standards and procedures. Disciplinary proceedings. Advertising and media relations guidelines. Concession guidelines. Budget process and financial guidelines. Important phone numbers, websites, and resources. 5. Risk management plans. Event planning and risk assessment procedures. Safety procedures and guidelines. Medical emergencies and emergency situations. Safety and liability guidelines. Crisis response plans. Rules for actors and stakeholders. 6. History of the organization. Historical information. Calendar of regular events. Previously approved brown link event forms. Event evaluations. Contracts. Budgets and financial records. Insurance policies. Link(s) to programs/national organization. 7. Appendix. Flink event orchestra. Risk management matrix. Incident report forms. Event forms. Behavior agreement forms. Contract forms. Travel forms. Financial forms. Exemption forms.

(continued)

Table 3.15 (continued)

Suggestions	Structure
Author (2021)	1. Index 2. Summary 3. Introduction 4. Reference documents 5. Update guidelines 6. Scope 7. Organizational congruence matrix 8. Version of the manual 9. Background 10. Objectives and attributions 11.Organizational structure 12. Functions 13. Risk management 14. Glossary of terms 15. References 16. Annexes

Source: Author (2021)

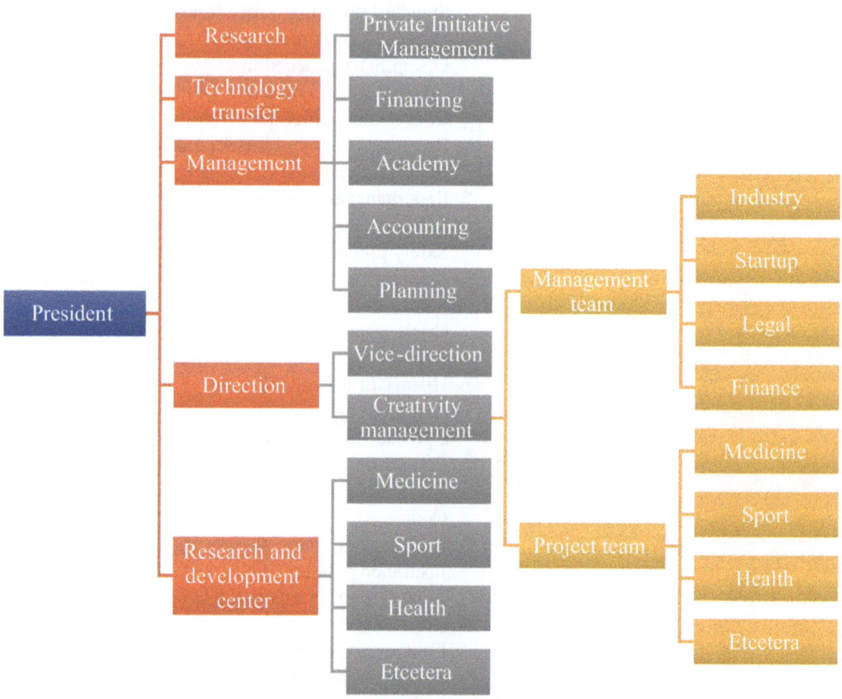

Fig. 3.16 Japan open innovation organizational structure. Source: Author (2021), taken from the strategic organization of open innovation (University of Tsukuba, 2021)

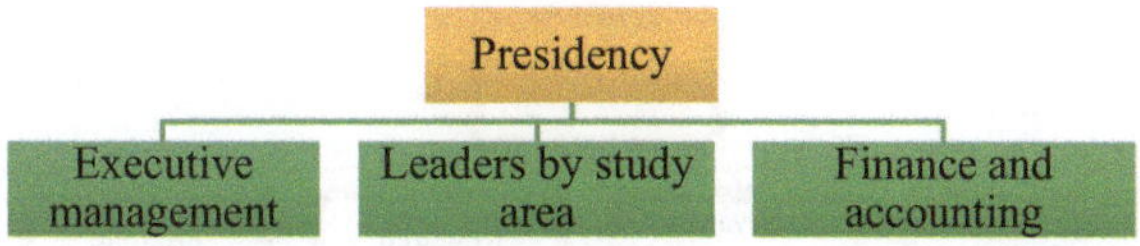

Fig. 3.17 General organizational structure of *Greater Manchester Combined Authority (GMCA)* England. Source: Author (2021), taken from local business and community services (Greater Manchester Combined Authority, 2021)

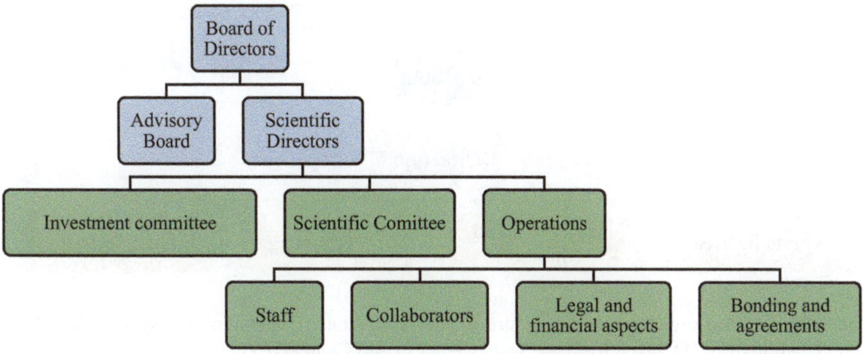

Fig. 3.18 General organizational structure of Fundación Kaertor, Spain. Source: Author (2021), taken from the Kaertor Foundation Task Force (Kaertor Fundation, 2021)

collaborate with the management and development of entrepreneurship projects and/or link with the private, public, and social sectors.

To understand, in a general way of the Fig. 3.22, the tasks of the main areas of an innovation and entrepreneurship ecosystem, it is presented in the following Table 3.16.

On the other hand, to ensure the alignment of the *EOE* structure according to Fig. 3.23, it is suggested to develop a congruence matrix to observe their interaction, which will pay to the organization chart and position card as appropriate. It is important to suggest that the *EOE* and its job schedule are suggested to be developed under the principle of freedom of thought, creativity, and exploration of knowledge.

3.1.4.2 Conformation of the Advisory Council of the Innovation and Entrepreneurship Ecosystem

According to the organizational structure presented in Fig. 3.22 in which the figure of an advice is shown, it is considered important as part of the strategies to properly design this figure since it will be decisive in decision-making and relationships abroad. Therefore, it is suggested to define and distinguish the types of advisory councils, as well as their general functions and the roles of each member, to end with the proposal of this body for the ecosystem.

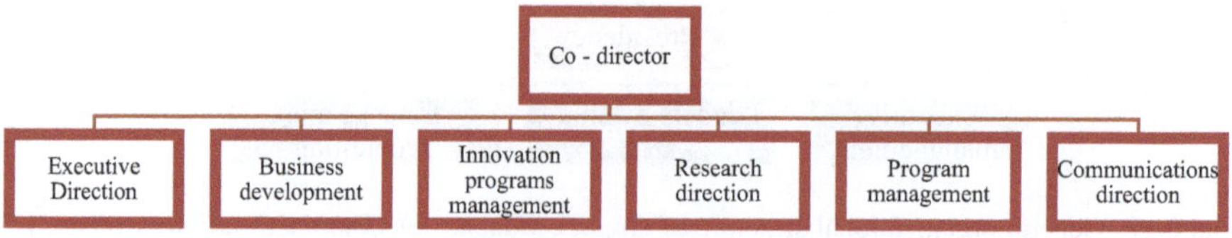

Fig. 3.19 Innovation ecosystem – *Massachusetts Institute of Technology (MIT)*, United States. Source: Author (2021), taken from the MIT Innovation Initiative (Massachussets Institute of Technology, 2021)

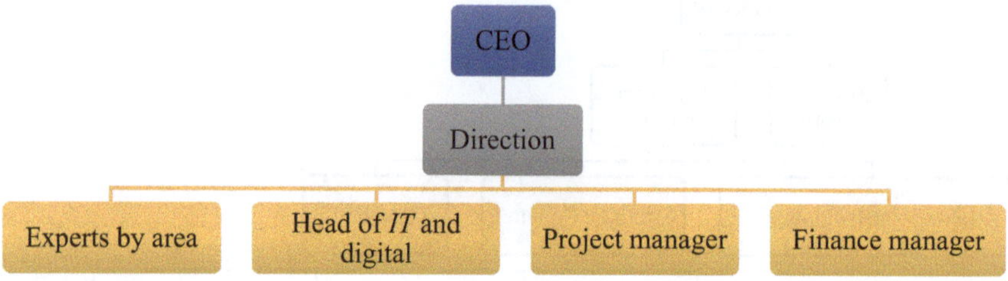

Fig. 3.20 General organizational structure of the Testa Center Innovation Ecosystem, Sweden. Source: Author (2021), taken from the Testa Center (Testa Center, 2021)

Fig. 3.21 General organizational structure of Paths-Up in the United States. Source: Author (2021), taken from the Texas A&M Engineering Experiment Station (Paths – UP, 2021)

An advisory council is a structure and a method of collaboration for organizations to commit to the objectives of the ecosystem and to serve as a link with external councils (Advisory Board Centrer, 2021). On the other hand, Broetje (2020) points out that an advisory council is a structure that is made up of specialists who collaborate with decision-making based on their experience and knowledge of the environment (innovation and entrepreneurship ecosystems) and provides advice. It is clear that an advisory council is a body that is added to the scope of the mission and vision of the ecosystem so that, given the importance of this figure within the ecosystem, an advisory council fulfills an important role in the development of each specific objective, strategy, and goal, so it must be composed of diverse and committed advisors who will work to provide feedback to the rest of the members of the board and to the stakeholders on the design, implementation, evaluation, continuous

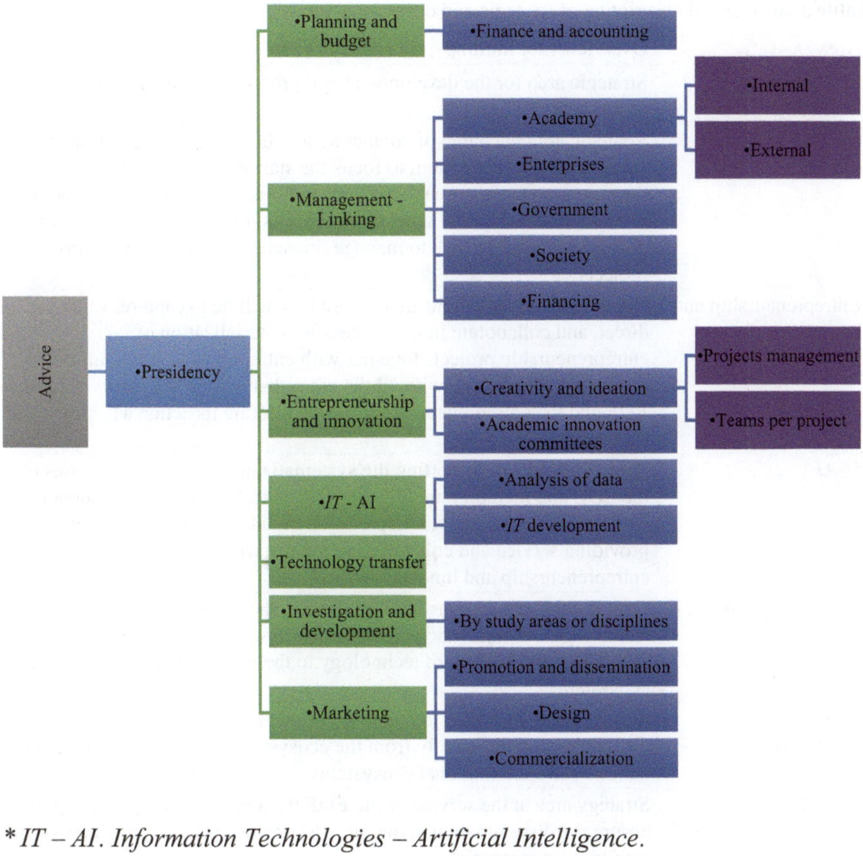

Fig. 3.22 Proposal for the organizational structure of the innovation and entrepreneurship ecosystem (*EOE*). Source: Author (2021). **IT-AI, information technologies-artificial intelligence*

improvement, and review of the strategic planning of the ecosystem, as well as the training and monitoring of the *EOE* results. The members of the advisory council must be made up of representatives of enterprises, academia-research, and society, whose occupational field is directly related to the activities of the ecosystem. They should also be made up of stakeholders with experience and knowledge as appropriate to the advice. To identify the advisory council, it is important to know its diversity and objectives. For this, the types of advisory councils are presented in Table 3.17.

While it is true that the council provides different perspectives, knowledge, and experience that collaborate for decision-making, what is its purpose, functions, roles, and responsibilities? Derived from the foregoing, and to collaborate in the delimitation of said council, the following definitions are presented:

- Purpose: The purpose of most advisory councils is to support the organization in obtaining new knowledge and advice to solve business and operational prob-

Table 3.16 General description of strategic and operational areas

Area	Overview (not limiting)
Planning and budgeting	Strategic area for the development and proposal of planning and budget of the *EOE*
Management and linkage	Strategic area in charge of contacting and linking the actors of interest for and with the ecosystem to focus the stakeholders or at the request of the entrepreneurship area to manage and link the participation of actors in entrepreneurship and innovation projects. In the same way, given its dynamics, it will be able to manage financing for entrepreneurship projects.
Entrepreneurship and innovation	Operational and strategic area whose task will be to capture, value, direct, and collaborate in the successful materialization of entrepreneurship projects together with entrepreneurs. It will have a horizontal relationship with all the areas that will be at the service of the *EOE* and the entrepreneurship projects, limiting its action as appropriate.
IT-AI	Area in charge of supporting the systematization of all the processes of the *EOE* and including intelligent systems techniques such as support for decision-making and interpretation of data analysis, as well as providing service and collaborating mainly with the area of entrepreneurship and innovation
Technology transfer	Operational area responsible for ensuring the appropriation of technology and innovation created according to copyright, in addition to facilitating the transfer of technology to the interior and exterior of the ecosystem
Research and development	Strategy area dedicated to collaborating with applied research to companies coming mainly from the ecosystem and from local, regional, national, and international ecosystems
Marketing	Strategy area at the service of the *EOE* the area of entrepreneurship to ensure the dissemination, dynamic, and creative promotion of ecosystem activities as appropriate

Source: Author (2021)

lems, as well as to explore new opportunities by stimulating meetings with experts. The advisory council is not a decision-making body; rather, it provides up-to-date knowledge, critical thinking, and analysis to give credibility and confidence to decision-makers in organizations. The advisory council is different from a governing board or a board of directors, so its functions are defined as an advisory body (Advisory Board Centrer, 2021; Broetje, 2020).

- Profile of the board members:
  - Expert in your field of study.
  - Business leader.
  - Reliable and frank person.
  - Outstanding skills.
  - Honest and open to dialogue and criticism.
  - Multidisciplinary.
  - Committed to local, regional, national, and international development.

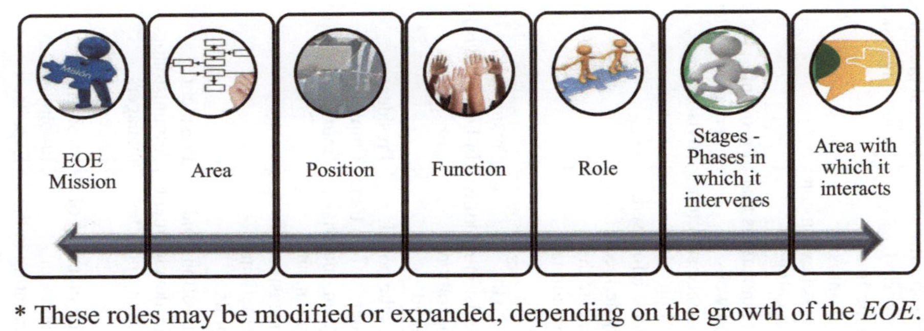

Fig. 3.23 Congruence in the support of the project through the organizational structure. Source: Author (2019). *These roles may be modified or expanded, depending on the growth of the EOE

Table 3.17 Types of advisory councils

Type	Description	Integration	Author
Advisory board for the business sector	It integrates an independent president, statute, and protocols of structured meetings with annual evaluations of its economic impact. These types of advisory boards are used in the birth of enterprise.	President Expert advisors Managers	Advisory Board Centrer, 2021
Project advisory board	It is formed with a specific purpose and for a period generally with a lifetime between 3 and 8 months. They focus on market expansion and short-term planning.	Internal president Expert advisors	City of Vancouver (2020)
Corporate advisory board	It is created in organizations that have a formal and well-articulated governance structure such as a board of directors. These councils have a focused scope and clearly defined protocols to delineate the national and international operation.	President Internal and external advisors	
Local advisory councils	Provides support to the presidency for decision-making and advises on operational activities in the field	President In-house advisors	Pennsylvania Department of Education (2020)
Occupational advisory councils	Body that advises the board, administration, and staff on their planning, work team, materials, safety and evaluation, and control and risk measures. To comply with international standards and norms	President Employees Entrepreneurs	Nova Scotia School Advisory Council (2020)
Professional advisory boards	Advises middle positions and collaborates in the development of secondary planning policies and strategies	President Administrators / managers Experts	
Advisory councils for participatory planning	Collaborates in the planning of certain strategic areas in addition to collaborating in the design of processes for the fulfillment of operational tasks	President Employees Experts	
Advisory boards for strategic planning	Collaborates with the development of long-term strategic plans, in addition to specifying the processes that collaborate in the fulfillment of the strategies	President Administrators and managers Representatives of the social, business, government, and academic sectors	

Source: Author (2021)

- Outstanding academic training.
- Scientific training (desirable).

• General roles and responsibilities (Advisory Board Centre, 2021; City of Vancouver, 2020):

- Chairman of the board:

  Establish the structure of the advisory council.
  Evaluation of the board members.
  Facilitate planning and monitoring through meetings with the council.
  Contribute to the achievement of the objectives and facilitate the results to the board of the council through results indicators.
  Advise decision-makers of the *EOE*.

- External adviser:

  Have the knowledge and experience in the themes of the ecosystem and its operation in the field.
  Experience in problem-solving.
  Contribute to the fulfillment of the objectives.
  Advise and give recommendations to the council through knowledge and evidence.
  Make strategic presentations and promotion of ecosystem activities, without compromising strategic information.

- Internal adviser and stakeholders:

  Support the decision-making of ecosystem projects.
  Provide knowledge of the context and operation in the field.
  Make objective critical suggestions.
  Collaborate in advice for decision-making.

- For all members of the advice:

  Represent the interests of the innovation ecosystem and the *EOE*.
  Stay informed of strategic and operational activities.
  Make recommendations to internal and external stakeholders.
  All members must have the voting rights to conclude points of agreement.
  Organize and coordinate presentations and external communications.
  Follow the policies of the university and the innovation ecosystem and entrepreneurship.
  Collaborate with administrative activities of the *EOE*'s usual projects or investigations carried out by the council itself.
  Prepare and distribute agendas for informal meetings (work sessions and meetings).
  Propose content for the strategic dissemination of the council's activities.
  Follow up on the council's resolutions.
  Develop an annual work plan at the beginning of each year.

Develop an annual activity report at the end of each year.

On the other hand, according to Broetje (2020), in the business environment and as such, the innovation and entrepreneurship ecosystems require highly qualified work teams and time allocated for their performance, so it is necessary to create values in the entities that make up the ecosystem, one of the most important being the advisory council. In this sense, it is important to mention some of the motivations that encourage candidates to join said council, some of which are the following:

- Collaborate in the construction of the ecosystem with social benefit.
- Passion for business, entrepreneurship, and social development.
- Desire to support the initiatives of entrepreneurs and their context.
- Integrate into the dynamics of the innovation-entrepreneurship ecosystem.
- Expand your professional networks.
- Extend your knowledge in the field.
- Share your experience.
- Keep your knowledge up to date.

In this same dynamic, according to BoadSource (2016), for an advisory council to be successful, it must comply with the following suggestions:

- Be prepared to allocate time and resources.
- Make sure you know exactly what you want from the advisory council.
- Take the time and research to find the right council members.
- Prepare council members for the advice they will provide, through introductory courses.
- Support the council with properly developed meeting agendas, support material, and facilitation of meeting conditions.
- Create communication mechanisms and spaces for dialogue between the council, stakeholders, and decision-makers.
- Periodically evaluate the performance of the board to identify opportunities for improvement and, where appropriate, determine if it is aligned with the fulfillment of the objectives.
- Maintain an informed and prepared council through continuing education and training.

After reviewing the previous information and given the importance of this body, Table 3.18 presents a general (non-limiting) proposal for the integration of the ecosystem advisory council.

According to Table 3.18 and after the objective review of the board, a minimum of 3 members and a maximum of 11 are recommended, distributed as follows:

- Four members.
  - Chair (1).
  - Vice-chair (1).
  - Adviser-expert representatives of the local business sector aligned with the mission and vision of the ecosystem (1).

Table 3.18 Conformation of the advice in the innovation and entrepreneurship ecosystem

Position[a]	Responsible	Attribution
President	Rector of the university where the *EOE* is established	Voice and vote
Vice-chair	President of the *EOE*	Voice and vote
Secretary	In charge of entrepreneurship and innovation	Voice and vote
Directors	Expert representative of the local business sector aligned with the mission and vision of the ecosystem	Voice and vote
Directors	Expert representatives of the sector of local social organizations aligned with the mission and vision of the ecosystem	Voice and vote
Directors	Academic representatives and university research aligned with the mission and vision of the ecosystem	Voice and vote
Directors	Representatives of the local government sector aligned with the mission and vision of the ecosystem	Voice and vote

Source: Author (2021)

[a]It is important to note that this body is limited to making suggestions to decision-makers, and at no time will its advice be a decision-making

- Ten members.
  - Chair (1).
  - Vice-chair (1).
  - Vocal (1).
  - Adviser-expert representatives of the local business sector aligned with the mission and vision of the ecosystem (2).
  - Adviser-expert representatives of the local social organizations sector aligned with the mission and vision of the ecosystem (2).
  - Adviser-academic representatives-university research aligned to the mission and vision of the ecosystem (2).
  - Adviser-representatives of the local government sector aligned with the mission and vision of the ecosystem (2).

The size of the advice will depend on the complexity with which the innovation and entrepreneurship ecosystem evolves, so its integration could increase, decrease, or stabilize.

3.1.5 Ecosystem Activity Schedule

According to Table 3.19, the general schedule suggested in the proposal is projected for 9 years, a time that is planned for the local innovation and entrepreneurship ecosystem to reach maturity. However, the phases, stages, and tasks must be cyclical to encourage and progressively increase the materialization of entrepreneurships and their sustainable success (main objective of the ecosystem) and in turn accelerate their development and growth as time progresses. This is to allow the entry of entrepreneurship proposals and the formation of clusters of the locality on a

Table 3.19 General schedule of activities

Tasks	Year 01		Year 02		Year 03		Year 04		Year 05		Year 06		Year 07		Year 08		Year 09	
	1	2	1	2	1	2	1	2	1	2	1	2	1	2	1	2	1	2
Phase 1. Birth of the innovation ecosystem	X	X	X	X	X	X	X	X										
Stage I. Planning	X																	
Define the mission and vision	X																	
Investigation of the current state	X																	
Development of objectives, goals, strategies, and indicators	X																	
Development of the organizational manual	X																	
Defining the schedule	X																	
Stage II. Sources of financing without return on investment		X																
Obtaining financing		X																
Systematization of processes		X																
Establish mechanisms, policies, and procedures for stakeholder participation		X																
Stage III. Call and reception of entrepreneurship projects	X	X																
Meeting with stakeholders	X																	
Identification of strategic sectors	X																	
Design of calls		X																
Opening of calls		X																
Dissemination of calls		X																
Reception of projects		X																
Stage IV. Selection of projects		X																
Indicator design		X																
Reception, evaluation, and selection		X																
Publication of results		X																

Tasks	Year 01		Year 02		Year 03		Year 04		Year 05		Year 06		Year 07		Year 08		Year 09	
	1	2	1	2	1	2	1	2	1	2	1	2	1	2	1	2	1	2
Feedback of results																		
Stage V. Project implementation			X	X	X	X	X	X										
Manage participation of experts and researchers			X															
Allocation of funding			X															
Measurement of partial results			X	X	X	X	X											
Measurement of results							X	X										
Valuation of remuneration to the ecosystem							X	X										
Stage VI. Closure of phase 1			X	X	X	X	X	X										
Valuation to unleash entrepreneurship								X										
Impact assessment								X										
Information generation and information analysis		X	X	X	X	X	X	X										
Phase 2. Evolution of the innovation ecosystem-entrepreneurship									X	X	X	X	X	X	X	X	X	X
Stage I. sources of financing with return on investment									X	X								
Establish mechanisms and procedures for participation									X	X								
Opening of spaces for information dissemination									X	X								
Stage II. Call, reception, and selection of established projects/companies											X	X	X	X	X	X	X	X
Presentation of projects											X							
Invitation to investors											X							
Investors submit proposals											X							
Systematization of intelligent processes and systems											X							
Information analysis											X	X	X	X	X	X	X	X
Selection of projects												X						
Selection of investors												X						

(continued)

Tasks	Year 01		Year 02		Year 03		Year 04		Year 05		Year 06		Year 07		Year 08		Year 09	
	1	2	1	2	1	2	1	2	1	2	1	2	1	2	1	2	1	2
Stage III. Anchoring rounds and closing of phase 2											X	X	X	X	X	X	X	X
Integrate ecosystem companies into a cluster												X	X					
Request and systematization of information from companies in the ecosystem											X	X	X	X	X	X	X	X
Opening of financing rounds per year														X	X	X		
Evaluation of results and impact											X	X	X	X	X	X	X	X

Source: Author (2021)

permanent basis. In this sense, the *EOE* based on the operation may include activities or repeat any of the stages or phases depending on the results, the financing, and the capacity to operate it.

In the same way, in the schedule, a financing without return or a significant grade of risk is proposed in each phase, in which investors do not receive their capital and therefore profits. This is because in the first phase, it is required to give new entrepreneurships an opportunity, with the uncertainty that they may go bankrupt or close. However, already in the second phase or advanced stages of phase 1 and after the valuation of the profits and performance that the *EOE* values and that does not put the operation of the company at risk, mechanisms may be established to return the capital and in your profit case. Already in the second phase and at the request of enterprises already established with more than 3 years of permanence in the market with healthy accounting and financial balances (preferably those from the ecosystem), it will be possible to participate in projects in which said enterprises require sources of financing to accelerate your development or expand your market. For this, priority will be given to actors and entities that participated in the first phase and exhibited their capital to support the birth of enterprises. It is important to mention that both in phase 1 and phase 2, all the details of said participation should be included in the policies and regulations, in addition to the corresponding assessment through data analysis and use of intelligent systems so that decision-making is well-founded and transparent for the actors involved. Another objective of the schedule and as such of the ecosystem is to protect the interests of the entrepreneur, since it starts with the tasks of the ecosystem and through regulatory mechanisms to protect their ideas and creativity through patents, copyrights in favor of the entrepreneur or the main author, as well as establishing regulatory, transparent, and reliable mechanisms to give certainty to investors and entrepreneurs. The recommendation that within the schedule included in the detailed assessment tasks, schemes and mechanisms that measure the progress of entrepreneurships and enterprises, their contribution to the community, their contribution to caring for the environment, as well as their collaboration with the ecosystem with the In order to convert the phases and stages into a virtuous cycle in which, on the one hand, constantly, either semi-annually or annually, support new ventures and, on the other hand, project and collaborate with their acceleration and growth at the local, regional level, and National and international.

3.2 Stage II. Funding Sources without Return of Investment

At this stage, there are **several models** similar to the present proposal, such as the KTH Innovation Stockholm in Sweden (2021) through the Swedish technology enterprise, which supports entrepreneurs (students, researchers, the general population) to develop their ideas of entrepreneurship, and with the commercialization process, it also supports them with processes related to patents, contracts, linkage, and management, in addition to linking sources of financing to allow the materialization of the undertakings.

Another similar case is that of the *EIC* Accelerator of the European Union (2021), based on a combined financing model through investment of public and private capital with the aim of accelerating the creation of new enterprises and to accelerate the growth of existing companies. Another case is in Switzerland, through the Ministry of Industry, Employment, and Communication (2021), which, through academic programs in universities and public programs related to the culture of entrepreneurship, can raise funds to fund entrepreneurship projects of the general population, as long as these are linked and supported by universities or incubators to ensure the design and development of the business plan and justify the product or service to be generated.

This stage aims to obtain resources to finance entrepreneurship projects and encourage disruptive innovation, which require seed capital to materialize. However, after national and international experience, being able to ensure that the entrepreneurship project materializes is complicated since there is a risk of losing 100% of the capital, after the failure of the enterprise. For this reason, the *EOE* will be assuming co-responsibility with the entrepreneur to ensure as far as possible the creation, permanence, growth, and development of said enterprise.

To achieve this, it is suggested to apply the principles of:

- Sustainability: Promoting investment with long-term economic and social impact.
- Public, private, and social collaboration: Through collaboration that seeks to involve stakeholders to potentiate and increase the seed capital destined for entrepreneurship projects.

Linked to results: Systematically seek the achievement of results that guarantee the correct application of resources.

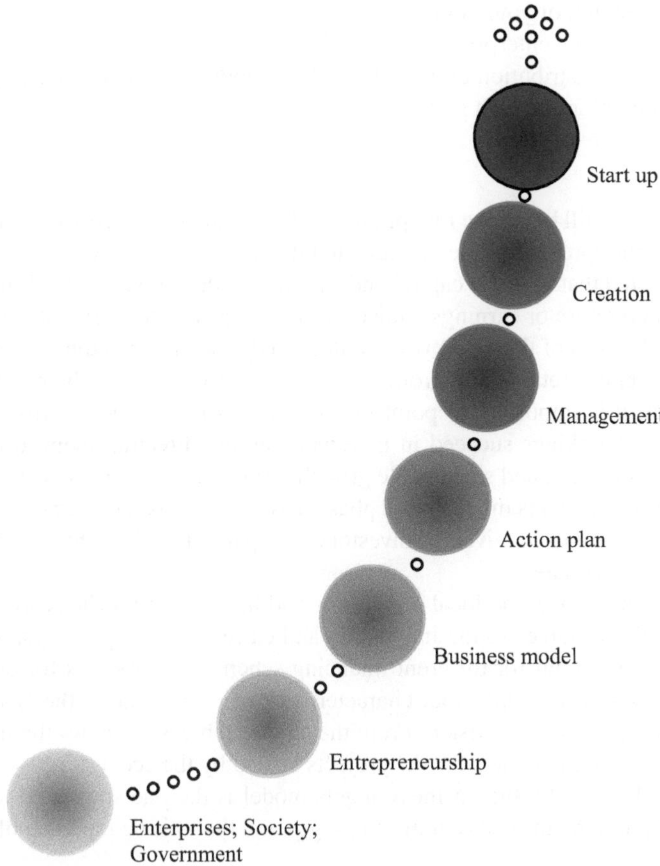

Fig. 3.24 Destination of seed capital. (Source: Author, 2021)

According to Fig. 3.24, the capital that was raised will be used in the creation, startup, and permanence of the venture, for a period of 3 months, with the possibility of expanding it depending on the returns and profits obtained by the created enterprise.

To give the funder certainty about the application of the resources, decisions will be made through the council in accordance with the corresponding regulatory framework in addition to the fact that through the development of an information system the processes are made transparent, and the accounting and financial health status of the enterprises created as appropriate is shown. Similarly, it is suggested as far as possible and with the voluntary consent of the parties, the signing of a collaboration agreement between the funder and the *EOE* that stipulates the scope, rights, and obligations. The collaboration agreement between the investor/funder and the *EOE* is suggested, among other things, to stipulate the following:

- Know the destination of your contribution.
- Know the status of the enterprise.
- Know the rules of distribution or allocation of the amount to the undertakings.
- Rights and obligations of both parties.
- Duration of the agreement.
- Among others.

As could be seen, still being the first phase, the funder does not have direct intervention with the entrepreneur or the venture, and it is only informative.

It should be noted that with the capital and earnings of the amount funded in this phase 1, there is no return or earnings. However, it is suggested to carry out evaluations of the health status of the enterprise monthly, and now in which the enterprise stabilizes and generates returns and profits, it will be valued to ensure the return of capital. However, it is important to point out that in this phase, the priority is to ensure that the undertakings succeed in materializing and directing them to their permanence, development, and sustainable growth. From phase 2 of the ecosystem, the contributions-investments made in said phase may receive a percentage of profit. At this stage, priority will be given to investors who participated in phase 1. Said phase 2 will be detailed later.

On the other hand, given the local conditions and the criteria for the search for financing to supply resources to the innovation and entrepreneurship ecosystem, a search has been carried out for different financing schemes and models for enterprises, in which, given the contextual characteristics of each locality, the type of financing business angels is suggested. From the above, Table 3.20 shows the internal and external financing models for the projects hosted by the ecosystem.

According to Table 3.20, the business angels model is the one suggested to be used in this first phase by the ecosystem. It is suggested that this be made up of the following local actors:

- Businessmen.
- Civil society organizations.
- University where the *EOE* is located.
-

It is recommended to sign collaboration agreements between the ***EOE*** and the **business angels**, where the obligations and responsibilities between both actors are stipulated.

On the other hand, in the suggested financing scheme through funding for innovation and entrepreneurship, the minimum initial amount to fund is suggested to be calculated by the average number of entrepreneurship projects and the average expenses and costs of the undertakings (INEGI, 2014; INADEM, 2018). To give

Table 3.20 Financing schemes and/or models (non-limiting)

Type of financing	Description	Advantages	Disadvantages
Internal	Own resources	You have access to the amount immediately.	In this stage of entrepreneurship, resources are limited and compete with the basic needs of the entrepreneur. If the venture fails, the amount is lost. There is a risk of using the amount for other activities.
	Cash flow	At this stage, it does not apply.	At this stage, it does not apply.
	Profits generated	At this stage, it does not apply.	At this stage, it does not apply.
	Among others	At this stage, it does not apply.	At this stage, it does not apply.

(continued)

Table 20 (continued)

Type of financing	Description	Advantages	Disadvantages
External	Business angels/ investors	You have access to the amount immediately. In this first phase, there is no commitment to return the amount by the entrepreneur. They are susceptible to refund (through tax strategies). Business angels, apart from capital, bring experience, knowledge to the project, and a network of contacts. They can also facilitate access to other financing alternatives.	There is a risk of losing 100% of the amount awarded.
	Microcredits (public and private)	You have access to financing in the short term	If the venture fails, there is an obligation to cover the debt. There is the possibility of underutilizing the amount for other activities.
	Government programs	There is no commitment to return the amount if the project fails.	It takes between 6 and 12 months to be delivered with a lag of between 6 and 12 months. The model requires partnerships.
	Lease	You can reduce taxes.	Higher financial cost Loss of assets
	Issuance of shares	At this stage, it does not apply.	At this stage, it does not apply.
	Commercial debt	At this stage, it does not apply.	At this stage, it does not apply.
	Financing with inventories	At this stage, it does not apply.	At this stage, it does not apply.
	Negotiable obligations	At this stage, it does not apply.	At this stage, it does not apply.
	Crowdfunding	Existing fundraising platforms have access to many potential investors.	It is necessary to achieve 100% of the financing objective. Disclosure of the idea before it has been developed
	Marketplace	Reduced capital raising costs Obtaining synergies because of the collaborative model Greater security for the investor	If the entrepreneur is not advised, he can lose the capital.
	Grant advances/ donation	It has no financial cost for the social or entrepreneurial organization.	They are voluntary, so they cannot be the only way to finance.
	TFF (trusted people, family, friends)	More flexible financing alternative No financial cost	Can lead to personal problems
	Capital	They advise and provide credibility with third parties.	Implies a temporary transfer of ownership
		Have experience in industries	They could include clauses that commit entrepreneurs.

Source: Author (2021), taken from Moreno (1998) Financial Planning, Pérez et al. (2016). Bases for a financing structure model in Latin American SMEs. Accenture Financing Models (2018)

security to the amount to be funded, it is suggested to carry out pilot tests of the phases to be able to correctly calculate the initial amount.

Derived from the above, at this stage, two initial rounds of funding begin (Cremades, 2018; Cardiff Lexington Corporation, 2020; Upcounsel, 2020):

- Pre-seed. This is the capitalization stage for an enterprise that starts operations. Those interested in its financing investigate the enterprise. Normally, they are relatives or acquaintances of the entrepreneur who participate in this round. Also involved are angel investors, who often participate in these early rounds as well. The variant that is sought in this proposal is that funders belonging to the ecosystem are integrated.
- Round seed. In this round, the definition, adjustment, or adaptation of the product to the market, purchase of raw materials, key contracts, and product development is sought. Angel investors also take part in this round. In the same way, the integration of funders of the ecosystem is also sought.

Normally, in the pre-seed and seed stages, several characteristics are displayed as shown in Table 3.21.

It is important to reiterate for this project, it is suggested to include funders of the ecosystem reiterating that in this phase 1, there will be no return on investment, so all the capital is high risk.

Table 3.21 Seed rounds deployment

	Phase 1 – stage II. Sources of financing without return on investment	
Type	Pre-seed	Seed
Type of investor	Funders/actors/stakeholders of the innovation ecosystem-entrepreneurship Friends and family Angels in early stages of entrepreneurship Startup accelerators	Funders/actors/stakeholders of the innovation ecosystem-entrepreneurship Angels Early-stage venture capital
Stage of the enterprise	Pre-product or pre-service Final prototypes	Positive signs of market acceptance Indications of permanence of the startup
Increased expenses	Commissioning Prototype development Base infrastructure Hiring of work team	Development of products or services The operation shows signs of exceeding the financing

Source: Author (2021), adapted from Pre-Seed to Series C: Startup, explanation of financing or investment rounds (Crunchbase, 2020)

3.3 Stage III. Call and Reception of Entrepreneurship Projects

To be inclusive with all the entrepreneurs of the university and the locality, semester or annual calls will be launched at the beginning for the reception of entrepreneurial projects, which will be open to any entrepreneur without any distinction, giving opening to the creativity and inventiveness of the participants.

On the other hand, it is reiterated that the integration of Intelligent Systems and Information Systems are a core part in the management and operation of ecosystems, and this stage is not the exception, so it is suggested that in the call and reception, all projects are entered into the information system by the corresponding actor, which will allow the generation of real-time information on indicators, comparatives, and qualifications, among other items. This will have multiple effects such as transparency in the process, providing information to evaluators, placing alerts, and identify qualifications, among others. At the same time, the information generated will serve as an input to intelligent systems to project and/or predict the success of the undertakings and support the decision-making of the stakeholders involved, among other activities and processes.

Returning to the issue of the calls, it is suggested that the following sections be integrated into these with the intention that the entrepreneurs themselves capture the information, and the reception of these is transparent for the *EOE* (see Table 3.22).

According to Table 3.22, it is important to mention that each item must be designed and substantiated in detail within the *EOE*, depending on the local context, as well as the delimitation and information that is of interest to collect for the *EOE*, which will serve as a means of input for the argumentation of the projects and their evaluation with the experts. For this, it is important to develop the procedures that support said activities and information to be generated, which will ensure their transparency in real time. On the other hand, given that this process must be systematized, practically, the operational work of reception of projects, the rules of operation, and other mechanisms related to the call and reception should not generate activities by the *EOE*, except receipt notifications (see Fig. 3.25).

3.4 Stage IV. Evaluation and Selection of Entrepreneurship Projects

At this stage, qualitative and quantitative indicators play a central role since through these, it is possible to assess the projects and in turn select those with the highest score as beneficiary projects. For this, it is important to define the general weightings, as well as the actors that will intervene in their capture. As can be seen in Table 3.23, the following general weighting and the actor involved are suggested.

As can be seen in Table 3.23, the entrepreneur and the expert enter the evaluations of each qualitative and quantitative indicator corresponding to the project according to their role. The maximum value of the total of the indicators is 50% for each actor and type (qualitative and quantitative). In this sense, the detailed quantitative indicators are shown in Table 3.24. As can be seen, they are grouped into 10 blocks and each one with its own indicator and score. These indicators are suggested to be transparent for the entrepreneur and evaluator so that they form part of the capture and evaluation process (respectively). This means as the entrepreneur captures his project, he must evaluate himself. Once you finish capturing the information of your project in the *information system (IS)* and therefore the capture of the indicators, the *IS* will be storing the information in a database, without showing partial results.

On the other hand, the qualitative indicators shown in Table 3.25 will be assigned by the entrepreneur and evaluator through the *information system (IS)* at the time of making the evaluation. In this sense, these indicators require evaluations and interpretations and value judgments by the actors involved, with the corresponding evidence; therefore, the evaluator must have access to all the project information through the information system.

Table 3.22 Information structure for the call and reception of projects

Document	Item	Description
Call for innovation-entrepreneurship	Introduction	Integrate the following information: Headers with the logos of the sponsor, s`
	Objective of the call	Briefly develop the objective of the call
	Who is it addressed to?	Describe the actors to whom the call is addressed
	Suggested deliverables	What information they will be capturing in the information system
	General criteria	General explanation of the criteria to be applied when selecting projects
	Dates to consider	Include the dates: Aperture. Where the system is enabled for project capture. Closing. In which the system stops receiving projects. Publication. In which the results of the benefited projects are published.
	Final notes	This section includes important notes for participants, in addition to the reference or links to reference documents, such as terms of reference and user manuals, among others.

(continued)

Table 3.22 (continued)

Document	Item	Description
Terms of reference (linked to the call)/ reception of projects	Introduction	Integrate the following information Headers with the logos of the sponsor, stakeholders, ecosystem, and the *EOE*. Motto of the *EOE* and/or ecosystem. Date of publication of the information. Indicate to which call the terms of reference are linked.
	Criteria and information to be contained in the proposals	Explanatory memorandum. Resume. Cover letter. Extensive project. Entrepreneur information. Contact details. Project title. Project description. Background. Hypothesis. Objectives. Goals. Methodology. Budget. Expected results. Work team. Schedule of activities. Available infrastructure. Conclusion. Bibliography.
	Characteristics of the project	To support entrepreneurs, references and help links should be placed to facilitate the understanding of each item.
	Duration of the project	Indications of how long the project will be supported, which is suggested to be 3 to 6 months
	Financing amounts	Indicate that the amounts are conditional on the available funds
	Audits and field visits for follow-up	Note that the projects that are benefited are committed and obliged to allow the *EOE* to carry out audits and field visits to corroborate the development of the project.
	Public communication of knowledge	Allow the publication of information derived from the project, ensuring that confidential or strategic information that puts the project at risk is not compromised.

(continued)

Table 3.22 (continued)

Document	Item	Description
	Transparency	Indicate that it is the obligation of the beneficiaries, to make the amounts and their destination transparent, the above through reports that must be captured in the information system. On the other hand, provide through the system, transparency in the entire flow of reception of projects.
	Intellectual property and copyright	Point out that they must respect the copyright and intellectual property of third parties, as well as protect those that derive from the project according to its origin.
	Commitment letter	Integrate a commitment letter from the entrepreneur.
	Sanctions	Indicate that any action that violates the principles and values of the *EOE* and the ecosystem will be sanctioned in accordance with the *EOE*, where appropriate request advice from the board for the final decision.
	Deliberations	Note that the resolutions will be defining and unappealable, if and only if the process is transparent through the information system.
	Freedom of creativity and thought	The call and its terms of reference should stimulate the freedom of creativity and thought of the participants.
	Inclusion	Note that all projects can be captured without any distinction, allowing the inclusion and participation of stakeholders.

Source: Author (2021)

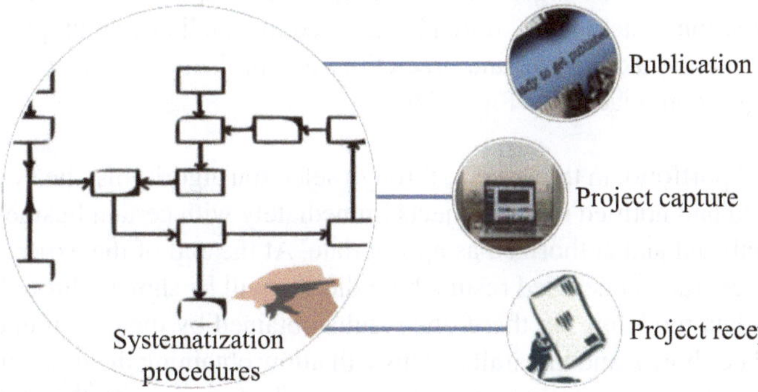

Fig. 3.25 The procedures and their systematization core in the publication, capture, and reception. (Source: Author, 2021)

It is important to highlight the degree of systematization, since at the end of the capture of the project by the entrepreneur, the evaluation session will be enabled for the expert. In this evaluation process since it is required to be evaluated by an expert depending of the selected sector, it is suggested that the information system and through the management-linkage area in coordination with the entrepreneurship and innovation area, it was possible to have a prior portfolio of experts, to evaluate the entrepreneurship projects (prior agreement between the parts).

Table 3.23 Qualitative and qualitative indicator scores

Description	Quantitative (maximum values) (%)	Qualitative (maximum values) (%)
Enterprising	50	50
Expert	50	50
Average	50	50
Final grade: Averages (qualitative + quantitative)	100	

Source: Author (2021)

The means to be able to carry out the capture and evaluation of the project is suggested by the *information system (IS)* based on the business rules that must previously be configured by the *EOE*, coming from the call and terms of reference. This will allow the process to be carried out in a dynamic, intuitive, clear, simple, didactic, and user-friendly way, to facilitate its use and reduce the risks in the capture of information and therefore in the generation of results. On the other hand, it is suggested to integrate *artificial intelligence (AI)* who, through intelligent systems such as neural networks, genetic algorithms, or another technique, will take the inputs that the information system threw (already captured the qualitative and quantitative evaluations of mentioned actors), and predictions and projections of success or failure of the projects are made (see Fig. 3.26).

Having said portfolio, in the system, through selection algorithms, the evaluators can be assigned and notified of the projects immediately with certain business rules previously analyzed and authorized as appropriate. At the end of the expert assessment, all the general and detailed results by indicator will be shown, through the *IS* and dynamic data modeling. In these, the results obtained by the entrepreneur and evaluator will be shown, and in parallel. This will allow obtaining the final qualification with which the project(s) can be listed and ranked along with the rest of the projects. In this way, it will be possible to select and, where appropriate, notify the beneficiary entrepreneur and entrepreneurial project, as well as the publication of the results and feedback of all the projects received, and as such ensure the initial

Table 3.24 Quantitative indicators

Concept	Sub concept	Percentage (%)	Maximum (%)[b]
Project type	Private – social	4	4
	Private	4	
	Social	3	
	Government - smart cities	3	
Economic sector	Agro-industrial	2	2
	Foods	2	
	Information and communication technologies	2	
	Automotive	2	
	Aerospace	2	
	Mining	2	
	Renewable and clean energy	2	
	Biomedicine	2	
	Biotechnology	2	
	Other	1	
Gender equity	The team consists of 50% (H) and 50% (M).	3	3
	The team is made up of most of a single gender.	1	
Intercultural	The project is made up of at least one person belonging to an ethnic group, a community originally from the town.	1	1
	The project includes people from another locality, region, or country.	1	1
Internal	The project is made up of active students from the town.	2	2
	The student studies at the university to which the *EOE* belongs.	2	2
Commissioning time	3 months	5	5
	6 months	2	
Budget	The entrepreneur collaborated with more than 50% of the budget.	5	5
	The entrepreneur collaborated with 25–49% of the budget.	3	
Schedule	The schedule is clear and does not exceed 6 months to be implemented.	3	3
Freedom	The project does not respond to interests other than the entrepreneur.	2	2
	There is freedom of thought, creativity, ideation, and work	2	2
	Economic/market.	2	2

(continued)

Table 3.24 (continued)

Concept	Sub concept	Percentage (%)	Maximum (%)[b]
Socioeconomic indicators – Innovation (local, regional, national)[a]	Average interest rate (last 5 years)	2	2
	Average change in the exchange rate against the dollar (last 5 years)	2	2
	Average inflation (last 5 years)	2	2
	Average unemployment rate (last 5 years)	2	2
	Average growth in gross domestic product (last 5 years)	2	2
	Average human development index (last 5 years)	2	2
	Global innovation index average (last 5 years)	2	2
	Global competitiveness index average (last 5 years)	2	2
Total		–	50

Source: Author (2021)

[a]Socioeconomic indicators will apply to all projects and will be configured and captured annually by the *EOE*

[b]It is important to mention that the evaluation indicators presented are, for example, it is suggested that the *EOE* contextualize them to the locality and readjust the weightings and even eliminate, modify, or add indicators to enrich the evaluations. It is important to reiterate that the results of the qualitative and quantitative indicators will be presented until the evaluator finishes

Table 3.25 Qualitative indicators

Concept	Sub concept	Percentage (%)	Maximum (%)[a]
Multidisciplinary	Includes more than two disciplines	3	3
	Includes a single discipline	2	
Sustainable	The project covers one of the 17 sustainable development goals.	3	3
	The project is entirely circular economy.	3	3
Methodologies	The project shows the methodology for the achievement of the project objective and collaborates with the obtaining of positive performance of the organization.	3	3
Clusters	The project is part of a cluster of projects, as part of its production and/or consumption chain.	3	3
Innovation	The project includes patents/copyrights.	3	3
	The project is original and/or covers a significant improvement.	2	2
	The entrepreneurship project is considered as disruptive innovation.	3	3
Budget	The budget is clear and shows the scope of the objective.	3	3
Schedule	The schedule is clear and does not exceed 6 months to be implemented.	2	2

(continued)

Table 3.25 (continued)

Concept	Sub concept	Percentage (%)	Maximum (%)[a]
Impact	The project achieves in its proposal to generate sustainable products or services.	3	3
	The project generates value for local society.	2	2
	The project includes collaborations with social entrepreneurship projects.	3	3
Social responsibility	Collaborates with social actions as part of its organizational philosophy, where it collaborates with the social development of the locality	2	2
Business plan	Structure of the environment: Minimum viable product, alternative product Catalog SWOT analysis – Strengths, opportunities, weaknesses, threats describe the target audience; know how often your product and/or service is purchased; competition detected and study of competitors; market research; competitive advantages segments and customer relationship; key activities and resources or alliances: Customer profile; priority map space map – Technology, business, trends, needs, prototype	2	2
	Financial structure: Projected 3-year pro forma income statement; projected 3-year pro forma balance sheet; projected 3-year pro forma cash flow; break-even point analysis; scenario analysis; sources of financing – Own and external income	2	2
	Ideological structure: Definition of the project; company name; mission; vision; values; commitment	3	2
	Human resources: Organization chart; cedula of posts; determine the cost of the template	2	2
	Marketing structure: Strategic planning; price of your product and/or service; payment plans; sales force; distribution channels; communication channels; generation of strategic indicators; logo and brand; consumer behavior	2	2
	Executive summary: Business concept; financial factors; financial needs; current business position; report on key achievements; reached	2	2
Total		–	50

Source: Author (2021)

[a]It is important to mention that the evaluation indicators presented are, for example, it is suggested that the *EOE* contextualize them to the locality and readjust the weightings and even eliminate, modify, or add indicators to enrich the evaluations. It is important to reiterate that the results of the qualitative and quantitative indicators will be presented until the evaluator finishes

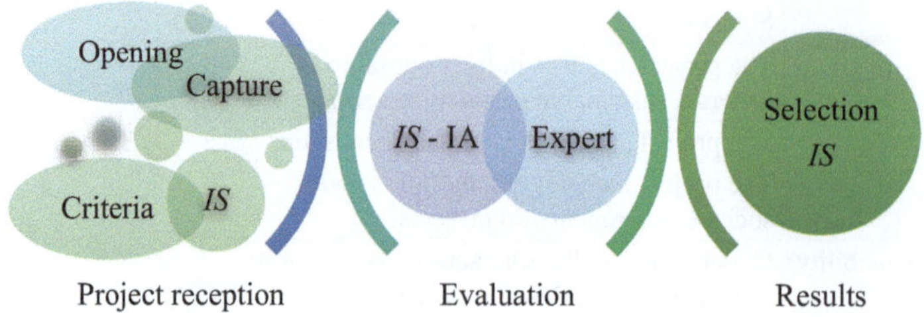

Fig. 3.26 Selection process. (Source: Author, 2021)

financing of the venture. It is important to note that the credibility percentage of intelligent systems in this type of process is more than 95%, with an error factor of 5%, according to the research carried out by Patino et al. (2020), which guarantees the use of said systems in predicting the success of the undertakings, which will serve as a reference and not as part of decision-making. Finally, and as part of quality control and to reduce risks in this project selection phase, the *EOE*, through a significant and valid sample, will be verifying the results to ensure that the criteria are met and established.

3.5 Stage V. Implementation and Startup of Entrepreneurship Projects

Perhaps the most challenging stage of the ecosystem since its main objective is to collaborate with the materialization of entrepreneurships that manage to remain, grow, develop, and evolve. This cover is the culmination of what was planned and valued by the experts. In this, the entrepreneurships become an enterprise and must be starting formal operations. The most important role in this phase oversees the entrepreneur, who assumes the role of owner of the enterprises, and through which all the decisions of the enterprises pass.

The *EOE* and the ecosystem as such will support and serve as an advisor to the now owner of the enterprises for a limited period.

As can be seen in Fig. 3.27, phase one covers 4 years; however, this does not mean that enterprises are benefited for 4 years. Rather, they will be advised by the ecosystem and gradually these companies must become "independent." To explain this, the following processes are presented once the venture is selected and financed (see Fig. 3.28):

- 3–6 months. The ecosystem constantly advises the owner of the enterprise (formerly an entrepreneur) to suggest strategic activities and reduce risks, among other issues. The objective is to prepare the owner to attend to the administration

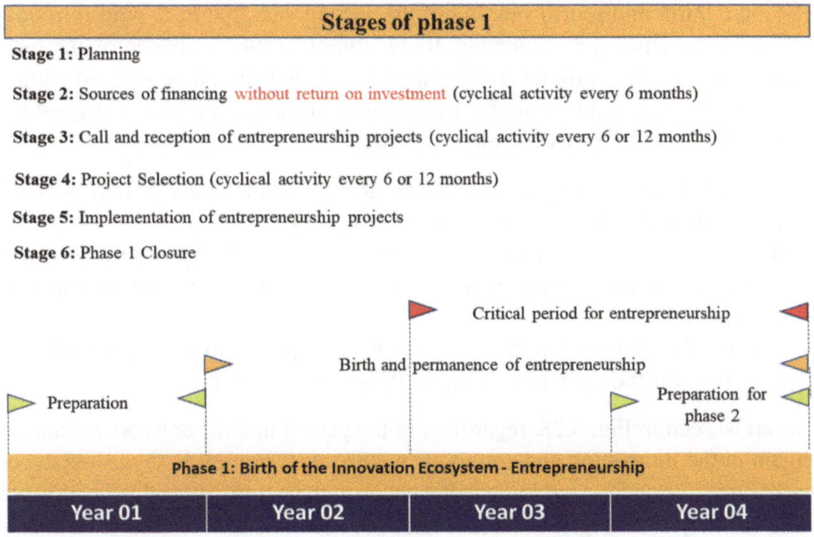

Fig. 3.27 Stages of phase 1 of the ecosystem. (Source: Author, 2021)

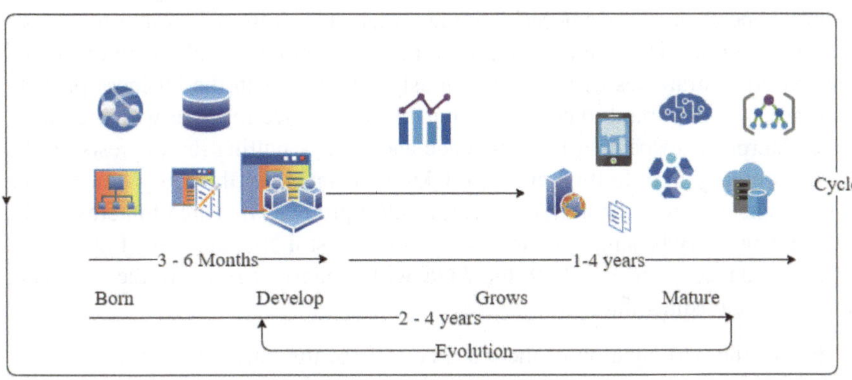

Fig. 3.28 Advice – independence of the employer. (Source: Author, 2021)

and operation and, together with his work team, to stabilize the enterprise. This activity will remain for 3 months as a recommendation, unless the *EOE* and the owner decide to extend it for another 3 months at most. In this period, the *EOE* will be supported through information systems, statistics, and systematized indicators to constantly measure the performance of the company, this through information that the new enterprise provides to the *IS* in a systematic way.

- First year. After the first 3 or 6 months, the *EOE* will gradually detach from the enterprise. That is, it will stop advising the entrepreneur, leaving the owner to make the decisions "independently." However, for purposes of monitoring and analyzing the performance of the enterprise, it is suggested that it continue to provide information to the *EOE* in a systematic way, upon prior agreement.

- • Second, third, and fourth year. As of the second year, the *EOE* stops providing advice to the employer, achieving 100% complete independence of the enterprise. Information continues to be shared for statistical and ecosystem learning purposes. Also, depending on the performance of the company, it is suggested to perform the analysis to assess the following:
  - Formally include it as part of a cluster derived from the ecosystem after validation of its capabilities, products, and services.
  - Assess whether the entrepreneur wishes to include the enterprise in the dynamics of the second phase and as such accelerate its development or growth.
  - Suggest donations from the company to the ecosystem to support new ventures (not for the operation of the *EOE* or the ecosystem).

As can be seen in Fig. 3.28, regardless of the period that the enterprise continues to remain in the innovation and entrepreneurship ecosystem, it is suggested to continue sharing experiences and knowledge between the enterprise and the ecosystem, which does not put strategic information at risk, without neglecting its own mission and vision.

An important part of the advisory role of the *EOE* and support of the ecosystem is to provide as much as possible tools, links, experts, and knowledge to guarantee the initial operation of the enterprise to the owner, at least from 3 months to a maximum of 6 months. This implies suggest to the owner commercial, operational, and administrative strategies that were previously established in the business plan. In this sense, it is important to define the dynamics of advice together with the owner of the enterprise, respecting independence and always putting the interests of this and his company first. In this sense and taking advantage of the ecosystem and the possible clusters formed within it, services and/or products that are of interest to the new company may be suggested to ensure its successful operation (see Fig. 3.29).

In accordance with Fig. 3.29, the *EOE* will suggest or reiterate the following actions to the businessman:

- Manage the participation of the research staff of the university where the *EOE* operates/internal or external experts to participate in the project. It is important to define your collaboration through participation agreements and policies.
- Researchers, teachers, and participating experts are required to have a download of hours for research work to collaborate with the entrepreneurship project prior to the generation of participation policies.
- The enterprise will have an economic collaboration for 3 months or a maximum of 6 months, established in the format of capture and participation of the calls by the then entrepreneur.
- During the next 6 or 9 months, the collaboration of the *EOE* will decrease, according to the results obtained by the enterprise, in coordination with the now entrepreneur.

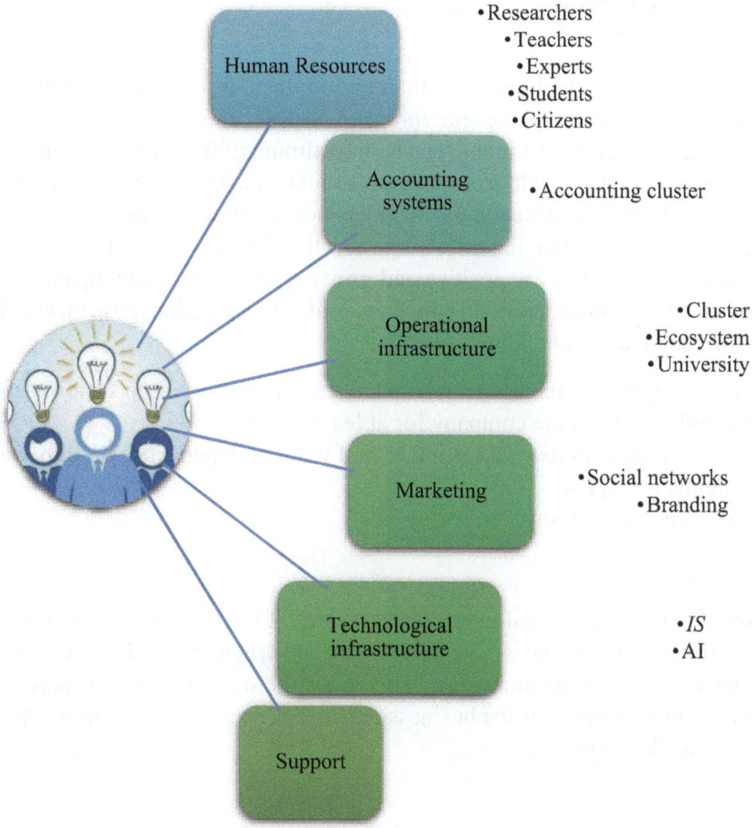

Fig. 3.29 Example of the services or products that you can link and/or advise the new enterprise. (Source: Author, 2021)

- On a fortnightly and/or monthly basis, the health status of the company will be assessed, through the monitoring of indicators such as performance and profits, among others, to support decision-making or reduce the risks of failure.

Although it is true that the first phase of the ecosystem does not contemplate return on investment, given that there is the possibility that enterprise may have an acceleration and natural growth of less than 3 years, the *EOE* will carry out monthly evaluations, analysis, and interpretations of the enterprises now (previously entrepreneurship) already operating, to observe their behavior, and in case there is the possibility of any remnant of the profits that does not put the operation, growth, and development at risk of the enterprise. A percentage of these profits will be suggested to the entrepreneur, which it is recommended to allocate to the ecosystem only for funding another entrepreneurship. It is suggested that, for the analysis of monthly information, processes be systematized to optimize the resources allocated to this process as well as to guarantee the transparency, timeliness, and accessibility of information to the interested parties.

3.6 Stage VI. Phase 1 Closure

Stage IV of closure is nothing more than giving the company independence, to be managed and operated by the entrepreneur (before entrepreneur). This closure phase may take place after 3 months up to a maximum of 6 months. This means that the entrepreneur will be able from now on to make his own decisions without the advice of the *EOE*. The decision of the independence of the company in this phase is suggested to be based on the following (non-limiting) assessments:
The returns for 6 months are positive and growing, and this is accompanied by the increase in the enterprise's profits, which guarantee its operation, growth, and development in the medium and long term.

- That the net profits manage to guarantee the medium-term operation, development, and growth of the company for at least 1 year.
- The enterprise, with its own resources and without dependence on third parties, operate the enterprise.
- Among other evaluations.

> Given the mission and vision of the ecosystem, if the entrepreneur makes the decision to close this phase, he can do so even when the *EOE* indicators or suggestions do not recommend it. This since the only person in charge and owner of the enterprise is the businessman and as such, it will be necessary to respect his decisions.

It is important to mention that at this stage, like the rest, it is cyclical in the sense that through constant monitoring (through *IS* and *IA*), the stages of those companies that cannot guarantee their operation can also be closed, and the indicators to be evaluated indicate that its growth is not promising, but on the contrary, they generate an economic deficit for the enterprise. This means suggesting to the entrepreneur to close it, and on the other hand, the *EOE* and ecosystem will stop advising the enterprise and will demarcate from commitments not without first generating, together with the businessman, a report on the causes and phenomena presented, which will be the basis for suggesting the closure of the enterprise.

To protect the interests of the ecosystem and its stakeholders, all agreements, conventions, and minutes and all possible scenarios in which the parties involved are aware and in agreement should be included to avoid conflicts or misunderstandings.

References

Accenture. (2018). *Modelos de financiamiento*. Obtenido de https://www.accenture.com, recovered March 25, 2019.

Advisory Board Centrer. (2021). *What are advisory boards roles & responsibilities?* Obtenido de https://www.advisoryboardcentre.com/what-are-the-advisory-board-roles-and-responsibilities/, recovered July 23, 2021.

Al-Mubaraki, H., Muhammad, A., & Busler, M. (2015). Measuring innovation: The use of indicators in developed countries. *World Journal of Entrepreneurship, Management and Sustainable Development, 11*(3), 220–230.

ANUIES. (2019). *Anuarios Estadísticos de Educación Superior*. Obtenido de http://www.anuies.mx/informacion-y-servicios/informacion-estadistica-de-educacion-superior/anuario-estadistico-de-educacion-superior, recovered January 15, 2020.

Astebro, T., & Michaela, J. (2005). Predictors of the survival of innovations. *Journal of Product Innovation Management, 22*(3), 322–335.

Avdar, S., & Aydin, A. (2015). An empirical analysis about technological development and innovation indicators (world conference on technology, innovation and entrepreneurship). *Procedia – Social and Behavioral Sciences*, 1486–1495.

Basberg, B. (1987). Patents and the measurement of technological change: A survey of the literature. *Research Policy, 16*, 131–141.

Bayarçelik, E., & Taşel, F. (2012). Research and development: Source of economic growth. *Procedia – Social and Behavioral Sciences*, 744–753.

Belitz, H., Clemens, M., von Hirschhausen, C., Schmidt-Ehmcke, J., Werwatz, A., & Zloczysti, P. (2011). An indicator for national systems of innovation – Methodology and application to industrialized countries. *Discuss. Pap. Dtsch. Insitut Wirtsch*, 1–27.

Bloch, C., & Bugge, M. (2013). Public sector innovation – From theory to measurement. *Structural Change and Economic Dynamics, 27*, 133–145.

BoadSource. (2016). *Advisory councils nine keys to success*. Obtenido de https://www.rivernetwork.org/, recovered May 10, 2021.

Broetje, T. (2020). *Understanding the role of advisory boards*. Obtenido de https://www.cfoselections.com/perspective/understanding-the-role-of-advisory-boards, recovered July 12, 2021.

Brown. (2009). *Change by design: How design thinking transforms organizations and inspires innovation*. Harper Business.

Brown, & Wyatt. (2010). *Design Thinking for social innovation, Stanford social innovation review*. Obtenido de http://5a5f89b8e10a225a44ac-ccbed124c38c4f7a3066210c073e7d55.r9.cf1.rackcdn.com/files/pdfs/news/2010_SSIR_DesignThinking.pdf, recovered January 05, 2019.

Buesa, M., Heijs, J., & Baumert, T. (2010). *Research Policy, 39*, 722–735.

Bureau of career – Iowa Department of education. (2020). Advisory Councils. CTE Advisory Councils, 1–27.

Caird, S., Hallett, S., & Potter, S. (2013). The Open2-Innova8ion tool – A software tool for rating organizational innovation performance. *Technovation*, 381–385.

Carayannis, E., & Campbell, D. (2019). *Smart quintuple helix innovation systems. How social ecology and environmental protection are driving innovation, sustainable development and economic growth*. Springer.

Cardiff Lexington Corporation. (2020). *Understanding A, B, C, fundraising stages*. Obtenido de https://cardifflexington.com/content/general/whitepapers/Understanding+ABC+Funding+Modified++Rev.pdf, recovered January 02, 2021.

Cavdar, S., & Aydin, A. (2015). An empirical analysis about technological development and innovation indicators (world conference on technology, innovation and entrepreneurship). *Procedia – Social and Behavioral Sciences, 15*, 1486–1495.

City of Vancouver. (2020). *Guidelines for advisory bodies*. Obtenido de https://vancouver.ca/docs/council/Guidelines%20for%20Advisory%20Bodies%20February%202020.pdf, recovered July 28, 2021.

Cooper, R. (1990). Stage-gate systems: A new tool for managing new products. *Business Horizons, 33*(3), 44–54.
Cooper, R. (1999). From experience: The invisible success factors in product innovation. *Journal of Product Innovation Management, 16*(2), 115–133.
Cremades, A. (2018). *How funding rounds work for startups*. Obtenido de https://www.forbes.com/sites/alejandrocremades/2018/12/26/how-funding-rounds-work-for-startups/?sh=3e44767a7386, recovered January 02, 2021.
Crunchbase. (2020). *The ultimate guide to raise capital for a startup*. Obtenido de http://about.crunchbase.com/wp-content/uploads/2019/10/Ultimate-guide-raising-startup-capital.pdf, recovered January 2, 2021.
De Felice, F., & Petrillo, A. (2013). Key success factors for organizational innovation in the fashion industry. *International Journal of Engineering Business Management, 5*(27), 1–11.
De Medeiros, J., Ribeiro, J., & Cortimiglia, M. (2014). Success factors for environmentally sustainable product innovation: A systematic literature review. *Journal of Cleaner Production, 65*, 76–86.
Dewangan, V., & Godse, M. (2014). Towards a holistic enterprise innovation performance measurement system. *Technovation*, 536–545.
Dodgson, M., & Hinze, S. (2000). *Research & Evaluation, 8*(2), 101–114.
Dziallasa, M., & Blinda, K. (2019). Innovation indicators throughout the innovation process: An extensive literature analysis. *Technovation*, 3–29.
Education and Culture. (2017). *Best practices & pedagogical methods in entrepreneurship education in Europe*. Francia: Quality of Entrepreneurship Programmes in Europe.
Entrepreneur. (2018). *Tu Plan de Negocios paso a paso*. Obtenido de https://www.entrepreneur.com/article/269219, recovered February 02, 2019.
European Commission. (2021a). *EASME – Executive Agency for SMEs*. Obtenido de https://wayback.archive-it.org/12090/20210412123959/https://ec.europa.eu/easme/en/, recovered March 4, 2021.
European Commission. (2021b). *SME support & innovation*. Obtenido de https://ec.europa.eu/easme/en/, recovered August 11, 2021.
European Innovation Council. (2021). *European innovation ecosystem*. Obtenido de https://eic.ec.europa.eu/, recovered July 10, 2021.
Fleuren, M., Paulussen, T., Dommelen, P., & van Burren, S. (2014). Towards a measurement instrument for determinants of innovations. *International Journal for Quality in Health Care, 26*(5), 501–510.
Franklin, E. (2009). *Organización de empresas*. McGraw-Hill.
Gallardo, E., Molano, G., Gutiérrez, E., & Urbina, C. (2019). *Plan estratégico de difusión y diseminación*. Obtenido de https://acacia.red/wp-content/uploads/2019/08/Plan_estrat%C3%A9gico_de_difusi%C3%B3n.pdf, recovered July 10, 2021.
Government of Spain. (2017). *Programa Emprendimiento Universitario*. Obtenido de http://www.ipyme.org/es-ES/EmprendimientoUniversitario/Paginas/ProgEmpUniversitario.aspx, recovered January 22, 2019.
Greater Manchester Combined Authority. (2021). *Obtenido de Organización – Quienes somos*: https://www.greatermanchester-ca.gov.uk/who-we-are/ , recovered July 11, 2021.
Griffin, A., & Page, A. (1993). *Journal of Product Innovation Management*, 291–308.
Hart, S., Hultink, E., Tzokas, N., & Commandeur, H. (2003). *Journal of Product Innovation Management, 20*, 22–36.
Henríquez, S. (2020). Mecanismos de vinculación. Obtenido de http://vinculacion.ucsh.cl/mecanismos-de-interaccion/, July 10, 2021.
Hittmar, S., Varmusa, M., & Lendela, V. (2015). Proposal of evaluation system for successful application of innovation strategy through a set of indicators. *Procedia Economics and Finance*, 17–22.
INADEM. (2018). *Guía de trámites – The National Institute of the Entrepreneur (INADEM)*. Obtenido de https://www.inadem.gob.mx/guia-de-tramites/, recovered February 22, 2019.

INEGI. (2014). *Censos Economicos 2014*. Obtenido de http://www.beta.inegi.org.mx/app/saic/default.aspx, recovered February 17, 2018.

Ivanova, C.-I., & Avasilcăi, S. (2014). Performance measurement models: An analysis for measuring innovation processes performance. *Procedia – Social and Behavioral Sciences*, 397–404.

Kaertor Fundation. (2021). *Organization chart*. Obtenido de http://kaertorfoundation.org/en/the-team/, recovered July 12, 2021.

Kato, M., Okamuro, H., & Honjo, Y. (2015). *Journal of Small Business Management*, 114–128.

Kim, S.-K. (2014). Explicit design of innovation performance metrics by using analytic hierarchy process expansion. *International Journal of Mathematics and Mathematical Sciences*, 1–7.

Klaus, S. (2019). *The global competitiveness report*. World Economic Forum.

Kline, S., & Rosenberg, N. (1986). The positive sum strategy: Harnessing technology for economic growth. *International Journal of the Economics of Business, 8*(3), 343–364.

Koc, T. (2007). Organizational determinants of innovation capacity in software companies. *Computers and Industrial Engineering, 53*, 373–385.

Kramis, J. (1994). *Sistemas y procedimientos administrativos: metodología para su aplicación en instituciones privadas y públicas*. Universidad Iberoamericana.

Lester, D. (1998). Critical success factors for new product development. *Research-Technology Management, 41*(1), 36–43.

Massachussets Institute of Technology. (2021). *MIT innovation ecosystems*. Obtenido de https://innovation.mit.edu/about/team/, recovered July 11, 2021.

Mendes Luz, L., Carlos de Francisco, A., & Piekarski, C. (2015). Proposed model for assessing the contribution of the indicators obtained from the analysis of life-cycle inventory to the generation of industry innovation. *Journal of Cleaner Production, 96*, 339–348.

Moreno, A. (1998). *Planeación financiera*. Universidad de Sonora.

Nova Scotia School Advisory Council. (2020). *School Advisory Council*. Obtenido de https://www.iata.org/contentassets/01e197ea66384f27a9e763d151ae2d7d/advisory-councils-rules-and-regulations.pdf, recovered November 20, 2020.

OECD. (2021). *OECD science, technology and innovation Outlook 2021: Times of crisis and opportunity*. Obtenido de https://doi.org/10.1787/75f79015-en, recovered June 17, 2021.

Oyelaran-Oyeyinka, B., & Adebowale, B. (2012). University-industry collaboration as a determinant of innovation in Nigeria. *Institutions and Economies, 4*(1), 21–46.

Palmberg, C. (2006). *Technovation*, 1253–1267.

Paths – UP. (2021). *Innovation ecosystem team*. Obtenido de https://pathsup.org/people/innovation-ecosystem-team/, recovered July 12, 2021.

Patino, I., Hernández, J., & Vallejo-trujillo, S. (2020). Enterprise dimension of the e-government: Background of a genetic algorithm to collaborate with local economic development. *Journal of Theoretical an Applied Information Technology, 98*(6), 935–947.

Pennsylvania department of Education. (2020). *Establishing and operating effective local advisory*. Obtenido de https://www.education.pa.gov/Documents/K-12/Career%20and%20Technical%20Education/Teacher%20Resources/Advisory%20Committee%20Guidelines/Establishing%20and%20Operative%20Effective%20Local%20Advisory%20Committees.pdf, recovered July 23, 2020.

Pérez, J., Sattler, S., Bertoli, M., & Domingo, D. (2016). Bases para un modelo de estructura de financiamiento en las PyME Latinoamericanas. *Contabilidad, 16*, 179–214.

Pervan, S., Al-Ansaari, Y., & Xu, J. (2015). Environmental determinants of open innovation in Dubai SMEs. *Industrial Marketing Management, 50*, 60–68.

Raja, M., & Wei, S. (2015). *Tékhne – Review of Applied Management Studies, 13*, 25–33.

Ries, E. (2013). *El método Lean Startup*. Pearson.

Rodríguez, J. (2002). *Estudio de sistemas y procedimientos administrativos*. ECASA.

Sánchez, J., Casado, L., & Bastidas, A. (2019). Consumer neuroscience techniques in advertising research. *Sustainability, 13*, 2–20. https://doi.org/10.3390/su130315897

Sawang, S. (2011). Key performance indicators for innovation implementation: Perception vs. actual usage. *Asia Pacific Management Review, 16*(1), 23–29.

Slater, S., Mohr, J., & Sengupta, S. (2014). Product. *Innovation and Management*, 552–566.

Testa Center. (2021). *Acerca del Staff*. Obtenido de https://testacenter.com/staff/, recovered July 13, 2021.

Texas A&M University. (2019). *Operations manual guie for organizations*. Texas A&M University.

Therrien, P., & Mohnen, P. (2003). How innovative are Canadian firms compared to some European firms? A comparative look at innovation surveys. *Technovation, 23*, 359–369.

Tipping, J., Zeffren, E., & Fusfeld, A. (1995). Assessing the value of your technology. *Research-Technology Management, 38*(5), 22–39.

Tohidi, H., & Jabbari, M. (2012). Providing a framework for measuring innovation within companies. *Procedia Technology*, 583–585.

Torrisi, S., Gambardella, A., Giuri, P., Harhoff, D., Hoisl, K., & Mariani, M. (2016). Used, blocking and sleeping patents: Empirical evidence from a large-scale inventor survey. *Research Policy, 45*(7), 1374–1385.

Tsai, W. (2001). Knowledge transfer in intraorganizational networks: Effects of network position and absorptive capacity on business unit innovation and performance. *The Academy of Management Journal*, 996–1004.

Tseng, C.-Y., & Wu, L.-Y. (2007). Innovation quality in the automobile industry measurement indicators and performance implications. *International Journal of Technology Management*, 162–177.

University of Tsukuba. (2021). *Organizational chart*. Obtenido de https://oiso.tsukuba.ac.jp/en/chart/, recovered July 11, 2021.

Upcounsel. (2020). *Funding round meaning: Everything you need to know*. Obtenido de https://www.upcounsel.com/funding-round-meaning, recovered January 03, 2021.

Veugelers, R., & Cassiman, B. (1999). Make and buy in innovation strategies: Evidence from Belgian manufacturing firms. *Research Policy, 28*, 63–80.

Yang, C., Zhang, Q., & Ding, S. (2015). An evaluation method for innovation capability based on uncertain linguistic variables. *Applied Mathematics and Computation*, 160–174.

Chapter 4
Phase 2. Evolution of the Innovation and Entrepreneurship Ecosystem

4.1 Stage I. Sources of Financing with Return on Investment

According to Kulicke (2020) in an ecosystem of innovation and entrepreneurship, for enterprises to have access to financing, the enterprise must be formally established so that at the time of starting operations, it can cover the operation of the enterprise or, failing that, convince the investors for their participation through a network of contacts, such as the Austrian program AplusB ScaleUp (2021), where through AWS (Austria Wirtschaftsservice Gesellschaft mbH (aws) – promotion bank of the Austrian federal government), which provides pre-seed financing, this allows to benefit new enterprises through links with research and universities. Another type of financing is given through incubators that manage to link the entrepreneur with university researchers, as do some universities in the United States, Israel, and the United Kingdom. In the latter, the incubators adjust the entrepreneurship projects together with universities, and through the accelerator of the projects are funded. Similarly in Toronto, Canada, through MaRS Discovery District (2021), Toronto, it offers a wide range of infrastructure and service programs adapted to the needs of startups and new enterprises, where it is worth highlighting the support to the ecosystem through entrepreneurs, investors, researchers, and government representatives. The objective of this ecosystem is to create a highly innovative environment to boost creativity. It has supported just over 1200 companies based on knowledge, research, and innovation in the following areas: clean technology, health, and financial technology, among others. Something interesting about this ecosystem is that through the actors of the same ecosystem and companies that are born in it, they fund new enterprises, to the extent of raising just over 3 billion dollars. This without a doubt is an incentive to entrepreneurs; however, they must go through certain filters and enrichment of their entrepreneurship projects before being accepted and partially or fully funded.

I. Patiño-Galván, *Innovation and Entrepreneurship Ecosystems*, Innovation, Technology, and Knowledge Management,
https://doi.org/10.1007/978-3-031-24517-6_4

There are also nonprofit organizations around the world, private banks, universities, innovation parks, innovation ecosystems, business incubators, and government entities, among others, that offer funding, management, and mentoring services aimed mostly at existing companies, said entities that offer the crowdfunding service as can be seen in Table 4.1.

Taking the foregoing as a reference, this stage responds to the need of local enterprises (previous letter of intent and interest) that require financing to accelerate their development and growth to expand their market, create new business units/spin off, and modernize their infrastructure, among other reasons, and whose purpose is to increase sales and profitability, optimize resources, or, failing that, stabilize the enterprise. For this, it is suggested that the *EOE* open two calls on demand, one to formalize the interest of the enterprise to receive financing and the other closed call to invite companies or entrepreneurs to participate as funders/investors.

- In the specific case of financing sources in this phase 2, the return on investment is contemplated to difference of the phase 1. However, it is important to previously design rules and a regulatory framework and systematize all the activities involved to guarantee transparency and timeliness of the information. For this, it is suggested to consider the following points:
- Create a list of enterprises requesting financing, as well as a list of legally recognized and established entrepreneurs or enterprise (legal entities and individuals) who wish to participate as investors. Said list will be kept restricted only to the participants, with the *EOE* being the entity that guarantees confidentiality in co-responsibility with the employer/enterprise.
- All processes, meetings, and information that are generated in this dynamic must be systematized and regulated. To document the agreements or dialogues, make the processes transparent (without putting the confidentiality of the information at risk). This is to serve decision-making and for the generation of indicators.
- It is important to mention that priority will be given to request financing to enterprises that have been created in the ecosystem in its phase 1 (applicants and funders) as well as to give them priority to be part of the enterprises to request capital. However, if there are enterprises that operate in the locality and even if they have not entered the dynamics of the ecosystem, but require financing, they must submit their intention to the advice council, and other criteria to be considered at this stage, the above putting the interests of economic and social development of the region first, without deviating the mission and vision of the ecosystem.
- It is suggested to design indicators to measure all the participants (enterprise(s) requesting financing and company(s) that will provide financing, subjects interested in participating in the dynamics). Once designed, the participants will be asked to provide information that will contextualize the participants interested in both roles.

Table 4.1 Enterprise's funding

Name	Place	Description	Link
OurCrowd (2021)	Canada/ United States	Offers the funding service to existing and new companies with interest rates below the market	OurCrowd investments
ACFA (2021)	Africa	The *African Crowdfunding association (ACFA)* is an industry association that operates as a *self-regulatory organization (SRO)* that promotes transparency and good governance in the crowdfunding industry, as well as serving as a binding body for financing.	Home – *ACFA* (africancrowd.org)
Find Crowd Funding (2021)	Israel	It offers services to finance projects of existing enterprise, in addition to allowing you to train as an investor and support other projects in the region.	ISRAEL Crowdfunding Opportunities – Top Funding Offerings based in ISRAEL (findcrowdfunding.com)
National Crowdfunding & Fintech Association – NCFA (2021)	Canada	It is a financial innovation ecosystem that provides education, market knowledge, industry management, networking, opportunities, and financing services. It works closely with industry, government, partners, and affiliates to create a financial industry. It is a decentralized body which is committed to global stakeholders that collaborate in incubating projects and investments in fintech, alternative finance, crowdfunding, finance, payments, digital assets, and tokens, blockchain, cryptocurrencies, REGTECH, and INSURTECH.	Global Financial Technology and Innovation Ecosystem for Investors (ncfacanada.org)
Crowd funding Professional Association – CFPA (2021)	United States	It provides funding service with payment of commissions, in addition to providing education, resources, and assistance to the funder and the company requesting funds.	Crowdfunding Professional Association – CfPA – for all stakeholders in the crowdfunding community
Crowdfunding (2021a, b)	European Union	It supports investors and businesses to harness the potential of crowdfunding and make it easier for platforms to offer their services across the *European Union (EU)*.	Crowdfunding|European Commission (europa.Eu)
Birchal (2021)	Australia	It is a platform that allows you to join a portfolio of investors to fund international enterprises already created in the food sector.	Birchal – Invest in the brands you love – Equity Crowdfunding Australia

(continued)

Table 4.1 (continued)

Name	Place	Description	Link
Crowdfunding (2021a, b)	Latin America	Its objective is to provide entrepreneurs from anywhere in the world with a channel through which they can provide and obtain collective capitalization for any type of projects they wish to undertake.	Crowdfunding Latin America
Crowdfund.ca (2021)	Canada	Crowdfunding is responsible for raising money for ventures, through a series of procedures to ensure that the entrepreneur transmits his project so that it can be funded.	How it works|Crowdfund.ca|Crowdfunder Canada
	Mexico	It is an entity linked to the *institute technological of higher studies of Monterrey (ITESM)* to fund ventures, through donations. Its platform allows you to view project information to allow the collaboration of stakeholders.	Crowdfunding (tec.mx)

Source: Author (2021)

- Together and taking the *EOE* as the managing entity, it is suggested to design the regulatory framework for all actors, as well as to provide the freedom to the entrepreneur who requires financing to place clauses to protect the company, as well as freedom of decision, taking into consideration the regulations by which this phase will be governed.

> It is important to consider the points mentioned and others that arise in the dynamics of the design of indicators and regulatory framework, since these must be reflected and transmitted in the calls, terms of reference, and other information to be transparent in the processes.

Given that at this stage it is suggested to promote previous meetings with the participants, in order for the *EOE* to develop classification designs, calculations of performance, risk, and probability of return, in these meetings, it is possible to start from a base and, based on this, make adjustments with the main actors in particular with the enterprises that require financing and that given the phase will be willing to return the financing amount together with a percentage of profit or interest for the investor/funder that will give resources for financing. In this sense, it is suggested to establish policies that include a percentage of return for investors and the social sector. Finally, it must be reiterated that this stage already includes return on investment and profits on the amount invested in this second phase. It is suggested at the beginning to develop the classification of enterprises that require financing given the volume of startup that can be incorporated into this dynamic. Three classifications of

Table 4.2 Classification of enterprises to finance according to the interest rate and risk

Classification	Minimum quarterly interest rate	Risk	Amount requested[a]
AAA	15% above the quarterly bank interest rate	50–75%	Don't exceed more than 20% of your after-tax profits
AA	10% above the bank quarterly interest rate	25–40%	Don't exceed more than 10% of your after-tax profits
To	5% above the quarterly bank interest rate	5–12.5%	Don't exceed more than 5% of your after-tax profits

Source: Author (2019), taken from the good practices, suggestions of the Bank of Mexico and the bank and government annual interest rates del Banco de México (2020), Official Journal of the Federation (2018), Moodys (2021), Fitch (2021)

[a]If the requested amount is outside the suggested amount, the interest and risk rates may be modified depending on each enterprise

companies will be designed according to the quarterly interest rate to return the risk and the amount to request according to Table 4.2, in addition to meeting the criteria established in Table 4.3.

For the initial calculation of the yield, it is suggested to develop at least three formulas considering the following non-limiting variables (Banco de México, 2020; Comisión Nacional Bancaria y de Valores, 2020; Moodys, 2021):

- Opportunities:
  - Average increase in profits.
  - Growth expectations.
  - Market behavior.
  - Total assets.
- Commitments:
  - Credits.
  - Operation.
  - Seasonality of cash flows.
- External (seasonality and behavior for at least 3 years):
  - Local and regional GDP.
  - Inflation.
  - Exchange rate.
  - Competitiveness index.
- Performance annual reals:
  - Real annual returns.
  - Probability of payment.
  - Returns with risk.

Table 4.3 Criteria for classification of companies applying for financing

Classification	Qualitative criteria	Quantitative criteria
A	Be legally constituted in the Federal Taxpayers Registry as a natural or legal person. Be up to date in the fulfillment of tax obligations. Have valid digital stamp certificates. Not to be suspended in the register of importers Have the legal use or enjoyment of the property where it has operations. Have your accounting in electronic media. Have at least 50% of its organizational structure constituted by female gender. Not having active loans or debts Be an exporter showing the records and cédulas/permits to market. Have insurance for your operation.	Have at least 5 years operating with average profitability at 5% and percentage of positive variation of their profits on average or greater than 5%. Can pay Have cash flow with a balance in favor. Have operating flow that allows to cover interest, commissions, and debts in the short, medium, and long term. Increasing liquidity levels over the last 3 years Positive leverage and efficiency financial ratios, above the industry average Positive historical behavior of payments within the innovation and entrepreneurship ecosystem (in case of having incurred in previous funding of phase 2)
AA	Be legally constituted in the Federal Taxpayers Registry as a natural or legal person. Be up to date in the fulfillment of tax obligations. Have valid digital stamp certificates. Not to be suspended in the register of importers Have the legal use or enjoyment of the property where it has operations. Have your accounting in electronic media. Have at least 50% of its organizational structure constituted by female gender. Not having active loans or debts It has insurance for its operation.	Have at least 3 years operating with average profitability at 2% and percentage of positive variation of their profits on average or greater than 2.5% Can pay Have cash flow with a balance in favor. Have operating flow that allows to cover interest, commissions, and debts in the short and medium term. Liquidity levels decreasing in the last year Positive leverage and efficiency financial ratios, on average of the sector Positive historical behavior of payments within the innovation ecosystem–entrepreneurship (in case of having incurred in previous funding of phase2)

(continued)

Table 4.3 (continued)

Classification	Qualitative criteria	Quantitative criteria
AAA	Be legally constituted in the Federal Taxpayers Registry as a natural or legal person. Be up to date in the fulfillment of tax obligations. Have valid digital stamp certificates. Not to be suspended in the register of importers Have the legal use or enjoyment of the property where it has operations. Have your accounting in electronic media. Have at least 50% of its organizational structure constituted by female gender. Not having active loans or debts	Have at least 3 years operating with average profitability at 0.5% and percentage of positive variation of their profits on average or greater than 1%. Count on the ability to pay in the short and medium term. Have positive cash flow. Have operating flow that allows to cover interest, commissions, and debts in the short and medium term. Liquidity levels decreasing in the last year Positive leverage and efficiency financial ratios, below the sector Positive historical behavior of payments within the innovation ecosystem–entrepreneurship (in case of having incurred in previous funding of phase2)

Source: Author (20), taken from the Registry in the Certification and Classification Scheme of Companies of the Ministry of Finance and Public Credit (2021), Bank of Mexico (2020), Official Journal of the Federation (2018), Moodys (2021), Fitch (2021)

- Calculation of quarterly, semiannual, or annual risk (all aligned to losses or profits, which will be known after the months and years of life of the enterprise within the ecosystem).
- Include time variables vs percentage.
- The values are annual.
- On a monthly basis, the histogram analysis of the assets, normal distributions, and correlational analysis of the variables must be carried out.
- Systematize it and include regression analysis and neural networks for the projection of information.
- Consider using the following methods for calculation and projection:
  - Asset evaluation.
  - Probability analysis.
  - Monte Carlo Analysis/Scenario Analysis.
  - Time series.
  - Quantitative analysis integrating descriptive and inferential statistics.
  - Sensitivity analysis.
  - Diagnostics and predictions using artificial intelligence.
  - Among others.

On the other hand, although Table 4.2 shows the classification by quarterly interest rate and risk percentage, it is important to point out that those enterprises that require financing must meet the following (non-limiting) criteria shown in Table 4.3.

Table 4.4 Investor criteria

Classification[a]	Qualitative criteria
A	Be legally constituted in the Federal Taxpayers Registry as a natural or legal person. Be up to date in the fulfillment of tax obligations. Have your accounting in electronic media. Not having active loans or debts Belong to the innovation ecosystem with at least 3 years Participate as a funder in the first phase of the innovation and entrepreneurship ecosystem for at least 3 consecutive years. How much bank associated with your legal registry with funds for funding that demonstrates activity for at least 1 year Positive historical behavior of funding within the innovation ecosystem–entrepreneurship for at least 3 consecutive years
AA	Be legally constituted in the Federal Taxpayers Registry as a natural or legal person. Be up to date in the fulfillment of tax obligations. Have your accounting in electronic media. Not having active loans or debts Belong to the innovation ecosystem with at least 2 years Participate as a funder in the first phase of the innovation and entrepreneurship ecosystem for at least 2 consecutive years. How much bank associated with your legal registry with funds for funding that demonstrates activity for at least 1 year Positive historical behavior of funding within the innovation ecosystem–entrepreneurship for at least 2 consecutive years
AAA	Be up to date in the fulfillment of tax obligations. Have your accounting in electronic media. Not having active loans or debts Participate as a funder in the first phase of the innovation and entrepreneurship ecosystem for at least 2 consecutive years. How much bank associated with your legal registry with funds for funding that demonstrates activity for at least 1 year Positive historical behavior of funding within the innovation ecosystem–entrepreneurship for at least 2 consecutive years

Source: Author (20), taken from the Registry in the Certification and Classification Scheme of Enterprise of the Ministry of Finance and Public Credit (2021), Bank of Mexico (2020), Official Journal of the Federation (2018), Moodys (2021), Fitch (2021)

[a]It is suggested that given the importance of funding, if there is any other donor who does not enter the categories but expresses their intention, this will be valued by the council and if their category is approved, it would be B

On the other hand, legal entities or individuals who wish to participate as investors in phase 2 must meet the criteria established in Table 4.4 before starting the funding rounds.

The criteria included in Tables 4.2, 4.3, and 4.4 must be systematized by the *EOE* and captured by the requesting entity and the investor/funding entity with their respective voucher. The *EOE* will review the information as informative to guarantee the validity of the information. If any additional information is required, it will be requested from the corresponding entity.

It is suggested the participation of a banking or financial service entity (as far as possible created in the ecosystem) serves as a binding entity only for the corresponding deposits. This is in order to cover the legal regulatory framework and corresponding bank transactional registry. In this way, the *EOE* is separated from that activity, as well as its follow-up, leaving the collection, accounting, and payment tasks derived from these sources of financing to the companies (applicant and funder) and to the bank or financial services entity.

Upon agreement between the parties, the *EOE* will limit itself to requesting from the banking entity information on indicators of the participating enterprises/subjects for the classification of the companies, noting that the inclusion of the banking entity is not for account management and banking services. It is only to serve as support and to comply with the regulatory framework for the transactions that will be carried out in the amounts and transactions that are most convenient for the interested parties.

4.2 Stage II. Call, Reception, and Selection of Enterprises

The stage of calls, reception, and selection of companies that request funding will operate differently from the first phase, since enterprises in this phase are already operating, are stable, and require financing to grow, develop, or stabilize, so they must demonstrate their profitability and profits and justify the reason for requesting financing in two moments. The first moment is through their participation in the corresponding calls and their respective load of information that the call requires according to Table 4.5, and the second moment is through a face-to-face or online exhibition where the *EOE*, the funders/investors, and the financial entity that will serve as the binding agent for the deposits that may be made are present. At this second moment, funding rounds will be named, which will be detailed in the following subtopic.

According to Table 4.5, it is important to mention that all the information captured by the company is suggested to be kept confidential and will only be available to the legal person who confirms their interest in participating as an investor and is selected in accordance with their call (see Table 4.6). To ensure this process, said call will be simultaneously disseminated to legal persons who wish to participate as investors/funders to ensure that they meet certain criteria. Finally, it is important to point out that the information system will automatically assign the enterprise category (A, AA, or AAA) under certain criteria. As a result of the above, Table 4.6 shows the call structure and terms of reference for investors.

Table 4.5 Structure for the convocation and reception of enterprises in need of capital

Document	Topic	Description
Call for funding of enterprises	Introduction	Integrate the following information: Headers with the logos of the sponsor, stakeholders, ecosystem, and the *EOE* Motto of the *EOE* and/or ecosystem Date of publication of the information Integrate the applicable general regulatory framework Areas involved in the ecosystem Productive sectors for which the call is intended Brief explanation of the call and stakeholders
	Objective of the call	Briefly develop the objective of the call
	Who is it addressed to?	Describe the type of enterprises to whom the call is addressed
	Suggested deliverables	Indicate in a general way the information will be capturing in the information system the companies that require funding
	General criteria	General explanation of the criteria to be applied when selecting projects
	Dates to consider	Include the dates: Aperture. In which the system for the capture of enterprise information is made. Closing. In which the system stops receiving requests from interested companies. Publication. In which the results of the enterprises that move to the next stage are published.
	Final notes	This section includes important notes for participating enterprise, in addition to the reference or links to reference documents, such as terms of reference and user manuals, among others.

Document	Topic	Description
Terms of reference (linked to the call)/reception of applications	Introduction	Integrate the following information: Headers with the logos of the sponsor, stakeholders, ecosystem, and the *EOE*. Motto of the *EOE* and/or ecosystem. Date of publication of the information. Indicate to which call the terms of reference are linked.
	Criteria and information that must be contained in the proposals to request funding	Explanatory memorandum on why they require financing. Executive curriculum of the director of the company including the objectives achieved and main challenges. Cover letter oriented to your contribution to the ecosystem. Extensive project. Enterprise background. Balance sheet and income statement for the last 2 years. Contact details. Description of the destination of the funds. Background. Objectives, goals, and strategies in which the requested amount will have consequence or benefit. Methodology for the achievement of objectives. Expected results. Work team. Schedule of activities where the use of the requested amount is included or associated. Products or services offered. Target market. 5-year sales projections (including supply and demand charts and break-even point) Conclusion. Recommendations.
	Characteristics of the terms of reference	To support enterprises, references and help links should be placed to facilitate the understanding of each item.
	Funding amounts	Indicate the amount they require, the time of return, and interest rates (prior to this point, the enterprise must have meetings with the *EOE* to estimate these numbers).

(continued)

Table 4.5 (continued)

Document	Topic	Description
	Transparency	Because all information will be captured in the information system, transparency of information is ensured, as appropriate. However, in this phase information, security measures will be included, according to the interested parties. On the other hand, transparency will be provided through the information system in all the flow of reception of projects as appropriate.
	Intellectual property and copyright	All copyrights and intellectual property derived from the amount will be solely and exclusively the property of the company requesting the funding.
	Commitment letter	Integrate a letter of commitment from the company through its representative or administrator.
	Sanctions	Indicate that any action that violates the principles and values of the *EOE* and the ecosystem will be sanctioned in accordance with the *EOE*, where appropriate request advice from the board for the final decision.
	Deliberations	Note that the resolutions will be defining and unappealable, if and only if the process is transparent through the information system, preserving in some cases access through information security methods.
	Freedom of creativity and explore	The call and its terms of reference should stimulate the freedom of creativity and thought of the participants, and willingness to participate.
	Inclusion	Note that all applications may be captured, without any distinction, allowing the inclusion and participation of interested parties.

Source: Author (2021)

Once the investor is selected, only certain information about the enterprise(s) that requires funding will be shown to serve the investor's decision-making. It is important to note that through algorithms, statistics, and the use of artificial intelligence, and considering the category of investor (A, AA, or AAA), certain enterprises will be automatically recommended depending on the information captured in the call. At the end of accounts, the investor may select those companies where he wishes to participate. However, given your investor category (A, AA, or AAA), certain options or information will be blocked.

According to Tables 4.5 and 4.6, each item must be designed and substantiated in detail within the *EOE*, depending on the local context, as well as the delimitation and information that is of interest to collect for the *EOE* and the ecosystem.

On the other hand, those participants who meet the requirements and supporting documents will be selected. The *EOE*, through the information system, will group

Table 4.6 Structure for calling and receiving investment/funding enterprises

Document	Topic	Description
Call for investors	Introduction	Integrate the following information: Headers with the logos of the sponsor, stakeholders, ecosystem, and the *EOE* Motto of the *EOE* and/or ecosystem Date of publication of the information Integrate the applicable general regulatory framework Areas involved in the ecosystem Productive sectors for which the call is intended Brief explanation of the call and stakeholders
	Objective of the call	Briefly develop the objective of the call.
	Who is it addressed to?	Describe the type of enterprise, legal entities, or individuals to whom the call is addressed.
	Suggested deliverables	Indicate in a general way the information will be captured in the information system by moral or natural persons.
	General criteria	General explanation of the criteria to be applied at the time of the selection of investors
	Dates to consider	Include the dates: Aperture. In which the system for capturing information from investors is opened. Closing. In which the system stops receiving requests from investors. Sending private notification. In which the results of the selected investors will be notified.
	Final notes	This section includes important notes for investors, in addition to the reference or links to reference documents, such as terms of reference and user manuals, among others.

(continued)

Table 4.6 (continued)

Document	Topic	Description
Terms of reference (linked to the call)/receipt of application to be an investor	Introduction	Integrate the following information Headers with the logos of the sponsor, stakeholders, ecosystem, and the *EOE*. Motto of the *EOE* and/or ecosystem. Date of publication of the information. Indicate to which call the terms of reference are linked.
	Criteria and information that must be contained in the proposals to request funding	Explanatory statement of why they need to participate as an investor Curriculum of the representative of the enterprise or legal person Cover letter oriented to your contribution to the ecosystem Include the investment amount, along with the statement that supports that amount. Legal registry
	Characteristics of the terms of reference	To support investors, references and help links should be placed to facilitate the understanding of each item.
	Investment amounts	Indicate the total amount required to invest and the estimated return time and interest. The latter will be capped according to the capabilities of the applicant company, although in the funding rounds these can be modified.
	Transparency	Because all information will be captured in the information system, its transparency is guaranteed, as appropriate. However, information security measures will be included, according to the interested parties. Moreover, transparency will be provided through the information system in the entire flow of project reception as appropriate.
	Intellectual property and copyright	All copyrights and intellectual property derived from the amount invested will be solely and exclusively the property of the enterprise requesting the funding.
	Commitment letter	Integrate a letter of commitment from the investor through its representative or administrator.
	Sanctions	Indicate that any action that violates the principles and values of the *EOE* and the ecosystem will be sanctioned in accordance with the *EOE*, where appropriate request advice from the board for the final decision.
	Deliberations	Note that the resolutions will be defining and unappealable, if and only if the process is transparent through the information system, preserving in some cases access through information security methods.
	Freedom of creativity and thought	The call and its terms of reference should stimulate the freedom of creativity and thought of the participants, and willingness to participate.
	Inclusion	Note that all applications may be captured, without any distinction, allowing the inclusion and participation of interested parties.

Source: Author (2021)

the participants to notify their participation by digital means, as well as initiate the corresponding process for the facilitation of information from the participants in a strategic way, so that investors know the offer and express interest by any startup(s), as well as providing information to investors' startups. It is important to note that by common agreement and under regulations, it will be stipulated that information may be provided to investors and startups to avoid conflicts of interest and facilitate decision-making. From the interest samples, you will be shown statistical information, projections, and information estimates.

> All information, projections, estimates, graphs, dynamic tables, and other information must be shown through the information system by profiles, passing through information security filters and access logs.

4.3 Stage III. Investment/Funding Rounds

> At this stage, it is suggested to define with the interested parties the investment amounts required by the enterprises/startups with the participating investors, as well as document the agreements, taking as reference the corresponding calls. In this phase 2, all responsibility and decision-making rests with the owner of the enterprise that requires the capital.

On the other hand, according to the Australian AGTECH (2018), Shirshikov (2019), and Cardiff Lexington Corporation (2020), the investment/funding rounds are characterized by the need for capital of already established enterprises with proven capacity and stability, and which require investments to grow, develop new product lines, or improve existing ones and market growth, among others. To obtain said financing, funding rounds called A, B, and C are established (which may be extended to more rounds as required), where enterprises with the capacity to invest place funds to cover the capital needs of the applicant companies. It is carried out to obtain profitability by assuming different risks, which are previously established, and which can be adjusted at the time of carrying out the negotiation dynamics. It is important to note that enterprises with a need for capital can raise funds in the various rounds as needed. To appreciate the characteristics of the funding rounds, Table 4.7 is presented.

According to Table 4.7, the objective of each round is to avoid having a lot of capital at risk, to be able to make the market distinction between the indicated collection rounds, when raising capital is essential to maximize the exposure of the enterprise. Enterprise to sources of investment and the return of this together with returns are viable and more secure. The process at each stage works essentially the same, the difference being risk tolerance or risk mitigation that attracts different investors looking for different returns on their investment. In each series, investors will make different proposals, to the startup that requires the capital, based on risk/expected returns (Cardiff Lexington Corporation, 2020). In the same way, it can be observed as a symptom of the evolution of the ecosystem when more and more startups enter these investment schemes, where the participating companies are more stable, with a view to continuing to grow and expand their market. It is important to reiterate that it is suggested to give priority as investors in this stage and funding rounds to the investors/funders who participated in phase 1.

Now, how to operate the funding rounds? To answer the question, there are various entities in the market, some of which are cited below (Cardiff Lexington Corporation, 2020; Australian AGTECH, 2018; Ziyaad, 2018):

- For-profit intermediary funders. They serve as intermediaries where they charge commissions, and through which essential and limited information of any of the participants is shown. Through this, the transactions are carried out and the contracts are made, type of risk and returns.
- Nonprofit intermediary funders. These models present information on the enterprises that require the capital, and contact details, in addition to the contracts prior to accessing information.
- Intermediary hybrids. In these models, in addition to being for profit, unlike the previous ones, previous interviews are carried out with the entrepreneurs who require the capital and, if possible, interviews with investors. Through this dynamic, the investment amounts, returns, and contracts are formalized.
-

> In the case of this proposal, it is suggested that the *EOE* act as a nonprofit arbitrator to ensure that the essential rules are complied in accordance with the regulatory framework, respecting the autonomy of the interested parties.

For this, the following stages are generally suggested in each round (appointment):

- Before starting the round:
- Publication of the call, reception, and selection.
- Notification of participants (startups that require capital and interested investors).
- Grant access by profiles to the information system to share data, statistics, projections, behaviors, and other information that is useful for decision-making, restricting certain strategic information. This is important to be profiling investors and so that they express their interest in participating.

- In process (initiates the dynamics of the funding rounds):
- The *EOE* will schedule in a location located within the ecosystem a face-to-face and/or virtual interview between the owner of the company that requires capital and interested investors. This dynamic will explain the reasons of the owner of the enterprise requesting capital and the investors. This will allow to sensitize the actors and possibly reach agreements. It is important to note that before the inter-

Table 4.7 Fundings rounds A, B, and C

Series	Characteristics	Authors
A	The applicant enterprises Marketing becomes an increasingly strategically. New production and sales processes Market expansion	Crunchbase (2020)
	It is the first round of venture capital financing. The startup must have a developed product and a customer base, with a steady revenue stream. It is an ideal opportunity that allows startups to scale to different markets. A strategic plan that generates long-term benefits is required. Learn how fundraising works and start making early engagements with angel investors and venture capitalists. Series A funding comes primarily from angel investors and traditional venture capital firms, which are looking for startups with a strong business strategy that can turn their idea into a successful and profitable organization, allowing investors to reap the benefits of their investment. A single investor can serve as a basis, and once the startup has secured its first investor, it is easier to attract additional investors. Although angel investors prefer to invest during this stage, they tend to have much less influence than venture capital firms at this stage.	Cloudways (2021)
	This round provides financing for an enterprise to bring its product to a mass market and stabilize the company. At this stage, the startup has already developed a minimum viable product (*MVP*), tested the product, and found the right product for the market. However, in most cases, their operations are limited demographically or geographically, and a series A funding round allows them to reach a wider audience. In this round, valuation and fundraising statistics are analyzed. Angel investors are offering larger amounts of funding. Series A investors include accelerators and venture capital firms. Venture capital firms and startup accelerators are the main sources of series A investments. Startups join incubators and accelerators for seed funding and prototyping.	Shirshikov (2019)
	This stage requires having obtained some proof of concept. Investors are beginning to validate the data to see and analyze the startup's achievements. This may not be an income, but it is required to know the key metrics which give an indication of improvement and have a real idea of its potential. The capital of this round is usually about optimizing the business model. Previous investors may participate although at this stage, startups will begin to require the association of investors who can really help take the company to the next level. Series A investors are usually venture capitalists or angels. Potential series A investors will assess how seed money was used to assess the results. Other investor profiles that may participate in these types of rounds include family offices, private equity firms, and hedge funds.	Cremades (2018)

(continued)

Table 4.7 (continued)

Series	Characteristics	Authors
B	Startups ensure their ability to scale. Hiring of experts in strategic positions of the startup is required. The startup can potentially expand to different market segments. Initiates the development of new business units/spinoff.	Crunchbase (2020)
	Startups that go through the previous stages of startup funding (initial and series A funding) They have developed a substantial user base along with a steady stream of revenue. They have proven to investors that they can achieve success on a larger scale. Investors help startups expand their horizons by funding their market reach activities, increasing their market share, forming operational teams such as marketing, business development, and customer success. The series B funding stage allows startups to grow so that they can meet the diverse demands of their customers and compete in tight markets in terms of competition. It's typically run by the same characters from the A series, including a key anchor investor who helps attract other investors. The main difference is the addition of new venture capital that specializes in investing in well-established startups so that they can further exceed expectations.	Cloudways (2021)
	It is required to scale the business and expand your distribution channels. Startups focus on enterprise-grade solutions to grow the team, serve more customers, and build structures that keep the enterprise stable and growing. This is also the stage where venture capitalists are most valuable because they can offer financing and advice. They initiate the barriers to access the B rounds, since the startups must guarantee their permanence and growth. The increase in fundraising amounts and valuations of startups raising series B is the result of larger initial funding rounds. With the growth of innovation–entrepreneurship ecosystems, multiple enterprise-grade solutions enable faster scaling.	Shirshikov (2019)
	Startups are looking for venture capital. This stage is about building the enterprise and building on existing successes. Capital can be used to expand teams, expand geographically into new markets. Investors at this stage should be carefully chosen to make the leap to entrepreneurial levels. It begins to visualize the growth of startups and the progressive success of the innovation and entrepreneurship ecosystem.	Cremades (2018)

Series	Characteristics	Authors
C	Participation of private companies Venture capital to a medium scale Intervention of banks as investors Large-scale operations Normally the support that startups need to enter new international markets	Crunchbase (2020)
	Enterprises that come to this series should be on their growth path, looking for funds to help them build new products, reach new markets, and even acquire other underperforming startups. In this series, investors fund successful startups. They hope to receive a profit greater than the money they invest. At this point, companies that require financing are less risky. The startup has proven to be a success, so investors invest significant amounts of money in thriving startups to secure their own position as leading investors. Startups have a customer base, have earned stable revenue streams along with proven stories of their growth, and want to expand their operations on a global scale. If you have not achieved the above, then you are not yet ready for funding this series.	Cloudways (2021)
	This funding round is used to scale reach and operations nationally or internationally. This is the round in which most venture capital firms invest. Investors receive a smaller amount of capital at this stage because the company is generating enough revenue to scale operations and is now preparing for an initial public offering or acquisition. In both scenarios, overvaluation can hurt all investors, so this round is more conservative.	Shirshikov (2019)
	From this series, it is likely that there will be a sprint towards an exit or at least to increase market share and position. There is a high probability that there will be strategic acquisitions. This may be due to talent, elimination of competition, instant jumps in users and geographic coverage, and/or grouping several companies together to prepare for an exit through a purchase. At this point, we will work with the largest venture capital firms and perhaps even corporate investors. However, this can also be one of the most difficult rounds for startups that require capital. Investors are likely to be even more demanding and expect the due diligence process to be exhausting, intensive, and suspenseful.	Cremades (2018)
	This series has to do with scale and speed to maximize market share. One way to scale is to acquire competitors, suppliers, and/or distributors; another method is to expand into new markets. Investment banks, hedge funds, and private equity firms inject capital strategically, targeting companies to expand rapidly and drive significantly higher margins. This series tries to refine and scale quickly to achieve a larger footprint, possibly dominating a specific market.	Cardiff Lexington Corporation (2020)
	The innovation and entrepreneurship ecosystems see their objectives reflected with the good performance and growth of the startups. The valuation of startups is growing faster and faster. More and more often "unicorns" are born. It allows the ecosystem to grow and link to regional, national, and international ecosystems.	Ziyaad (2018)

Source: Author (2021)

view, the investors already had access to statistics of the applicant company and that in turn already knows the interested investors.
- Dynamic interview.

- Close.
- The closing of this dynamic is suggested to be given at the end of the interview, where the actors reach an agreement and are formalized at that very moment.
- It may be the case for security purposes, invite a third party (financial services enterprise or commercial banking) so that through this the transfers are made or, failing that, that the interested parties agree and formalize the processes of transfers.

Finally, it is suggested:

- The *EOE* will not be able to participate in the funding rounds as an investor.
- To guarantee as much as possible the diversification and distribution of the participants, it is suggested that the participation of the members be capped if and only if the percentage amount required by the enterprise is achieved; otherwise, it will be possible to accept participations that cover 100% of what is required. The final decision will be made by the enterprise requesting capital.
- At no time will the *EOE* be a collection agent.
- All operations without exception must be carried out electronically according to the interested parties.

4.4 Stage IV. Phase 2 Closure

The closing of phase 2 occurs when the funding rounds are exhausted. It is desirable that before the closing, the startup has managed to obtain more than 50% of the required amount of capital. In that sense, all the phases and their respective stages of this proposal are cyclical, for which an organization is required for the operation of the entire process by the *EOE*, where the use of information technologies, security of information, and artificial intelligence serve as a managing agent throughout the process, optimizing and making activities transparent and facilitating decision-making.

On the other hand, continuing with phase 1, the stages that comprised this phase 2 are shown as informative in Fig. 4.2. Stages of phase II of the ecosystem.

As can be seen in Fig. 4.2, the projection of the time shown in the stages is an approximation, since it depends on the operation and development of the operation of the ecosystem, so that according to its evolution, the period can be shortened or extended.

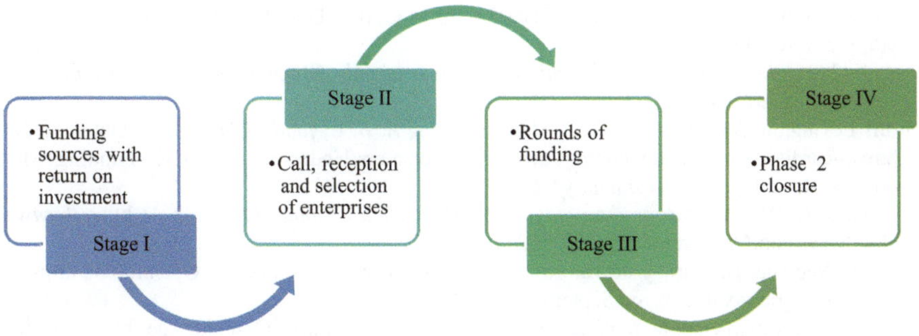

Fig. 4.1 Phase 2 stages. Source: Author (2021)

Phase 2 stages

Stage 1: Sources of financing **with return on investment** (cyclical activity every 6 or 12 months)

Stage 2: Call, reception and selection of established projects/enterprises (cyclical activity every 6 or 12)

Stage 3: Funding rounds and closing of phase 2 with return on investment (cyclical activity every 6 or 12 months)

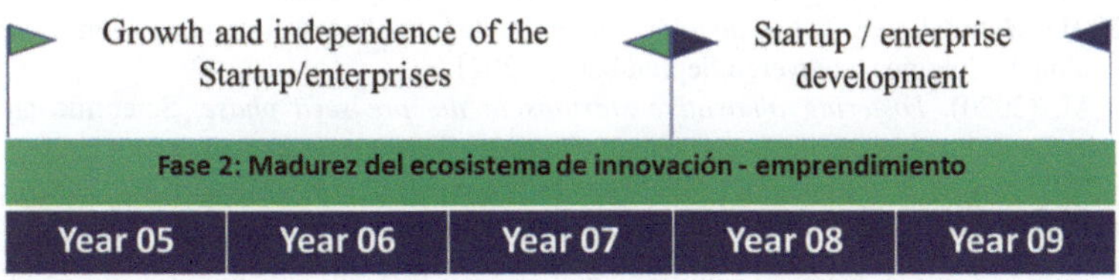

Fig. 4.2 Stages of phase II of the ecosystem. Source: Author (2021)

References

ACFA. (2021). *African Crowdfunding Association*. Obtenido de https://africancrowd.org/, recovered May 7, 2021.

Australian AGTECH. (2018). *Opportunities and challenges as seen from a US venture capital perspective*. Obtenido de https://finistere.com/wp-content/uploads/2018/10/Australian-AgTech-Opportunities-and-challenges-as-seen-from-a-US-venture-capital-perspective.pdf, recovered May 23, 2021.

Austria Wirtschaftsservice Gesellschaft mbH (aws). (2021). *Support by university-associated incubators: AplusB Scale-up in Austria*. Obtenido de https://www.aws.at/en/aws-aplusb-scale-up/, recovered August 10, 2021.

Banco de México. (2020). *Clasificadoras de Riesgo – Determinación de la tasa ponderada de fondeo interbancario con papel bancario*. Obtenido de https://anterior.banxico.org.mx/disposiciones/normativa/circular-3-2012/%7B60333E30-FC8B-94D3-E1D0-4AF8E3C75E90%7D.pdf, recovered September 09, 2021.

Birchal. (2021). *Invest in exciting Australian consumer brands*. Obtenido de https://www.birchal.com/, recovered May 7, 2021.

Cardiff Lexington Corporation. (2020). *Understanding A, B, C, fundraising stages*. Obtenido de https://cardifflexington.com/content/general/whitepapers/Understanding+ABC+Funding+Modified++Rev.pdf, recovered January 02, 2021.

Cloudways. (2021). *Startup funding stages you should know about*. Obtenido de https://www.cloudways.com/, recovered May 23, 2021.

Comisión Nacional Bancaria y de Valores. (2020). *Calificadoras de Valores*. Obtenido de https://www.cnbv.gob.mx, recovered September 20, 2021.

Cremades, A. (2018). *How funding rounds work for startups*. Obtenido de https://www.forbes.com/sites/alejandrocremades/2018/12/26/how-funding-rounds-work-for-startups/?sh=3e44767a7386, recovered January 02, 2021.

Crowdfund.ca. (2021). *What is crowdfunding?* Obtenido de https://crowdfund.ca/how-to-crowdfund, recovered May 7, 2021.

Crowdfunding. (2021a). *Crowdfunding Latinoamérica*. Obtenido de https://www.crowdfunding.lat/, recovered May 7, 2021.

Crowdfunding. (2021b). *Regulation on European Crowdfunding Service Providers (ECSP) for business*. Obtenido de https://ec.europa.eu/info/business-economy-euro/growth-and-investment/financing-investment/crowdfunding_en, recovered May 7, 2021.

Crowdfungind Professional Association. (2021). *The crowdfunding Professional Association*. Obtenido de https://cfpa.org/, recovered May 7, 2021.

Crunchbase. (2020). *The ultimate guide to raise capital for a startup*. Obtenido de http://about.crunchbase.com/wp-content/uploads/2019/10/Ultimate-guide-raising-startup-capital.pdf, recovered January 2, 2021.

Find Crowd Funding. (2021). *Best crowdfunding OFFERS in Israel*. Obtenido de https://www.findcrowdfunding.com/en/projects/country-il, recovered May 7, 2021.

Fitch. (2021). *Metodologías de Calificación*. Obtenido de https://www.fitchratings.com/es/region/mexico/methodologies, recovered September 24, 2021.

Kulicke, M. (2020). *Fostering innovative startups in the pre seed phase*. Scientific analysis Fraunhofer.

MaRS. (2021). *We help high-impact Canadian tech ventures grow and succeed*. Obtenido de https://www.marsdd.com/startup-services/, recovered August 21, 2021.

Moodys. (2021). *Metodologías de Calificación*. Obtenido de https://www.moodys.com/researchandratings/methodology/003006001/rating-methodologies/methodology/003006001/003006001/-/-1/0/-/0/-/-/es/mex/rr, recovered September 24, 2021.

National Crowdfunding & Fintech Association. (2021). *Global financial technology (Fintech) and funding innovation ecosystem for investors, companies and platforms*. Obtenido de https://ncfacanada.org/, recovered May 7, 2021.

OurCrowd. (2021). *Startup invest*. Obtenido de https://invest.ourcrowd.com/, recovered May 7, 2021.

Shirshikov, D. (2019). *Series A, B, C & D funding rounds explained*. Obtenido de https://fitsmall-business.com/series-a-b-c-d-funding/, recovered May 23, 2021.

Ziyaad, A. (2018). *London's lost innovators; understanding Brexit's effect on venture capital and startup investing in the UK*. The University of Texas at Austin.

Chapter 5
Conclusions

5.1 Expected Benefits

Based on the experience that innovation and entrepreneurship ecosystems have obtained in stages of development and growth, this proposal will allow the creation of a local ecosystem and through its evolution join wider-ranging ecosystems such as regional, national, and international ones, which will bring the benefit of increasing knowledge and its appropriation. There are also other benefits in the short, medium, and long term with the implementation of this proposal, such as:

- Academy dimension. University students, through projects that will be able to gradually integrate into the dynamics of the ecosystem, guided by teachers, researchers, and experts, and once the projects are mature, they will be able to transform themselves into enterprises, and this will strengthen their academic development.
- Research dimension and appropriation of knowledge. It will collaborate with the training of researchers, since the ecosystem through the creation of entrepreneurship and innovation projects will be able to integrate researchers in a multidisciplinary way and even evaluate projects derived from research to create startups. In addition to this, it will be possible to generate scientific production, derived from innovation projects such as: articles, books, congresses, patents, copyrights, technology transfer, and multidisciplinary projects, among others.
- Society, since they will be included in the ecosystem operation rules, that entrepreneurship and innovation projects have objectives aligned to the benefit of society, which are linked to the sustainable development goals. In addition to promoting the creation of startups that integrate circular economy, care for the environment, and consumption of renewable energies, the participation of civil society organizations will be stimulated for the creation of social startups guided

I. Patiño-Galván, *Innovation and Entrepreneurship Ecosystems*, Innovation, Technology, and Knowledge Management,
https://doi.org/10.1007/978-3-031-24517-6_5

by the ecosystem. Derived from the above, the sustainable development objectives with which it will be possible to collaborate are:

- Quality education and gender equality.
- Affordable and clean energy.
- Decent work and economic growth.
- Industry, innovation, and infrastructure.
- Sustainable cities and communities.
- Responsible consumption and production.
- Climate action.
- Alliances to achieve the objectives.

- Environment. It is suggested that as an ecosystem policy, projects include the use of renewable energy, caring for the environment, either in a progressive or complementary manner, in addition to encouraging the creation of enterprises that integrate the circular economy in all or part of their production processes.
- Government. This actor is suggested to collaborate and acquire experience in the prioritization and stimulation of the ecosystem, providing and supporting the registration of enterprises and incentives, guaranteeing the freedom of operation, and linking the ecosystem to be able to create companies. Additionally, in the ecosystem, they may be integrated into government projects proposed in the development plans, including collaborating with the creation and evolution of smart cities.
- Experts/researchers/academics. It is expected that as the ecosystem acquires experience and maturity, it will be possible to progressively count on the specialized infrastructure for the development of research and innovation applied to enterprises immersed in the ecosystem.
- Take advantage of the innate talent of local citizens. Perhaps the most important benefit is to give an outlet or hope to the talent of citizens so that they can materialize and polish their talent and increase their knowledge and experience, in addition to continuing to develop skills through entrepreneurship projects.
- Creation of enterprises. According to Eurostat (2020), an ecosystem observes its results through two areas, growth and development of specialized companies, and as this grows, their market and product diversification grow since they not only serve a local market but also a regional, national, and international market. In addition to this, the creation of companies oriented to intensive knowledge services and, on the other hand, to enterprises oriented to research and development can be concentrated.
- Economical. By creating enterprises and collaborating with the development and growth of existing ones in the locality, greater income is generated, payment of taxes, payment of competitive salaries, interaction with the purchase of raw materials, among other economic ties of the locality.
- Among others.

5.2 Future Works

The development of future works revolves around detailing each of the stages and phases, since in this work the general proposal is presented, presenting each stage and phase that integrates the birth and evolution of innovation ecosystems and local enterprises of such that the projected works will be the following:

- Detail each phase separately and its respective stages.
- Develop the profile, role, and responsibilities of the actors depending on the phase.
- Develop the transition from a local ecosystem to a regional, national, and international ecosystem.
- Potentialize ecosystems depending on their specialty.
- Present statistical works with results and their respective comparisons in the regional, national, and international context.
- Among others.

5.3 Conclusions

Social development contributes to the construction of strengthened and free societies, with values, principles, and sensitivity for the care of the environment. However, over time, increasingly complex and disintegrated societies are observed, which makes them vulnerable to problems such as poverty, insecurity, and pollution, among others, which, since they are not addressed with long-term solutions and in the absence of integration or involvement of all social actors, makes them grow far from being solved and in the long term contribute to the already damaged social decomposition.

To provide answers and solutions, different initiatives have been sought to solve present and future problems and thereby develop strategies to solve problems and achieve an impact on social reintegration. From this perspective, one of those initiatives are the innovation and entrepreneurship ecosystems that collaborate with the solution to these problems in the medium and long term, in addition to contributing to the integration and strengthening of societies through the generation of an environment that allows give outlet to the talent of citizens, and they can face current and future problems. The above, since these ecosystems, although they are a space for integration and collaboration for the creation of entrepreneurships and/or strengthening of existing enterprises, by interacting with actors such as the government, enterprises, academy, and social organizations, can collaborate to provide alternative solutions through the generation and appropriation of knowledge, take advantage of and polish the talent of its citizens and compete with other regions, among other advantages.

On the other hand, it is concluded that local innovation and entrepreneurship ecosystems are the first social space that collaborates in giving opportunity to the materialization of citizens' talent translated into startups, not without first getting interested actors to get involved and commit shortly, medium, and long term, collaborating with the birth, growth, and evolution of the ecosystem. It should also be aware that the construction and maturity of the local ecosystem is a long-term project where partial results are expected from the fourth year, and gradually from the ninth, depending on the degree of maturity that the actors acquire, and of the startups that are born, can develop and grow in the ecosystem. For this, it is important to be aware that there will be failures where more than 70% of the companies that are created will be forced to close according to the *National Institute of the Entrepreneur* (*INADEM*) (2018) and García (2015); however, the fact of having an ecosystem that collaborates with providing the minimum conditions for the birth of enterprises, and seeking their permanence, development, and growth, will undoubtedly generate experience and knowledge that will reduce the percentage of enterprise closings in the locality and, on the contrary, collaborate with its development and growth.

It is important to reiterate the commitment and roles of government actors, enterprise, academia, and, most importantly, the social sector, since through them the ecosystem can be born, grow, and evolve, where each actor knows their role and interaction and achieve openness to dialogue, confront ideas, debate objectively, and design the ecosystem that best suits the local society, putting collective interests first and seeking long-term social and economic development.

Another conclusion of this proposal is that the application of the two phases and their respective stages are cyclical and flexible in the sense that the operation and operating capacity of the *EOE* allow the change in the sequence of the stages, such as its openings according to the demand or the design of the ecosystem, and even more so in its birth stage, where learning and knowledge about the behavior of the actors are acquired, in addition to identifying weaknesses that can be addressed in the course of their birth, hence the importance of paying attention to all stages, those that allow the birth of the ecosystem, where the bases and foundations for its creation are generated, which will be reflected in its evolution.

5.4 Recommendations

The recommendations focus on collaborating with the generation of the conditions so that the talent of the local citizens can be polished and be materialized in undertakings.

- Carry out permanent evaluations on the development of the ecosystem, as well as the startups created, based on indicators.
- Carry out pilot tests to refine details in the design of the stages of phase one.
- Develop information systems integrating intelligent systems in all the processes of the innovation ecosystem to allow better management, transparency, and access to information for decision-making.
- Pay attention to stage one of phase one, as it will be an important part of the creation of the ecosystem.
- Identify the actors that will make up the town, who obey a certain profile.
- Integrate the social sector into strategic segments of the ecosystem.
- Involve local citizens in events on entrepreneurship from an early age to encourage the culture of entrepreneurship in collaboration with actors from that segment.
- Allow the ecosystem to evolve and specialize.
- Give an opportunity for the ecosystem to achieve its maturity and evolution, paying attention to the results obtained in each phase and stage.

References

Eurostat. (2020). *Business Demography Statistics and Mannheimer Unternehmenspanel*. Obtenido de ZEW calculations in Bersch and Gottschalk 2019 and EFI 2020. https://www.bertelsmann-stiftung.de/fileadmin/files/BSt/Publikationen/GrauePublikationen/Study_NW_Fostering_innovative_startups_in_the_pre-seed_phase_2021.pdf, recovered May 2, 2021.

García, L. (2015). Causas de fracaso en las MiPyME. *PyME y finanzas, 23*.

Instituto Nacional del Emprendedor – INADEM. (2018). *Las MiPyME en México: retos y oportunidades*. Obtenido de https://www.inadem.gob.mx/las-mipyme-en-mexico-retos-y-oportunidades/, recovered January 12, 2018.

Index

I. Patiño-Galván, *Innovation and Entrepreneurship Ecosystems*, Innovation, Technology, and Knowledge Management,
https://doi.org/10.1007/978-3-031-24517-6